WRITING CHOREOGRAPHY

A new contribution to studies in choreography, *Writing Choreography: Textualities of and beyond Dance*, focuses upon language and writing-based approaches to choreographing from the perspectives of artists and researchers active in the Nordic and Oceanic contexts.

Through the contributions of 15 dance–artists, choreographers, drama-turges, writers, interdisciplinary artists and artist–researchers, the volume highlights diverse textual choreographic processes and outcomes arguing for their relevance to present-day practices of expanded choreography. The anthology introduces some Western trends related to utilizing writing, text and language in choreographic processes. In its focus on art-making processes, it likewise offers insight into how performance can be transcribed into writing, how practices of writing choreograph and how choreography can be a process of writing with. Readers, such as dancers, choreographers, students in higher education of these fields as well as researchers in choreography, gain under-standing about different experimental forms of writing forwarded by diverse choreographers and how writing is the motional organisation of images, signs, words and texts. The volume presents a new strand in expanded choreography and acts as inspiration for its continued evolution that engenders new adapta-tions between language, writing and choreography.

Ideal for students, scholars and researchers of choreography and dance studies.

Leena Rouhiainen is Head of the Research Institute of the University of the Arts Helsinki, Finland, and Professor of Artistic Research at the university's Theatre Academy. She is a dancer and choreographer whose research interests lie in experimental writing, phenomenology and artistic research.

Kirsi Heimonen is University Researcher at the Research Institute of the University of the Arts Helsinki, Finland. Her background is in dance, choreography, somatic movement practices and experimental writing.

Rebecca Hilton is Professor of Choreography in the research area Site-Event-Encounter, at Stockholm University of the Arts, Sweden. As a performer, writer, pedagogue and researcher, she works to unfold relationships between embodied knowledges, oral traditions and choreographic systems.

Chrysa Parkinson is Professor of Dance and Head of the Subject Area Dance at Stockholm University of the Arts, Sweden. Her research focus is on performers' perspectives and authorship.

WRITING CHOREOGRAPHY

Textualities of and beyond Dance

Edited by Leena Rouhiainen, Kirsi Heimonen,
Rebecca Hilton and Chrysa Parkinson

Routledge
Taylor & Francis Group

LONDON AND NEW YORK

Designed cover image: Drawing and writing by Kirsi Heimonen and Leena Rouhiainen. Photo by Jan Rosström ©

First published 2024
by Routledge
4 Park Square, Milton Park, Abingdon, Oxon OX14 4RN

and by Routledge
605 Third Avenue, New York, NY 10158

Routledge is an imprint of the Taylor & Francis Group, an informa business

British Library Cataloguing-in-Publication Data
A catalogue record for this book is available from the British Library

ISBN: 9781032502144 (hbk)
ISBN: 9781032501987 (pbk)
ISBN: 9781003397427 (ebk)

DOI: 10.4324/9781003397427

Typeset in Galliard
by codeMantra

CONTENTS

ACKNOWLEDGEMENTS

Writing Choreography: Textualities of and beyond Dance is the off-spring of the editors' life-long work in and passion for dance and choreography. What first triggered the collaboration between them was the *Artistic Doctorates in Europe: Third Cycle Provision in Dance and Performance* (ADiE), an Erasmus+ funded project they contributed to between 2016 and 2019 (www.artisticdoc-torates.com). After the project ended, they continued their exchange becoming more and more curious about one shared interest. In their recent artistic and research activities, they all have, in different ways, engaged with writing and language-based processes in choreography and have witnessed others doing so as well. This interest and awareness led to the book proposal for Routledge that resulted in the volume at hand.

We thank all the contributing authors, whose singular approaches to the topic offer invaluable insight into the practices of expanded choreography. Without their efforts, this volume would not have come into being nor would it be as rich as it has turned out to be. We are appreciative of the support Routledge has given us in compiling the book. Our express thanks go to Steph Hines, who kept us updated about the publishing process and tirelessly responded to all our queries.

We are likewise grateful to the reviewers of this volume who provided the volume with appreciated rigor through their constructive commentary. Our specific thanks also go to the institutional environment we work in, namely the University of the Arts Helsinki and the Stockholm University of the Arts, that provided us with working time to write and edit the book.

1

INTRODUCTION

Leena Rouhiainen, Kirsi Heimonen, Rebecca Hilton
and Chrysa Parkinson

Here the four editors talk about writing and choreography, and co-authoring this introduction.

One editor (OE): Might we start with this quote from Yvonne Rainer:

> What the body can say without verbal language is limited, which is why I so frequently used language in my dances … to tell stories mostly. I would speak or project texts and later used more elaborate scripts, including multi-media.
> (Jayamanne, Kapur, and Rainer 1986 as reported by Dempster 1995, 22)

Or this?

> […] choreography is just a frame, a structure, a language where much more than dance is inscribed.
> (Jérôme Bel as reported by Bauer 2008, 42)

Another editor (AE): I guess it's also a lot about what you consider writing and how you write. The *how* of the what … I like what poet Imamu Amiri Baraka says about writing machines:

> If I invented a word placing machine, an 'expression inscriber,' if you will, then I would have a kind of instrument into which I could step & sit or sprawl or hang & not only use my fingers to make words express feelings but elbows, feet, head, behind, and all the sounds I wanted, screams, grunts, taps, itches….
> (Baraka 1971, 156)

DOI: 10.4324/9781003397427-1

AE: All three of these quotes capture aspects of the subject, but there are so many ways to consider it, and as William Forsythe (2012, 201) says, "To reduce choreography to a single definition is to not understand the most crucial of its mechanisms: to resist and reform previous conceptions of its definitions."

AE: Yes, choreography currently is a dynamic, mutable, even uncontainable art form and when we talk about choreography in this volume, we are definitely talking about it as something that continues to move and manifest beyond the framework of what some might call dance, or *a* dance.

AE: As in expanded choreography?

AE: Exactly, Anna Leon (2022, 23) describes expanded choreography as a "non-centralised network of practices and ideas probing what *else* choreography may be;" this seems reasonable to me.

AE: And the particular "what *else*" this volume is exploring or "probing" are practices of writing choreography; after all "graphia" denotes writing.

AE: And chorea signifies dance, which all we editors and contributors have backgrounds in, at the same time as we are all somehow working with textualities of and beyond dance.

AE: Hmmm, chorea can also denote a chorus, or a group dance so what if we collectively author this introduction; so that multiple things become a single thing — a simple surface with complexity underneath?

AE: That would work; in fact, some of us have co-authored so often over the years that sometimes I can't even remember who wrote what.

AE: I really like it when that happens, it animates me.

AE: So, it's decided! Our multiple voices will now intermingle to form an expanded yet single authorship, which will situate the motifs, threads and themes we are exploring in this volume. Here we go:

Editors in Polyphonic Unison (EiPU): Conveying textual approaches to choreography, this volume proposes different ways in which language, text and writing inform current choreographic practice. *Writing Choreography: Textualities of and beyond Dance* engages with choreography in the expanded field of transdisciplinary processes, moving with and beyond the conventions of dance. In these practices, forms of writing organise the actions of human and more-than-human performers in various settings. While the production of writing and text are anthropocentric processes, language-based exposition has only recently (in the historic scheme of things) become central to choreographic artists. It is our experience that in daily practice in the fields of dance, choreography and artistic research, there is a growing interest in the ways experimentations with writing and reading inform the processes and performance of choreography. This volume shares a spectrum of processes and practices that range in scale from local to international, from artistic to pedagogic, and from intimate to historic. In observing and discussing the work of seminal international choreographers, as well as reflecting on our own work and that of peers and colleagues, we decided that a volume focusing on textual approaches to choreography would be a relevant addition to the field.

Our curatorial process began with extending invitations to dance-artists, choreographers, dramaturges, writers, interdisciplinary artists and artist-researchers whom we knew were working in the area of expanded choreography and whose work had an existing relationship to reading, writing, text and language. The invitation:

> We are inviting you to contribute to the anthology *Writing Choreography* by submitting one of the following: 1) an experimental, performative or poetic choreographic text with the opportunity of utilising alternative layouts and images, 2) an essay describing your practice of choreographic writing performed in other formats than printed paper, again with the opportunity of including portions of experimental text and images, or 3) a more scholarly article about timely conceptions and approaches to choreographic writing. While including concrete examples of materials in choreographic writing, please also respond to one or more of the following questions when composing your contribution: How in your view does choreography write? With what methods, tools and materials does it do so? Who writes in choreography, and for whom does choreography write? What does choreography write on, what turns choreography into writing or vice-versa, with what or whom does choreography write? When does choreography not write? In the end, what is writing in choreography? How does choreographic writing expand our conceptions about writing? What role does reading play in the above-mentioned questions?

The volume has contributions from 15 authors, including us. In addition to this introduction, a contextualising chapter and a poetic conclusion, it consists of ten chapters presented in a three-part structure: *Transcribing performance into writing*; *Practices of writing that choreograph*; and *Choreography as writing with*. The three sections interweave practically oriented chapters with more theoretical ones, a conscious editorial attempt to keep practice and theory in dialogue with, rather than separate from one and other. It may be useful to note that some contributions or parts of the chapters are concrete pieces of textual choreography and others are more *about* textual choreography, reflecting the many different approaches to the theme.

In the contextualising chapter, we the two of the co-editors, Leena Rouhiainen and Kirsi Heimonen, approach the volume's themes from a dance studies perspective, with a specific focus on Western dance art. We unfold a history of textual choreography as experienced from a periphery, detailing how writing, text and language-related international practices have informed and influenced Finnish choreographic practice over the past 50 years. In exploring the volume's themes, the chapter lays out some of the ways in which writing choreography has manifested over time and place, locally and internationally.

Part 1, *Transcribing performance into writing*, includes various approaches to transcription as method, including a performance text, an entanglement of choreographic and writing practices, a past choreography as a future film and visual documentation of a planetary pas-de-deux as a form of choreoreading. These contributions each play with experimental and expanded forms of writing and reading, introducing new language-based ways in which choreography performs.

In the dance theatre work of Australian choreographer Vicki Van Hout, talking and writing, moving and choreographing, culture and community, the personal and the political, all combine to create a coalition of coexistences, with no one language or style or genre ever subsuming another. Her contribution to this volume explores relations between choreography, dance history, orality and literacy as well as speaking to the complexity of relations between contemporary art and traditional cultural practices, which inspire, situate and complicate her creative processes. Verbatim transcriptions of a live performance are accompanied by her reflections on the ways speaking/dancing/writing/choreographing and contemporary/traditional/indigenous/colonial/political/personal perspectives converge in her work; she asks, whose dance is this anyway and what does it mean, make and do, to claim authorship, to perform, to own and to write choreography?

Interdisciplinary artist alys longley's contribution considers textual choreography through reflecting on her previous artistic and collaborative work. Proposing writing as a form of movement and exploring the performative characteristics of language, the chapter entitled *The place where the actual and fictional touch, the place where a language flicks channels* discusses how language and writing informed two performance processes, namely h u m a t t e r i n g (2022) and Mistranlation Laboratory (2019). In contemplating choreographic composition, longley is interested in playing with and probing textuality via practices of erasure, striking out, experiments with font settings, alternative page layouts, concrete poetry, drawing and image generation. She works in the expanded art field, softening the disciplinary constraints of both choreography and writing.

Performer, choreographer and pedagogue Jennifer Lacey's text takes shape as a film treatment — a proposal for a not-yet-made film — which relates in detail a choreographic situation that has already happened. She writes to permanently record the ephemerality of a situation that was both social and choreographic, moving her studio practice from stage to page, simultaneously documenting a past and proposing a future. She roams through these pasts, presents and futures via a free-wheeling, footnoting practice, which reveals the "worlds within worlds, times within times, places within places" present in the cultural and artistic practices of the various communities of dance people she encounters. Lacey depicts ways in which her practices of writing — in relation to studio, stage and page — inform, inflect and affect the before(s), during(s) and after(s) of her choreographic practice.

Simo Kellokumpu's chapter, *Invitation: choreoreading EXOXƎ* emerges from their post-doctoral artistic research process. Referring to hyper-reading, a notion coined by James Sosnoski, they invite readers to attune to their bodies in specific ways while reading their article. Choreoreading is made concrete when Kellokumpu addresses the reader as a performer in collaboration with the textual artwork, guiding awareness towards the bodily practice of reading, the situatedness, the tempo, the tracking of the eyeballs, etc. Forwarding hyper-reading via choreoreading has led Kellokumpu to reflect on issues of composition in relation to attention, and to exploring the many potential selves we each harbour. Kellokumpu looks to queering choreographic conventions by speculating on ways that practices of science-fiction-ing and outer space-ing might generate an alternative choreographic-being-in-the-world.

Part 2, *Practices of writing that choreograph*, offers experimentations with various writing formats considered *as* choreography. These include a letter, email correspondence, a ship's log and a restaging of historical figures' journals. Through these trans-compositional processes, the authors commune with absences and presences, with real and imagined interlocuters. These texts highlight how practices of embodiment and embeddedness both slip from and exist through writing, sometimes purposefully and sometimes inadvertently becoming choreography.

Choreographer and researcher Lynda Gaudreau has a dedicated letter-writing ritual, which anchors her artistic research practice. In her article, a personal letter to Saint Hildegard of Bingen is interwoven with e-mail correspondence between the author and her good friend Barbara De Coninck. A strong and sudden emotional experience, had while standing in front of a painting by Vincent Van Gogh, leads her to ask guidance from Hildegard. The correspondence between the friends recounts some personal history, addresses issues rising from the event at the museum and shares various fragmented ponderings on art making, destruction, disagreement and freedom inspired by specific philosophers and theorists. Gaudreau's letter writing invokes and attunes with her chosen saint, a practice which traverses multiple times, spaces and ideas. The practice of writing again and again to somebody, knowing you will never receive a response, urges the author toward questions of art-making as orientation, as transmission, as speculation, as hopefulness.

Performer, choreographer and writer Amaara Raheem's textual choreography draws on experiences she had during an artistic residency on a cargo ship travelling from Vancouver to Shanghai. The journey takes 24 days. Her search for relevant compositional and choreographic strategies through which to explore the immersive intensity of the experience included devising ways to move with and communicate with her fellow traveller, the crew and the ship itself. She created multiple archives of words, acts and gestures, collected via practices of conversing, spying and eavesdropping, and through studying and copying the ship's logbook. She finds that merely residing in the ship is unsustainable, and through her relational practices of residing-with, she explores processes of change, changing and being changed. The article *Logging: expedition and encounter* recounts in detail the embodiments, experiences and experiments had on, in and with the ship and its denizens. Raheem's performative textual choreography frames this transformative experience, and shares her agile, reflexive, in situ practice wherein choreography writes and writing choreographs.

Dramaturg and writer Martin Hargreaves contributes *Notes on betrayal*. The result of a performative writing practice that involves letter writing, fabulation and restaging, Hargreaves uses Susan Sontag and Jean Genet's own writings to queer their genealogies and choreographically "put them in touch." His evocations exceed, and betray, the historical figures he calls forth in a playful, erotic chaos of misfires, and not-not true stories.

Part 3, *Choreography as writing with*, addresses choreography and writing in collaboration with other human and more-than-human agents. The collected articles explore these themes via poetic texts sewn onto fabric, processual interweaves of writing, drawing and speaking, and the politics and poetry embedded in a co-authored, site-specific textual choreography. These contributions explore collaborative endeavours in relation to other artists, places and things, interlinking writing with other expressive media, materials and environments not necessarily associated with either literature or choreography.

Marie Fahlin's *Cicatrix textus II* has been created in a solitary process of sewing. Fahlin pierces her materials' surfaces with needle and thread, creating a kinetic writing that leaves a scar where language might have been. Each of the three choreographies in this work participates in its own reading through sensual logics and deviations, undertows and overlays that seem to simultaneously create and mend rifts in the fabric of sense-making.

In their chapter, the trio Emma Cocker, Nikolaus Gansterer and Mariella Greil revisit their collaborative artistic research project, *Choreo-graphic Figures*, offering insights into and examples of experimental textual practices situated at the interstices of choreography, drawing and writing. The chapter *Choreo-graphic writing: towards more-than-one means of inscription* is accessible in two ways: in this volume, as an article sharing and reflecting on their collaborative process, and via a link to their exposition on the Research Catalogue, a free online platform. The Research Catalogue exposition introduces and/or performs concrete textual outcomes of the choreographic writing processes generated by the trio. The article discusses the rich methodology that inscribes the thinking-feeling-knowing, which characterises their artistic practice, doing so from the different perspectives of the three collaborators. Their article highlights the inventive cross-artform and multi-medial opportunities textual choreography makes possible.

In their duet, *The choreographic politics of a staircase*, Heimonen and Rouhiainen introduce their score-based approach to co-authored site-specific textual choreography. They present the outcome of their choreographic writing in relation to their exploration of the staircase at Parliament House in Helsinki. They discuss the political dimensions of generating both the text and the choreography itself, highlighting the significance of framing an open-ended process. They also share insights regarding the project's collaborative and site-specific characteristics. Here, they call on André Lepecki's notion of choreopolitics as a practice of freedom. Commitment, dedication and repetition are central to the duo's politics of choreographic practice, and the invitation here is for readers to continue to perform the choreography through the reading of the published texts. Emerging from a collaborative endeavour by the duo, their textual choreography extends into the public realm, providing an opportunity to continue enacting alternative choreographic futures.

The volume ends with a poetic response to the theme of *Writing Choreography* generated by us, the four co-editors, produced via a textual choreography score, developed by Rouhiainen and Heimonen. In *Choreographic aftermath* the focus is on is on enabling the absent presence or present absence of dance–artists, choreographers, dramaturges, writers and interdisciplinary artists engaging in inscribing choreography on the page. In so doing, the co-choreographed piece writes an appreciation of the different bodies, places and approaches involved in this volume.

OE: This writing process feels a bit like choreography.

AE: The unison?

AE: All of it, the singular surface, the plurality of voices, the complexity. The coming together to make something.

AE: The authorship becomes permeable, even questionable, like in a choreographic process. Like when you're dancing.

AE: Authorship and authorisation, signature and ownership — they come up when thinking through choreography and writing. Recognition, stability and continuity...

AE: Are you talking about permanence? And impermanence?

AE: Yes, the fading or staying stable is choreographic in and of itself. The relative permanence and impermanence of the medium you choose to write with choreographs.

AE: … and the dance itself writes: choreo graphy — χορεία γραφή

AE: Ah, transcribed performance becomes writing, practices of writing choreograph, and choreography writes with.

EiPU: Yes!

References

Baraka, Imamu Amiri. 1971. *Technology and Ethos, Raise Rage Rays Raze: Essays Since 1965*. London: Random House.

Bauer, Una. 2008. "Jérôme Bel: An Interview." *Performance Research* 13(1): 42–48. https://doi-org.ezproxy.uniarts.fi/10.1080/13528160802465516.

Dempster, Elizabeth. 1995. "Women Writing the Body: Let's Watch a Little How She Dances." In *Bodies of the Text: Dance as Theory, Literature as Dance*, edited by Ellen W. Goellner and Jacqueline Shea Murphy, 21–38. New Brunswick, NJ: Rutgers University Press.

Forsythe, William. 2012. "Choreographic Objects / / 2008." In *Dance: Documents of Contemporary Art*, edited by André Lepecki, 201–203. London and Cambridge, MA: The MIT Press.

Leon, Anna. 2022. *Expanded Choreographies – Choreographic Histories: Trans-Historical Perspectives Beyond Dance and Human Bodies in Motion*. Bielefeld: Transcript Verlag.

2

MOTIFS AND INSIGHTS

Textual choreography, dance studies and local conditions in Finland

Leena Rouhiainen and Kirsi Heimonen

This chapter outlines some themes that could be understood to ground the orientation of textual choreography that the book *Writing Choreography: Textualities of and beyond Dance* addresses. It draws upon dance and performance studies in focusing on issues in progressive contemporary choreography from the perspective of Western dance art during the late 20th and early 21st centuries. The text touches upon such notions as North American postmodern dance, the textuality of dance, conceptual dance, expanded choreography and artistic research in detailing influences on, tendencies in and characteristics of textual choreography. In so doing, the chapter interlinks related insights and issues to the developments of dance art in Finland. It makes concrete the movement of transcultural influences in dance and how the conventions of dance and choreography evolve in local environments as hybrid forms and through different contemporaneities. Short vignettes by the authors play with words and themes to introduce the contents of each section. The chapter is meant to offer insight into the context from which *Writing Choreography* was initiated and to provide context for the other sections of the volume.

Introduction

In this chapter, we will discuss a selection of significant interlinks we perceive between choreography and language and writing and text from the perspective of Western dance as a performing art form. Whilst we might briefly note some earlier developments, our examination mainly relates to the choreography of the late 20th and early 21st centuries. We support the fact that choreographic history is a "collection of interlinked — but not linearly, smoothly connectible — paths" (Leon 2022, 27), which appear differently when observed from different

DOI: 10.4324/9781003397427-2

situational positions. As the authors of this book are mainly based in the Nordic and Oceanian contexts, *Writing Choreography* can be understood to be addressing Western dance art from its periphery. In the following, we will discuss some fragments of the related canon of dance and will include specific insights into developments in Finland. We, the authors of this Chapter, are white, middle-aged female dance–artists, choreographers and artist–researchers, who have worked in the context of the Finnish dance scene, mainly in Helsinki since the early 1990s. We both have experience in a range of approaches to contemporary dance, site-specific performance, somatic methods, improvisation and affiliated artistic research. Being aware of our privileged position, these practices inform the perspectives from which we write. We acknowledge that we are offering only a partial and schematic view of developments in choreography and that different geopolitical contexts have different kinds of related contemporaneities and experiences. In contextualising present-day practices and forms of writing choreography and discoursing with dance studies, we hope to advance its sphere by highlighting tendencies, issues and impacts. At the same time, we hope to offer relevant background information conducive to informing the other sections of the book. This chapter, therefore, is more theoretically oriented than many of the rest, which mainly speak from the practical perspectives of the dance–artists, choreographers, dramaturges, writers and interdisciplinary artists contributing to the volume.

Emergent horizons

Dance! Feet and legs fencing at the French Court. Express! Ephemeral and magnetising individual expression of the non-verbal reaches of corporeality. Act! Moving into a random avantgarde and workmanly everyday gestures. Partner! The intermix of diverse sources and contaminated genealogies form hybrid localities. Alter! Peripheries change traditions.

Deriving from the Greek words *choreia* and *graph*, etymologically the term "choreography" relates to movement, dance and rhythm, notions of space or region, as well as writing (Foster 2011). What is well established in the Western canon of dance art is the understanding that writing has been involved in the practices of choreography ever since European court ballet began its emergence in the early 16th century. Dancing masters in the Italian and French courts, who were quickly copied by those in other European countries, wrote dancing manuals. These guidebooks, containing both writing and drawing, were first about social dances and intended for the members of the court. Later, they described ballets that were performed by professional dancers on proscenium stages.

According to André Lepecki, the first version of the term "choreography" was coined by the French dance theoretician and dancing master Thoinot

Arbeau in his book *Orchésographie* from 1589, to denote "a technology that creates a body disciplined to move according to the commands of writing" (Lepecki 2006, 6). Arbeau's book included instructions for dancers, musicians and fencers, and was an innovation in dance notation at the time (Arbeau 1967; Cohen 1974/1977). In 1700, Raoul Feuillet published *Chorégraphie*, in which he introduced the dance notation system devised by Pierre Beauchamp, who was the principal dancing master in Louis XIV's court and supported the professionalisation of dance. Known as the Feuillet notation system, it allowed for a detailed inscription of the movements of different body parts, especially the feet and legs, as well as describing spatial movement patterns of dances. It was widely adopted in England and throughout Northern Europe allowing knowledgeable readers to develop required movement skills and learn dances without relying on the instruction of dancing masters. It also conveyed some teaching methods for professional dancers, something which began to be increasingly focused upon, and thus the gulf between social and concert dance widened (Cohen 1974/1977; Au 1988/1995; Foster 1998a). These developments in codifying, preserving and disseminating choreography had a foundational impact on the conception of dance in the West. Susan Foster points out:

> Even though construed as a language in Enlightenment thought, the body's gestures begin to signify that which cannot be spoken. This unique role of gesture prepares the way for a complete separation between dance and text that occurs in the early decades of the nineteenth century. Dance becomes imbued with a dynamic charisma, and text is assigned the ability to interpret and theorize about the ephemeral yet magnetizing presence of the dance.
>
> (Foster 1995, 234)

The above-mentioned anecdotes underline that, at the inception of the modern view on choreography, writing was important to the evolution of Western dance art. The understanding that choreography is the art of writing dances on paper is still significant for many of us, even if it is a definition that Foster (2011) surmises was last used by Rudolf Laban in his book *Choreutics* (1966). In line with the previous quotation, she also points out that the term "choreography" fell out of use in the 19th century, only to re-emerge in the early 20th century to denote processes of individual expression through movement and the act of creating dances (Foster 2011). This orientation was typical to what became known as "modern dance," a term that brings together two different genealogies, namely, American modern dance and German Ausdruckstanz.

Especially in the North American context, the 1960s witnessed another far-reaching change in the conception and production of dance. In an effort to establish dance as a contemporary art form, the predominantly white avantgarde in New York broke away from the conventions of ballet and modern dance. They viewed dance as an art form with the potential to act in and on the wider cultural field, an art form that could be critically investigated, actively reflected upon and de- and reconstructed. They championed experimentality and eschewed traditional modes of representation (Foster 1986; Monni, Järvinen, and Laakso 2022). The medium of dance itself was questioned, and new kinds of choreographic approaches emerged, including the use of improvisational chance, rule and task-based strategies. The vocabulary of dance was expanded to include everyday movements, the performance of which presented the actions themselves rather than aesthetic representations of them. What was of interest was a dissolution of the performer's self and achievements, presenting a more workmanlike image of the dancer. Through its anti-illusionary approach, dance performance could be perceived as an attempt to portray dance as theory. For instance, a dance performance could be conceptual, its choreography enacted through performers interpreting scores, tasks or rules, rather than via a series of preordained movements, temporalities and spatial relations. Another period-defining change was that dance was often presented in public spaces rather than being confined to the theatre. With these shifts, choreo-graphy began to involve the arrangement of movement in conjunction with a diversity of sources, such as sculpture, film and spoken and recorded text, providing dance–artists with opportunities to critically investigate and reflect on the form of choreography itself. Dance–artists had active ties with such progressive art phenomena as happenings and performance art practices, as illustrated by the work of Allan Kaprow, E.A.T and Fluxus among others (Foster 1986; 2011; Banes 1992; Kukkonen 2014; Monni, Järvinen, and Laakso 2022). Choreographers collaborated not only with dancers but increasingly with artists from other mediums "exploring interdisciplinary modes of performance between dance and theatre, video and film, lighting design, new digital media working with set designers and sculptors" (Foster 2011, 66). Additionally, visual artists like Robert Morris adopted the roles of choreographer and performer in their own works (Rosenthal 2011).

North American dance of the 1960s and 1970s has resonated strongly in contemporary Western dance contexts ever since, Nordic and Oceanic countries included. Related developments have had an impact on the textual choreography that this volume addresses. In the 1980s, dance critic and historian Sally Banes coined the term "postmodern dance" to depict some of the developments from this period. Banes uses examples drawn from the work of the Judson Theatre and Grand Union collectives to describe the characteristics of postmodern dance in contrast to the already-canonised American modern dance. She refers to minimalism, everyday movement, chance-methods and emerging somatic practices, such as release-technique and contact improvisation. Despite some dispute about "postmodern dance" as a term, in the international field of dance studies, it now refers specifically to the aforementioned North American developments in dance (Banes 1987; 1992; 1995; Kukkonen 2014; Järvinen 2018). However, in the Nordic countries, there was no such canonised modern dance tradition against which postmodern dance could evolve. In Finland, there were some individual modern dance–artists and groups active during this period but not enough to generate a strong professional modern dance scene with its own identity. Here, modern dance progressed and developed in relation to European and American influences. It developed through individual Finnish dance–artists first studying and working in these continents, then returning home to pursue their careers as well as through invited international artists teaching and performing in Finland (Kukkonen 2014; see also Laakkonen 2018).

It is worth noting that, in Finland, the term "postmodern dance" was first introduced in the 1980s at the same time as the term "contemporary dance" came into use. Since then, contemporary dance has been used as an overarching expression to denote modern, postmodern and new dance, as well as such theatrical dance that bears influences from German Tanztheater and Japanese Butoh dance (Hämäläinen 1999). Currently, the two terms are used interchangeably and have replaced a third term used at the time, namely, "new dance." It denoted a European approach to contemporary dance, which incorporated influences from North American postmodern dance. The term was popularised by a British magazine titled *New Dance* (1977–1986), which featured practices of dance that advocated body-friendly, sensation-based-movement methods, differing from the more externally motivated movement skills typical to conventional modern dance and ballet. It, likewise, introduced its readers to new critical perspectives, including feminist and Marxist thinking. British new dance was also influenced by practices of performance art, radical theatre and experimental film, as well as the thinking of European theorists, such as Roland Barthes, Michel Foucault and Jacques Lacan (Rouhiainen 2003; Kukkonen 2014; Järvinen 2017).

In the 1970s and 1980s, the influences of late-modern dance techniques, such as Hawkins and Cunningham, as well as work emerging from Amsterdam's School for New Dance Development, were important for progressing the dance field in Finland. In the late 1980s and early 1990s, Butoh dance also brought new insights through dance–artists such as Masaki Iwana and Anzu Furukawa, who performed, conducted workshops and created choreography for Finnish dance–artists and audiences. German Tanztheater, especially through the work of Pina Bausch, was much admired, impacting the work of many Finnish choreographers. Likewise, American-born choreographer Carolyn Carlson collaborated closely with Finnish dancer Jorma Uotinen at the Groupe des Réchèrches Théâtrales de l'Opéra de Paris and continued to invite many Finns to perform in her pieces through the years. In the 1990s she even directed the Helsinki City Theatre Dance Group for a few years. These developments led to a more intense investigation of the body, and from the 1980s onwards, sensitivity to its experiential stances became central to contemporary dance practices and processes. Corporeality, together with the non-verbal reaches of experience, became an increasingly central source of both content and meaning in Finnish dance contexts (Kaiku 1997; Rouhiainen 2003).

What needs underlining are the diverse ways in which the transcultural influences discussed above have contaminated each other and the local conditions in which they were forwarded. This implies that dance and choreography developed through hybrid forms in Finland (Korppi-Tommola 2012). Hanna Järvinen (2018, 223) notes: "Peripheries can be viewed not simply as places imitating the centres, but as hybrid places that change traditions, as freer spaces in which different approaches meet and impact each other."[1] In the intermix of influences and approaches, what can be argued is that, before the late 1990s, the use of language, text, writing and speech were not focal to either choreographic practice nor the performance contexts of contemporary dance in Finland.

The absent presence and textuality of dance

Note! Diversified bodies. The problem of presence: inscribed bodies writing heterochronic performance in the era of new postmodernism. Scribble! Deconstructed bodies. Professional theories of corporeality decode human existence and the commonplace. Register! Political bodies. A political pluralisation of the transcultural.

Until the 1980s, the most common methodologies for dance studies had been via history, movement analysis, anthropology and aesthetics. A work that first broke with these approaches was Susan Foster's *Reading Dancing* (1986). In it, Foster observes the meaning-generating and meaning-subverting forces in choreographic works. According to Ellen W. Goellner and Jacqueline Shea Murphy (1995, 2), it "demonstrated the congeniality of Roland Barthes' physical and dynamic concept of textuality to dance theory and analysis. Foster showed how dance, like literary text, goes down in 'language.'" Elizabeth Dempster (1995) argues that Foster's vision of the body's movement as an act of writing reminds us of the bodily grounds of reading, writing, dancing and watching dance. Additionally, since dances come into existence through bodies that both produce and reproduce them, dances are texts written of and through inscribed bodies. She opines: "If postmodern dance is a 'writing' of the body, it is a writing that is conditional, circumstantial, and above all transitory: it is writing that erases itself in the act of being written" (Dempster 1995, 33). Foster herself argues:

> When the body is allowed to develop a polyvalent significance, dance likewise becomes a practice or activity rather than a contained object. Its dancing-ness comes to the foreground so that dance proliferates from a single phenomenon into countless different forms for making meaning. The body, no longer the stylus, the parchment, or the trace, becomes the process

itself of signing, a process created mutually by all those — choreographers, dancers, and viewers — engaged in the dance. In this world of writing dancing, the body of this text could, as if in counterpoint with the writing body, leap off the two-dimensional page: it could turn, lunge, twist, kick, suspend...and with a final gesture — was it "Going my way?" or "Thumbs up"? — vanish.

(Foster 1986, 227)

The above view relates to the fact that, by the 1990s, the socio-cultural and political dimensions of embodiment, deconstruction and the linguistic turn, as well as the problem of representation became focal concerns of feminist theory, sociology, literary and cultural studies as well as philosophy and co-relatively of dance studies. Through the critical questioning of categories and conceptions related to embodiment, such as race, gender, identity, visuality and the gaze, what emerged was an understanding "that visual, temporal and nonwritten 'texts' such as dance, could provide" these issues with astute critical analyses (Goellner and Murphy 1995, 1; see also Kukkonen 2014). Identity, subjectivity and embodiment began to be understood as complex performative phenomena enacted in relation to their situational settings. Following these developments, some dance scholars have pointed towards a textual turn in dance (cf. Franko 2015; 2019; Lepecki and Morris 2019).

Dance scholars, such as Lepecki (2004a) specifically began to observe the problem of the presence of the body, which had previously been the discursive and ontological position through which dance had defined itself as an autonomous art form. He underlined that the body remains absent or only ambiguously present in the historical inscriptions of choreography and argued that this carries political implications for 20th-century dance practices and theories. Performed movement is never completely describable in words or images, and thus the body is only partially implied in choreographic notations. In his writings, Lepecki (2004b) repeatedly addresses this asymmetry between writing and dance that specifies dance's presence as a motion that escapes regulation and documentation. Lepecki even opines that it is this strange split between the body and presence that allows us to start addressing dance as a complex critical theory. He writes:

In capturing the evanescent dance, the scholar, the critic, the dance audience, even the dancer relies on a complex integration of sense-memories, associations, displacements, kinesthetic memories. Such is the inscription of the mnemonic traces of dance onto the body and the unconscious. But there is also an inscription of the dance onto the mnemonic mechanisms of technology, either through photography, film, the writing of the critic, or movement notation.

(Lepecki 2004a, 4)

Here, Lepecki discusses the complexity that characterises the absent presence of dance performance and its documentation by and for human bodies. He comes to underline that this complexity relates to a crisis in how to approach the visible dancing body and its endless referentiality. The presence of movement already slips into absence before it can be grasped by vision or language in any satisfactory way. Lepecki (2004a, 129) opines: "Before an absent presence and an absent movement, the problem dance puts before writing is of how movement and words can be placed under arrest. Dance confronts us with the impossibility of such a project." He agrees that choreography involves writing that aims at guaranteeing that dance's present is given both a past and a future but notes that it is in a constant "dissatisfaction before its own project" (Lepecki 2006, 125). He claims that choreographic writing aims at capturing dance that disappears in the act of its materialisation, it aims at capturing "irretrievable nows"(Lepecki 2006, 124). However, in his view, dancing and writing are co-dependent. They reshape each other via a sense of a shared, yet never fully graspable, ground (Lepecki 2004b).

The above relates to how dance can be considered both a means of malleable inscription and a (re)presentation of changing socio-cultural values and political issues. Foster (1998b, 5) suggests that choreography is a "tradition of codes and conventions through which meaning is constructed in dance." While choreographers sort, reject and construct physical images, they manifest a style of decoding prevailing choreographic conventions that determine how dances and bodily gestures mean what they do. In this sense, Foster observes that choreographers theorise corporeality. Choreographers engage with and fashion the body's semiotic field, and choreography can be considered a "theoretical act in which decisions made about the development and sequencing of movement entail a reflection on corporeal, individual, social and political identities" (Foster 2013, 27). Foster (2013, 27) proposes that choreography presents "a theory of what the body is, what it has been historically, and what it might become in the future."

* * * *

In the 1980s, the contemporary dance field in Finland became more professionalised. Several dance theatres, many of which are active to date, were founded in the 1970s. Commenting on recent developments, dance critic Irma Vienola-Lindfors wrote:

> The 1970s witnessed the burgeoning of tenacious free groups which have also received state subsidy — although not to a sufficient extent. The dance theatres *Raatikko* in Vantaa, *Rollo* in Helsinki, *Mobita* in Tampere and *Aurinkobaletti* in Turku, as well as the folkdance group *Katrilli* are at present clearing a path for the professionals in their field. The Helsinki City Theatre Dance Group, with Jorma Uotinen as artistic director, stands on a firm basis.
> (Vienola-Lindfors 1984, 10)

Since the 1970s, influential international dance companies performed at the Kuopio Dance festival and "in addition to high-class performances, [the festival] has yielded courses, for example, on which amateurs and professionals in the field have had a chance to get vital supplementary tuition" (Vienola-Lindfors 1984, 13–15). The first Finnish magazine focusing on dance, *Tanssi-lehti*, published its premiere issue in 1981. The National Dance Council was established in 1983, and dance finally received an official status in the national arts management system. Aside from the Ballet School of the Finnish National Opera and Ballet, professional education was made possible by the founding of the dance department at the Theatre Academy in Helsinki in 1983. It offered Master of Arts degrees in contemporary dance performance and choreography. The Theatre Academy earned the right to offer third-cycle education in 1988, which supported the development of various approaches to dance research in the following decade. In turn, Zodiak Presents was founded in 1986 by a critical group of dance–artists with backgrounds in new dance. These dance–artists were in search of a freer relationship with the body and identified more with ideas emerging from the visual arts, live and performance art, as well as experimental theatre rather than with the conventions of modern dance or ballet (Monni 2007). After ten years of work, the collective evolved into the governmentally supported Zodiak Centre for New Dance, which is still an influential venue for contemporary dance and performance in the country.

In the 1980s, books focusing on Finnish dance art and dance–artists were published with more frequency. They offered different perspectives on the evolution of Finnish modern and contemporary dance and included, for example, a book commemorating the 15th anniversary of the Kuopio Dance Festival entitled *Celebration of Dance* (Reunamäki and Patomäki 1984) and the visually ambitious volume *Uotinen The Art of Dance* (Miettinen et al. 1985), which portrayed choreographer Jorma Uotinen's work. An anecdote worth mentioning is that in his renown solo Jojo first premiered in 1979, Uotinen recited excerpts from Pablo Neruda's poetry while dancing. The 50th anniversary of the Union of Finnish Dance–Artists was celebrated through a published volume focusing on the developments in dance during the previous five decades (Arvola and Räsänen 1987). Riitta Repo (1989) published a study about the professionalisation of and education in dance in Finland. The developments mentioned in the previous paragraph and these publications point to the fact that, in the 1980s, discursive exchange around dance increased and played an important role in strengthening understanding of the art form and its potentialities.

Towards the end of the 1980s, and into the 1990s, Finnish dance was a heterochronic intermix, shaped by simultaneous, oppositional and referential interconnections between several different interests, tendencies and developments. Dance–artists of this period employed a variety of distinctly different expressive and aesthetic approaches to explore a range of processual relationships with the medium of dance. They also tested expectations of and relationships to dance audience(s) (Makkonen 2017). Dance–artists became interested in things critical theorists and philosophers had to say about the body, gender, politics and society, exploring them in relation to performing and choreography. New dance representatives, such as Sanna Kekäläinen, Kirsi Monni, Liisa Pentti and Riitta Pasanen, were especially curious about concurrent theoretical insights emerging from feminist theory, poststructuralism and phenomenology (Monni 2007; Kukkonen 2014). At the same time, the first doctoral studies in dance were published. Aino Sarje completed her doctoral dissertation in aesthetics at the University of Helsinki in 1994. It addresses Finnish conceptions of dance art in the 1980s on the basis of interviews from 100 dance–artists and experts (Räsänen 1994; Sarje 1994). Jaana Parviainen earned her doctoral degree in philosophy at Tampere University in 1998 with a dissertation entitled *Bodies Moving and Moved*, which explored the nature of the dancing subject and the dance work through a phenomenological perspective (Parviainen 1998). In 1999, Soili Hämäläinen was the first Doctor of Arts in Dance to graduate from the Theatre Academy with a dissertation exploring ways of teaching choreography (Hämäläinen 1999). By the end of the 1990s, several dance–artists and choreographers began their doctoral studies at the Theatre Academy, including Riitta Pasanen-Willberg, Leena Rouhiainen and Kirsi Monni.

This was the time when artistic research began to be debated more heatedly. The department of theatre studies at the University of Helsinki began to focus on performance studies, which impacted discussions in contemporary dance and theatre, and strengthened the field of performance and live art. Consequently, the programme in Live Art and Performance Studies was founded in 2002 at the Theatre Academy. At this time, community dance entered and expanded the field, impacting the professional identity of dancers and choreographers. Related socio-political debate concerning who is allowed to dance, and how dance is discussed and introduced in different social contexts also emerged (Heimonen and Kaiku 1999). All of this activity impacted the hybridisation of dance art as it moved beyond proscenium stages and out into society more broadly. Speech and projected text in performance began to be more commonplace in performance. In these respects, the Finnish dance scene could be understood to coincide with European trends. Lepecki (2004b) argued that, by the early 21st century, European contemporary dance, as a transcultural practice with choreographers from diverse training backgrounds, social and national contexts and conflicting aesthetic lineages, had moved from a theatrical to a performance paradigm. In this context, choreography became a field of trans-disciplinary creation "where the visual arts, performance art, political art meet performance theory" (Lepecki 2004b, 172).

At the beginning of the 21st century, in Finland, there was a renewed interest in the heritage and influences of American postmodern dance. For example, the work of postmodern dance luminaries Steve Paxton, Lisa Nelson, Yvonne Rainer and Deborah Hay were staged at the Kiasma Theatre and

Zodiak Centre for New Dance in Helsinki. However, in the broader Western dance context, there also was discussion about a new postmodernism in dance. The term highlighted the fact that, alongside the influences of American post-modern dance, things such as emotion, narrative, virtuosity and interpretation began returning as viable artistic approaches. Paradoxically, such things were eschewed by the original American postmodern dance movement. In any case, the continued use of hybrid forms, visible multiculturalism and the fusion of high and low culture all revealed the complexity of contemporary dance at this time (Reynolds and McCormick 2003; Kukkonen 2014). This was also evident in the Finnish dance scene. Over the past few decades, a diversity of thematics have informed dance performance: explorations of gender, ethnic, generational and cultural backgrounds, co-authorship and devising methods, digital technologies, other dance forms (folk, street, historic and culturally specific dances), other art forms (film, sound, performance art and the visual arts), the changing role and position of the audience (participatory perfor-mance) amongst others (Makkonen 2017). In Finland, and elsewhere in the Western world, the term "choreography" is currently applied to describe pro-cesses of structuring and regulating movement, not necessarily only the move-ment of human beings, in highly diverse situations, both within and beyond theatre dance contexts.

The discursivity of choreography and its expanded field

Recast! In the pulling apart of choreography and dance, object and text pose poignant problems. Contort! Complicated correspondences and limitless disorientation. Uproot! Transversal ideas redefine visual-auditive-sculptural practice in between communicative media. Transplant! Not-dance, a misnomer.

In current European contemporary choreography, a number of choreogra-phers incorporate philosophy and critical theory into their creative processes, utilising reading, writing and discussion as artistic methods. They simultane-ously experiment with choreographic practice and various communication me-dia, resulting in conventional performance-making being imbued with and/ or disrupted by concepts, texts and language in performance (Cvejić 2015; Monni 2022). This tendency relates specifically to conceptual dance and informs the recent approach of expanded choreography in association with such choreographers as Jérôme Bel, Xavier Le Roy, Boris Charmantz, Mårten Spångberg, La Ribot, Vera Mantero, Jonathan Burrows, Tino Senghal and Mette Edvardsen, amongst others. Anna Pakes points out:

These artists offer a reflexive engagement with the task of choreography, questioning its premises and results. They tend to eschew conventional dance virtuosity and choreographic structures. They often replace or supplement choreographed movement with dancers speaking or interacting with various kinds of object or text.

(Pakes 2019, 196)

Pakes (2019) unfolds the opportunities and problems the term "conceptual dance" invokes. She notes features that are similar to conceptual art, for example, those of self-reflectiveness and the use of irony. Interestingly, whilst artists affiliated with conceptual dance present their work at dance venues and festivals, they do so in ways that question audience expectations of dance. They typically evade virtuosic bodies and identifiable dance techniques, and the work often involves dancers speaking, something that can be considered a disruptive strategy in relation to a traditionally non-verbal art form. Anti-aestheticism is also a feature. Pakes implies that the idiosyncratic movement these choreographers utilise causes disorientation and thus no longer provides aesthetic pleasure for the audience. Conceptual dance does not, however, reject the physical medium, which differentiates it somewhat from conceptual visual art, which highlights the importance of the artistic idea over all else. Choreography requires perception in order to be appreciated, and choreography associated with conceptual dance can be understood as employing a physical medium in an extended sense. The extended medium, however, is where dance and choreography begin to separate into choreography that is dance, and choreography that is not dance. The later makes use of other means of presence, presentation and performance. The "pulling apart of choreography and dance within the art form is arguably part of a wider trend towards expanding the notion of choreography" (Pakes 2019, 201–203).

Pakes (2019) understands conceptual dance to be a genre, a mode of dance that performs an idea through engagement with questions of (de)materialisation, an approach consistent with conceptual art in its deployment of various other things, events or occurrences. Instead, Bojana Cvejić considers the term a misnomer. According to her, the term "conceptual dance" has never been introduced "in a programmatic way by makers of this work, i.e., the choreographers who are attributed the label" (Cvejić and Le Roy 2014, 145). Indeed, it is commonly received that these choreographers have denied the appropriateness of the term (Fabius 2012; Pakes 2019). Yet, according to Jeroen Fabius (2012), Cvejić acknowledges some similarities between conceptual art and what has been termed "conceptual dance." In her view, conceptual dance operates as a theory that is made manifest by practice, it is self-reflexive and interrogates the characteristics of the discipline, the apparatus of the theatre and the production of meaning in contemporary culture. It also addresses the frames of perception and operates as an institutional critique (Fabius 2012). Still, Cvejić (cf. 2015; 2018) argues that choreographers like Jonathan Burrows and Xavier Le Roy are not working conceptually, rather they pose choreographic problems. She presents a theoretical term "expressive concepts" which denotes how choreography might contribute to philosophical thinking concerning relationships between the body, movement and time. Here the experimental orientation of dance offers a practical framework for theorising embodiment, perception and other philosophical questions (Cvejić 2015; 2018).

Expanded choreography has come to be understood as choreography that is closely interlinked "with language and with the codes of visual-audial-sculptural practice" (Joy 2009, 12–13). It seems to have replaced the term "conceptual dance" and refers to the field of choreographic practice as it is undertaken beyond dance. In 2012, a much-cited conference titled *Expanded Choreography: Situations, Movements, Objects* introduced expanded choreography in the following manner:

> In the last few years the term "choreography" has been used in an ever-expanding sense, becoming synonymous with specific structures and strategies disconnected from subjectivist bodily expression, style and representation [...] Aesthetically, it is turning away from established notions of dance with its strong association with skill and craft, to instead establish autonomous discourses that override causalities between conceptualization, production, expression, and representation. At the same time, it is gaining momentum on a political level as it is placed in the middle of a society to a large degree organized around movement, subjectivity and immaterial exchange. Choreography is not a priori performative, nor is it bound to expression and reiteration of subjectivity, it is becoming an expanded practice, a practice that in and of itself is political.
>
> (e-flux Announcements, n.d.)

Whilst expanded choreography is an indefinable notion, it relates to experimental and progressive choreographic practice that is socio-politically engaged. According to Anna Leon (2022) the term "expanded choreography" implies both a core from which expansion may occur and the potentiality of limitless opportunity, perhaps even rendering the term choreography redundant. She notes:

> [...] expanded choreography may be seen as an encapsulation of the contemporary choreographic field's open-ness to re-definitions of choreography — what Bojana Cvejić has called "concept ouvert de chorégraphie [open concept of choreography]" — not only widening already-existing notions but also asking what else choreography can do, what else it can work with, what else it may be. To be sure, other terms could have played the same role. "Expanded choreography" has, however, the advantage of avoiding dichotomous negations — as in the binarity of "not-dance" — replacing them with an opening of potentials.
>
> (Leon 2022, 23)

Expanded choreography invites us to look at and experiment with what else choreography could be. It invites us to look at how else choreographers can approach choreography besides the known conventions of dance. It positions the choreographer as an investigator experimenting with diverse society-related questions and problems from the perspective of movement and performance. The open-endedness of expanded choreography also entails that its medial specification is dependent on the problem posed or question explored by each specific work (Cvejić 2018). With expanded choreography, we are also faced with new problems, as Cvejić poignantly expresses:

> [...] the choreographic ideas shift their objects out of dance, and so we might be forced to think another problem that the expansion of choreography choreographs for us: the new forms of entangling life and work that contemporary dance expresses once it leaves the theater that protects its relative autonomy as an artform.
>
> (Cvejić 2015, 231)

With these developments, writing and text, in different forms and modalities, have gained impetus and wield influence in the field of progressive dance. Choreographers further share and discuss the practical artistic processes of choreography in multiple and diverse artistic and increasingly academic contexts (Blades and Meehan 2018). A growing number of choreographers work with language-informed textual approaches, experimental forms of writing and artistic research. They regularly utilise scores, texts, words, writing and talking in their performances and perform philosophical and theoretical concerns and conceptions. They introduce their artistic processes and thinking through both online publishing and via traditional printed media (cf. Klien, Valk, and Gormly 2008; Burrows 2010; Rethorst 2012; Hay 2013; 2015; Manning and Massumi 2014; Forsythe 2016; Ingvartsen 2016a; 2016b; Longley 2016; Gansterer, Cocker, and Greil 2017; Kramer 2021). In recent years, a number of books about choreography that, to varying extents, also discuss language, text and writing have been published in the area of dance studies (cf. Lepecki 2010; Foster 2011; Joy 2014; Cvejić 2015; Pouillade 2017; Blades and Meehan 2018; Brown and Longley 2018; Pakes 2020; Butterworth and Sanders 2021).

Noteworthy is that the writerly, textual and language-based approaches forwarded in choreography have been offered an explorative arena through the academic research field of artistic research. Artistic research is conducted by artists, including choreographers, and encompasses artistic processes and outcomes employing "a variety of epistemological models as well as transdisciplinary, collaborative, and participatory practices" (Caduff and Wälchli 2019, 1). While not excluding more conventional conceptualisation and theorisation, artistic research emphasises that art practice involves a material form of thinking and that artistic articulation, in the form of artistic processes and artworks, conveys artistic knowing not articulatable through any other means. Therefore, along with published volumes of diverse kinds of reflective writing, the outcomes of artistic research in dance and choreography typically include performed dance and choreography.

Since the emergence of artistic research in Europe in the 1990s, especially in the Nordic countries, writing has been one of its most seriously debated issues (cf. Hannula, Suoranta, and Vadén 2014; Schwab and Borgdorff 2014). When understood as a form of knowledge production, artistic research has both utilised and questioned known forms of scholarly writing in an attempt to portray the artistic undertakings inherent in it. The inclusion of any explanatory text at all in artistic research has even been contested in an effort to substantiate the ownmost aesthetic and epistemological qualities of the art in question (Borgdorff 2012; Pérez Royo 2012; Mersch 2015). Artist–researchers most often employ inter- or transdisciplinary insights to interlinking art, theory and research practices, engaging multi-media formats of dissemination in order to do so. They creatively utilise and challenge spoken word and written text, integrating reflective appraisal or critique directly into the artworks themselves or in supplements to these works. Operating in between art and writing, these experimental methods of articulating artistic research have been dubbed hybrid texts (Schwab and Borgdorff 2014). In artistic research, writing has thus been conceived of "*as an operation of the 'in-between'*" unfolding itself in-between materiality and the intelligible" (Schäfer 2020, 87, emphasis in original). Finding approaches to writing and conceptualisation that convey the sensuous and material thinking inherent in artistic processes has been considered far more important for the field of artistic research than the construction of more conventional research methodologies (Rouhiainen, Anttila, and Järvinen 2014).

In order to adequately expose art and its contents, diverse literary forms, such as poetry, manifesto, text and image collage, procedural, fiction and fabulation writing have been experimented with and utilised in artistic research (Lilja 2015; Varto 2018; Caduff and Wälchli 2019). Some examples in and from choreography include performance writing, which experiments explicitly with ways writing might interact with other art forms, and performative writing, which underlines the kinds of performances texts themselves generate by involving readers as active co-authors and co-generators of the text. In *Performing Writing,* Della Pollock (1998, 80) asserts that "Performative writing operates metaphorically to render absence present," minding the gap between the known and the not-yet-known. She continues by noting that "The writer and the world's bodies intertwine in evocative writing, in intimate co-performance of language and experience" (Pollock 1998, 80). Artistic research in choreography also explores intertextuality, approaches to language-based arts, collaborative writing and electronic and media-sensitive writing. These modes and methods have supported artist–researchers in their aspirations to accommodate the not-yet-known as well as the processual, multimedial and trans-disciplinary features entailed in artistic research processes (Hilevaara and Orley 2018; Schäfer 2020; Language-based Artistic Research Group, n.d.). In the Nordic context, examples of choreographers forwarding experimental writing and/or textual choreography through the field of artistic research are Simo Kellokumpu (2019), Marie Fahlin (2021), Eleanor Bauer (2022) as well as the duo Heimonen and Rouhiainen (Rouhiainen and Heimonen 2021; Heimonen and Rouhiainen 2022).

Artistic research operates at the threshold of the writeable and the unwriteable and involves a movement of translation. As such, artistic research writing has a "theoretical and aesthetic potential beyond literary studies as well as literature itself — and that is — especially in times of an increasing functionalization and specialization of science and art — capable of providing valuable critical impulses" (Schäfer 2020, 93). This relates to choreography in that much of current progressive choreography is about establishing relationalities with different subject matters, practices, conventions and contexts. As argued above, it often is a critical and even theoretical practice that intertwines movement, action, thinking, writing and reading. Jenn Joy (2014, 15, 17) opines that "To speak of choreography or to speak choreographically is also to speak of history, of writing and of dancing as entangled forms" and characterises choreography as "a form of knowledge production and distribution, an economy of transversal ideas." She also recognises that "the writing implicit in choreography is already complicated by its many correspondences" (Joy 2014, 16). Writing has a significant preservative function and can offer retained inroads into the transience of the live performance of choreography. The reading of writing as choreography forwards open-ended interpretations or translations that have both immaterial and material implications for their readers. With this said, it is evident that current choreographic practice generates experimental problems which produce various (im)material forms of writing, voicing and theorising that disrupt conventional ways of perceiving and conceiving of embodiment, interaction, movement and material (Joy 2014; Cvejić 2016).

* * * *

Dance–artists and choreographers engaging with artistic research have advanced progressive thinking in choreography in Finland for almost three decades. Those artist–researchers, who have focused on the advancement of creative or experimental writing and text in dance and choreography, include Leena Rouhiainen (2010; 2017), Kirsi Heimonen (2009; 2021; 2022), Lynda Gaudreau (2020; 2021), Joa Hug (2020), Simo Kellokumpu (2020) and Jana Unmüßig (2021). Others have advanced critical conceptions of choreography by addressing the ageing dancer, a new, non-representational paradigm of dance, the impact of Alexander technique on spontaneous choreography, processual and participatory choreography, contextual choreography, developments in contact improvisation, choreography as a self-organising system as well as somatic choreography as a form of resistance (e.g., Pasanen-Willberg 2000; Monni 2004; Lahdenperä 2013; Thorsnes 2015; Törmi 2016; Mäkinen 2018; Orpana 2022; Turunen 2022). Some of these dance–artists and researchers presented their work at the 7th International Colloquium on Artistic Research in Performing Arts titled *Elastic Writing in Artistic Research* and arranged by the Theatre Academy, University of the Arts Helsinki in 2021 (CARPA7, n.d.). Several have engaged in the activities of the Special Interest Group of Language-Based Artistic Research supported by the Society of Artistic Research (Language-based Artistic Research Group, n.d.). All in all, these activities highlight that artist–researchers in choreography in Finland continue experimenting with and inventing new ways to convey choreography through words and texts.

Aside from artistic research and theoretical discussions around dance and choreography, the rise of accessible digital and social media has advanced a more variegated discourse about and around dance in Finland. Critical and urgent discourses in and on dance were forwarded by dance–artists themselves in contexts such as the online magazine *Liikekieli.com*. The magazine founded by dance–artists Thomas Freundlich and Valtteri Raekallio in 2004 closed down due to a shortage of resources in June 2023. While it existed, it aimed at filling the gap created by an increasing lack of dance reviews in local newspapers and also as a way to acknowledge the versatility and plurality of dance in Finland (Markkula et al. 2023). It is becoming evident in Finland and other Western dance contexts, that discourse no longer simply encircles a silent dance but instead permeates it in emergent ways. Olli Ahlroos (2016, n.p.) suggests that recently a linguistic turn has occurred within dance.

Present-day Finnish choreographers regularly incorporate speech and text in their performances. They are inspired by critical theory and philosophical conceptions which they address in their artistic and artistic research work. In 2018, *Liikekieli.com* published an issue on the relationship between choreography and text, highlighting the views of some choreographers working in this area. In it, Jenni-Elina von Bagh, who dialogues with philosophical concepts in her choreography, describes her interests:

> Thinking becomes articulated differently when placed beside bodily practice and vice versa: with theoretical thinking bodily practice inevitably gains new means of expression [...] I am interested in the shared resonance between philosophy and staged practice. I would like to call this a moment of translation, in which a philosophical concept turns into or becomes a scenic frame. [...] I am interested in handling philosophical concepts in performative and scenic settings, in which composition, impressions, transitions and collisions generate new comprehension and re-organise thinking.[2]
>
> (von Bagh 2018, n.p.)

In the same volume, Simo Kellokumpu (2018) discusses his choreographic approach through a neologism: choreo-orientation, in which he has moved from thinking about choreographic writing to forwarding a choreo-reading practice. He contemplates what happens to choreographic thinking, practice, body and movement when the choreographic potential of reading is observed. More specifically, he plays with shifting the reading of printed signs into the reading of the inter-relations between the body and its environment (Kello-kumpu 2018).

In engaging with language, writing and text, choreographers often choose to address timely societal questions and political and global crises. choreo-grapher Veli Lehtovaara addresses ecological issues via a mix of different art forms and media. His cross-artistic works contain speech, text, singing, move-ment and video, performed in a variety of public locations. They juxtapose relationships between linguistic and bodily expression underpinned by con-cepts drawn from critical theory and philosophy (SPACETIMELOVE, n.d.). Maija Hirvanen's choreographic approach is informed by performance studies and critical theory through the activation of formats such as the performance-lecture. She states that her "interests range from the relationship between art and different belief systems, collaborative processes within cultural practices and performance as collective memory to mechanisms of re-learning" (Maija Hirvanen — Choreographer, Artist, n.d.). Elina Pirinen utilises poems and texts she has written along with objects and materials to explore embodied experiences of feminism. Whilst engaging in intense physical activity, the per-formers often also speak and sing. Pirinen has developed a method she calls dark choreographic writing, a freely associative form of writing, exploring hard-core emancipation (Elina Pirinen, n.d.). During the last decade, Sonya Lindfors has actively campaigned against racism, and her artistic work addresses ideas of power, representation, black body politics and decolonial thinking. In 2009, she founded and continues to lead UrbanApa, an anti-racist and feminist art community designed to re-think what should be done and ways to do it. In her work as an artist and artistic director of UrbanApa, she utilises different per-formative and social formats including written publications as sites of empow-erment and radical collective dreaming (UrbanApa, n.d.; Sonya Lindfors, n.d.).

In conclusion

In the writing of this chapter, what has become most evident to us is the plethora of existing approaches to what could broadly be considered linguis-tically and textually informed choreography. We observe that what makes these different takes on the use of language, writing and text in choreography most interesting are the actual artistic questions that are addressed and the specific means, methods and materials through which this is done (Monni 2015). These approaches critically reorder choreography. They highlight choreographing as a process of politically underpinned change-making, especially when the questioning and material formation relates to current challenges of our societies and world.

In this chapter, we have gathered together different insights depicting different orientations and views which address both historic and recent developments in writing and choreography from various international and local vantage points. We have also situated some of these developments in relation to the field of artistic research. This collection of anecdotes and accounts about dance and choreography begins to chart, if only partially, some of the ways in which language, writing and text inform present-day choreography. We recognise that in expanding and redefining the field of choreography, writing in choreography takes inspiration from many sources beyond dance. More could be done to contemplate influences from other art forms and theoretical disciplines, considering, for example, bodily approaches to creative writing, écriture féminine, concrete poetry, procedural writing, artist publications, performance texts, dramaturgy and the like, but we leave that task to the artist–researchers of the future.

What also needs noting is that the term "contemporary dance" is currently being critically viewed. It is the contemporaneity the term refers to which is being questioned. The critique proposes a rethinking of the temporality of both a dance performance and contemporaneity of dance itself in ways that underline the complex relationships between past and present, appreciate different geopolitical locations, including power issues and identity politics, and acknowledge different human and more-than-human agents. The critique also relates to our incapacity to grasp our own times as certain historical periods. It encourages us to retain reflexivity and to be open to potentiality, recognising that we need some distance to value the implicit in the present from which the unforeseen emerges. The eclectic jumps and transcultural moves in the contents of this chapter are filled with gaps that will hopefully inspire the curious reader to inquire after alternative views. Following Lepecki (2012, 21), we believe that our fragmented account proposes interlinks across time, location and perspective, creating possibilities for "trans-historical and trans-geographic transformations [that] hopefully will reveal zones of generative resonances and dissonances, lines of convergence and divergences between texts, authors, choreographers, and artists." The following chapters of this book offer various perspectives which that testify to the fact that choreography as a language-based, writerly and textual practice, is a presence which can never quite be grasped, and a form which continually assumes unforeseen forms.

Notes

1 Translated by Leena Rouhiainen.
2 Translated by Leena Rouhiainen.

References

Ahlroos, Olli. 2016. "Haastatteluja nykytanssinkritiikistä ja sen tilasta." *Liikekieli.com*: n.p. Accessed April 15, 2023. https://www.liikekieli.com/uusi-alku-012016/haastatteluja-nykytanssikritiikista-ja-sen-tilasta/.

Arbeau, Thoinot. 1967. *Orchesography*. Translated by Mary Stewart Evans. New York: Dover Publications, Inc.

Arvelo, Ritva ja Auli Räsänen. 1987. *Tanssitaiteen Vuosikymmenet: Suomen Tanssitaiteilijoiden Liitto 50 Vuotta*. Helsinki: Suomen tanssitaiteilijain liitto.

Au, Susan. 1988/1995. *Ballet & Modern Dance*. London: Thames and Hudson.

Banes, Sally. 1995. *Democracy's Body: Judson Dance Theatre, 1962–1964*. Durham and London: Duke University Press.

Banes, Sally. 1992. "Is It All Postmodern? In What Has Become of Postmodern Dance? Answers and Other Questions by Marcia B. Siegel, Anna Halprin, Janice Ross, Cynthia J. Novack, Deborah Hay, Sally Banes, Senta Driver, Roger Copeland and Susan L. Foster. Ed. Ann Daly." *The Drama Review* 36(1) (T133 Spring): 58–61.

Banes, Sally. 1987. *Terpsichore in Sneakers: Post Modern Dance*. Middletown, CT: Wesleyan University Press.

Bauer, Eleanor. 2022. "Choreo | graphy: Artistic Research Project Documentation." PhD diss., Stockholm University of the Arts. Accessed March 3, 2023. https://www.researchcatalogue.net/view/1321770/1321771.

Blades, Hetty and Emma Meehan, eds. 2018. *Performing Process: Sharing Dance and Choreographic Practice*. Bristol: Intellect.

Borgdorff, Henk. 2012. *The Conflict of the Faculties: Perspectives on Artistic Research and Academia*. Leiden: Leiden University Press.

Brown, Carol and Alys Longley, eds. 2018. *Undisciplining Dance in Nine Movements and Eight Stumbles*. Newcastle upon Tyne: Cambridge Scholars Publishing.

Burrows, Jonathan. 2010. *A Choreographer's Handbook*. London and New York: Routledge.

Butterworth, Jo and Lorna Sanders, eds. 2021. *Fifty Contemporary Choreographers: Third Edition*. Abingdon and New York: Routledge.

Caduff, Corina and Tan Wälchli. 2019. *Artistic Research and Literature*. Brill Open. Accessed January 30, 2023. https//doi.org/10.30965/9783846763339.

CARPA7. n.d. Accessed April 14, 2023. https://sites.uniarts.fi/web/carpa/carpa7.

Cohen, Selma Jean, ed. 1974/1977. *Dance as a Theatre Art: Source Readings in Dance History from 1581 to the Present*. New York: Harper & Row Publishers by Dance Books LTD.

Cvejić, Bojana. 2018. "Choreography that Poses Problems." In *Contemporary Choreography: A Critical Reader, Second Edition*, edited by Jo Butterworth and Liesbeth Wildschut, 54–67. London and New York: Routledge: Francis & Taylor Group.

Cvejić, Bojana. 2016. "A Parallel Slalom from BADco: In Search of a Poetics of Problems." *Representations* 136(1): 21–35. Accessed February 2, 2023. https://doi.org/10.1525/rep.2016.136.1.21.

Cvejić, Bojana. 2015. *Choreographing Problems. Expressive Concepts in Contemporary Dance and Performance*. London: Palgrave Macmillan.

Cvejić, Bojana and Xavier Le Roy. 2014. "To End with Judgement by Way of Clarification." In *Danse: An Anthology*, edited by Noémie Salomon, 145–157. Paris: Les Presses du Réel.

Dempster, Elizabeth. 1995. "Women Writing the Body: Let's Watch a Little How She Dances." In *Bodies of the Text: Dance as Theory, Literature as Dance*, edited by Ellen

W. Goellner and Jacqueline Shea Murphy, 21–38. New Brunswick, NJ: Rutgers University Press.

e-flux Annoucements. n.d. "Expanded Choreography." Accessed March 15, 2023. https://www.e-flux.com/announcements/34425/expanded-choreography/.

Elina Pirinen. n.d. "Elina Pirinen – Dance – Artist – Music Maker." Accessed April 18, 2023. https://elinapirinen.com/project-type/texts/.

Fabius, Jeroen. 2012. "The Missing History of (not)conceptual Dance." In *Danswetenschap in Nederland*, deel 7, edited by Merel Heering, Ruth Naber, Bianca Niewboer, and Liesbeth Wildschut, n.p. Amsterdam: Vereniging voor Dansonderzoek. Accessed February 15, 2023. https://www.academia.edu/4060526/.

Fahlin, Marie. 2021. "Moving through Choreography: Curating Choreography as Artistic Practice." PhD diss., Stockholm University of the Arts. Accessed March 3, 2023. https://www.researchcatalogue.net/view/428263/428264.

Forsythe, William. 2016. "Choreographic Objects." Accessed May 15, 2021. https://www.williamforsythe.com/essay.html.

Foster, Susan Leigh. 2013. "Dancing and Theorizing and Theorizing Dancing." In *Dance [and] Theory*, edited by Gabriele Brandstetter and Gabriele Klein, 19–32. Bielefeld: transcript Verlag.

Foster, Susan Leigh. 2011. *Choreographing Empathy: Kinesthesia in Performance*. New York and London: Routledge.

Foster, Susan Leigh. 1998a. *Choreography Narrative: Ballet's Staging of Story and Desire*. Bloomington and Indianapolis: Indiana University Press.

Foster, Susan Leigh. 1998b. "Choreographies of Gender." *Signs: Journal of Women Culture and Society* 24(11): 2–33.

Foster, Susan Leigh. 1995. "Textual Evidances." In *Bodies of the Text: Dance as Theory, Literature as Dance*, edited by Ellen W. Goellner and Jacqueline Shea Murphy, 231–246. New Brunswick, NJ: Rutgers University Press.

Foster, Susan Leigh. 1986. *Reading Dancing: Bodies and Subjects in Contemporary American Dance*. Berkeley, Los Angeles and London: University of California Press.

Franko, Mark. 2015. *Dance as Text: Ideologies of the Baroque Body*. Oxford: Oxford University Press.

Franko, Mark, ed. 2019. *Choreographing Discourses: A Mark Franko Reader*. Abingdon: Routledge.

Gansterer, Nikolaus, Emma Cocker, and Mariella Greil, eds. 2017. *Choreo-graphic Figures: Deviations from the Line*. Berlin and Boston, MA: Walter de Gruyeter GmbH.

Gaudreau, Lynda. 2021. *The Almost Manual: On Asynchrony, Time Lapse, Choreography, and Extravagant Details in Life and Creative Process*. Nivel 16. n.p.: Theater Academy, Performing Arts Research Centre, University of the Arts Helsinki. Accessed March 23, 2023. https://taju.uniarts.fi/bitstream/handle/10024/7476/Nivel_16.pdf?sequence=1&isAllowed=y.

Gaudreau, Lynda. 2020. "A Letter to Ludwig Wittgenstein." *Dance Articulated, special issue CHOREOGRAPHY NOW* 6(10): 7–11. Accessed March 23, 2023. https://doi.org/10.5324/da.v6i1.3615.

Goellner, Ellen W. and Jacqueline Shea Murphy. 1995. "Introduction: Movement Movements." In *Bodies of the Text: Dance as Theory, Literature as Dance*, edited by Ellen W. Goellner and Jacqueline Shea Murphy, 1–20. New Brunswick, NJ: Rutgers University Press.

Hannula, Mika, Juha Suoranta, and Tere Vadén. 2014. *Artistic Research Methodology: Narrative, Power and the Public*. New York: Peter Lang Publishing.

Hay, Deborah. 2015. *Using the Sky: A Dance*. Abingdon and New York: Routledge.

Hay, Deborah. 2013. *My Body, The Buddhist.* Middletown, CT: Wesleyan University Press.

Heimonen, Kirsi. 2022. "The Touch of Words: Obscure Spatial Encounters." *Scriptum: Creative Writing Research Journal* 9(1): 1–30. Accessed February 26, 2023. https://jyx.jyu.fi/handle/123456789/79612.

Heimonen, Kirsi. 2021. "Walking in a Cage: Attuning to Atmospheric Intensities through Corporeality." *Choreographic Practices* 12(1): 47–66. Accessed February 26, 2023. https://doi.org/10.1386/chor_00028_1.

Heimonen, Kirsi. 2009. "Sukellus liikkeeseen – liikeimprovisaatio tanssimisen ja kirjoittamisen lähteenä." PhD diss., Theatre Academy, Acta Scenica 24. Helsinki: Theatre Academy. Accessed March 23, 2023. https://taju.uniarts.fi/bitstream/10024/6052/1/Acta_Scenica_24.pdf.

Heimonen, Kirsi and Jan-Peter Kaiku. 1999. "Tanssia kaikille – yhteisötanssin periaatteet ja käytännöt." *Teatterikorkea* 1: 30–31.

Heimonen, Kirsi and Leena Rouhiainen. 2022. "In the Shadows: Phenomenological Choreographic Writing." *Choreographic Practices* 13(1): 75–96. Accessed January 28, 2023. https://doi.org/10.1386/chor_00042_1.

Hilevaara, Katja and Emily Orley. 2018. *The Creative Critic: Writing as/about Practice.* Abingdon and New York: Routledge.

Hug, Joa. 2020. "Propositions for Unfinished Thinking: The Research Score as a Medium of Artistic Research." PhD diss., Performing Arts Research Centre, Theatre Academy, University of the Arts Helsinki. Accessed April 13, 2023. https://www.researchcatalogue.net/view/433112/596407.

Hämäläinen, Soili. 1999. "Koreografian oppimis- ja opetusprosesseista: kaksi opetusmallia oman liikkeen löytämiseksi ja tanssin muotoamiseksi." PhD diss., Teatterikorkeakoulu, Acta Scenica 4. Accessed April 13, 2023. https://taju.uniarts.fi/bitstream/handle/10024/6055/Acta_Scenica_4.pdf?sequence=1&isAllowed=y.

Ingvartsen, Mette. 2016a. "69 Positions." PhD diss., Stockholm University of the Arts and Lund University. Brussels: Stockholm University of the Arts and Lund University.

Ingvartsen, Mette. 2016b. "The Artificial Nature Series." PhD diss., Stockholm University of the Arts and Lund University. Brussels: Stockholm University of the Arts and Lund University.

Järvinen, Hanna. 2018. "Moderni, postmoderni vai nykytanssi: historijoitsijan vallankäytöstä." In *Postmoderni tanssi Suomessa,* edited by Niko Hallikainen and Liisa Pentti, 209–235. Helsinki: Taideyliopiston Teatterikorkeakoulu.

Järvinen, Hanna. 2017. "Democratic Bodies? Reflections on "Postmodern Dance" in the United States and Finland." *Nordic Journal of Dance: Rractice, Education, Research* 8(2): 18–29.

Joy, Jenn. 2014. *The Choreographic.* Cambridge, MA: The MIT Press.

Joy, Jenn. 2009. "An Introduction." In *The Art of Making Dances,* edited by Chase Granoff and Jenn Joy, 10–13. New York: The Kitchen and Abrons Arts Center's Artists Workspace.

Kaiku, Jan-Peter. 1997. "Murtumia ja moninaisuutta. Suomalaisen nykytanssin freelancekenttä 1980 ja 1990-luvulla." In *Valokuvan tanssi. Suomalaisen tanssin kuvat 1890–1997. Dance in Finnish Photography,* edited by Hanna-Leena Helavuori and translated by Jüri Kokkonen, 205–215. Oulu: Teatterimuseo ja Kustannus Pohjoinen.

Kellokumpu, Simo. 2020. "Towards Astroembodied Choreostruction: Deviating from Choreographing to Choreoreading." *Dance Articulated, special issue*

CHOREOGRAPHY NOW 6(10): 12–23. Accessed April 13, 2023. https://www.ntnu.no/ojs/index.php/ps/article/view/3616/3401.

Kellokumpu, Simo. 2019. "Choreography as a Reading Practice." PhD diss., Theatre Academy, University of the Arts Helsinki. Accessed March 3, 2023. https://www.researchcatalogue.net/view/437088/437089.

Kellokumpu, Simo. 2018. Lukeminen kirjoittaminen lukeminen kirjoittaminen. Koreografia ja teksti, liikekieli.com 2: n.p. Accessed April 4, 2023. https://www.liikekieli.com/koreografia-ja-teksti-2-2018/simo-kellokumpu-lukeminen-kirjoittaminen-lukeminen-kirjoittaminen/.

Klien, Michael, Steven Valk, and Jeffrey Gormly. 2008. *Book of Recommendations: Choreography as an Aesthetics of Change.* Ireland: Daghdha.

Korppi-Tommola, Riikka. 2012. "Virtauksia valloista: sukelluksia suomalaisen modernin tanssin amerikkalaistamiseen 1960-luvulla." In *Weimarista Valtoihin. Kansainvälisyys suomalaisessa tanssitaiteessa*, edited by Johanna Laakkonen and Tiina Suhonen, 83–111. Helsinki: Teatterimuseo.

Kramer, Paula. 2021. *Suomenlinna / / Groupius. Two Contemplations on Body, Movement and Intermateriality.* Axminster: Triarchy Press.

Kukkonen, Aino. 2014. "Postmoderni tanssi liikkeessä: Tulkintoja 1980-luvun suomalaisesta tanssista." PhD diss., University of Helsinki, Faculty of Arts, Department of Philosophy, History, Culture and Art Studies. Accessed March 1, 2023. https://helda.helsinki.fi/bitstream/handle/10138/135805/postmode.pdf?sequence=1&isAllowed=y.

Laakkonen, Johanna. 2018. *Tanssia yli rajojen: Modernin tanssin transnationaaliset verkostot.* Helsinki: Suomalaisen kirjallisuuden seura.

Lahdenperä, Soile. 2013. "Muutoksen tilassa: Alexander-tekniikka koreografisen prosessin osana." PhD diss., Teatterikorkeakoulu, Acta Scenica. Helsinki: Teatterikorkeakoulu. Accessed April 13, 2023. https://taju.uniarts.fi/handle/10024/6066.

Language-based Artistic Research Group. n.d. Accessed February 28, 2023. https://www.researchcatalogue.net/view/835089/835129.

Leon, Anna. 2022. *Expanded Choreographies–Choreographic Histories: Trans-Historical Perspectives Beyond Dance and Human Bodies in Motion.* Bielefeld: transcript Verlag.

Lepecki, André. 2012. "Introduction / / Dance as a Practice of Contemporaneity." In *Dance: Documents of Contemporary Art*, edited by André Lepecki, 14–23. London: Whitechapel Gallery. Cambridge, MA: The MIT Press.

Lepecki, André. 2010. "Zones of Resonance: Mutual Formations in Dance and the Visual Arts since the 1960s." In *Move Choreographing You: Art and Dance since the 1960s*, edited by Stephanie Rosenthal, 152–163. London: Hayward Publishing.

Lepecki, André. 2006. *Exhausting Dance. Performance and the Politics of Movement.* New York and London: Routledge Taylor & Francis Group.

Lepecki, André. 2004a. "Inscribing Dance." In *Of the Presence of the Body: Essays on Dance and Performance Theory*, edited by André Lepecki, 124–139. Middletown, CT: Wesleyan University Press.

Lepecki, André. 2004b. "Concept and Presence: The Contemporary European Dance Scene." In *Rethinking Dance History: A Reader*, edited by Alexandra Carter, 170–181. London and New York: Routledge Taylor & Francis Group.

Lepecki, André and Gay Morris. 2019. "Introduction." In *Choreographing Discourses: A Mark Franko Reader*, edited by Mark Franko, 1–13. Oxon and New York: Routledge.

Lilja, Efva. 2015. *Art, Research, Empowerment: The Artist as Researcher.* Regeringskansliet Stockholm: Elanders Sweden.

Longley, Alys. 2016. ""Skeleton Boat on an Ocean of Organs" and Other Stories: Understanding and Evoking Posthuman Relations Through Site-based Dance, Somatic Practices, Performance Writing and Artist-books." *Text and Performance Quarterly* 36(4): 229–249. Accessed March 28, 2023. https://doi.org/10.1080/10462937 .2016.1240827.

Maija Hirvanen – Choreographer, Artists. n.d. "Maija Hirvanen." Accessed April 15, 2023. https://www.hirvanen.net/maijahirvanen.

Makkonen, Anne. 2017. *Suomen Taidetanssin Historiaa.* Helsinki: Taideyliopiston Teatterikorkeakoulu. Accessed March 16, 2023. https://disco.teak.fi/tanssi/.

Manning, Erin and Brian Massumi. 2014. *Thought in the Act: Passages in the Ecology of Experience.* Minneapolis: University of Minnesota Press.

Markkula, Outi, Virva Talonen, Riina Hannuksela, Heini Tuoresmäki, and Lotta Halinen. 2023. "Tanssinverkkolehti Liikekieli.com pohtii toimintansa edellytyksiä." *Liikekieli.com:* n.p. Accessed April 15, 2023. https://www.liikekieli.com/ tanssin-verkkolehti-liikekieli-com-pohtii-toimintansa-edellytyksia/.

Mersch, Dieter. 2015. *Epistemologies of Aesthetics.* Berlin: Diaphanes AG.

Miettinen, Jukka O., Jorma Uotinen, David Mitchell, and Claude Le-Anh. 1985. *Uotinen: The Art of Dance.* Helsinki: Kirjayhtymä.

Monni, Kirsi. 2022. "Postmoderni spektri – tanssin uusia avauksia ja radikaaleja uudelleen määrittelyjä 1960 luvulle." In *Näkökulmia tanssitaiteen historiaan ja nykypäivään,* edited by Kirsi Monni, Hanna Järvinen, and Riikka Laakso, n.p. Taideyliopiston Teatterikorkeakoulu. Accessed March 28, 2023. https://disco.teak.fi/tanssin-historia/postmoderni-spektri-tanssin-uusia-avauksia-ja-radikaaleja-uudelleen-maarittelyja-1960-luvulla/.

Monni, Kirsi. 2015. "Diskursseja, identiteettejä, ontologioita." *Liikekieli.com:* n.p. Accessed April 15, 2023. https://www.liikekieli.com/diskursseja-identiteetteja-ontologioita/.

Monni, Kirsi. 2007. "Zodiakin kolme aaltoa. 20 vuotta kollegiaalisen taideyhteisön haasteita." In *Zodiak. Uuden tanssin tähden,* edited by Raija Ojala and Kimmo Takala, 60–83. Helsinki: Like.

Monni, Kirsi. 2004. "Olemisen poeettinen liike. Tanssin uuden paradigman taidefilosofisia tulkintoja Martin Heideggerin ajattelun valossa sekä taiteellinen työ vuosina 1996–1999." PhD diss., Theatre Academy, Acta Scenica 15. Helsinki: Teatterikorkeakoulu. https://taju.uniarts.fi/bitstream/handle/10024/6047/Acta_ Scenica_15.pdf?sequence=1.

Monni, Kirsi, Hanna Järvinen, and Riikka Laakso. 2022. "4. Tanssin postmodernismi (1960–1970)." In *Näkökulmia tanssitaiteen historiaan ja nykypäivään,* edited by Kirsi Monni, Hanna Järvinen, and Riikka Laakso, n.p. Taideyliopiston Teatterikorkeakoulu. Accessed March 28, 2023. https://disco.teak.fi/tanssin-historia/ luku-4/.

Mäkinen, Mirva. 2018. "Taiteellinen tutkimus kontakti-improvisaation arvoista somaesteettisen esityksen kontekstissa." PhD diss., Taideyliopiston Teatterikorkeakoulu. Accessed April 13, 2023. https://actascenica.teak.fi/makinen-mirva/.

Orpana, Mikko. 2022. "Choreographed by Situation: Self-Organizing Choreography and the Dancer's Agencement." PhD diss., University of the Arts, Theatre Academy, Performing Arts Research Centre, Acta Scenica 61. Accessed April 13, 2023. https://taju.uniarts.fi/bitstream/handle/10024/7557/Acta_Scenica_61. pdf?sequence=1&isAllowed=y.

Pakes, Anna. 2020. *Choreography Invisible: The Disappearing Work of Dance*. New York: Oxford University Press.

Pakes, Anna. 2019. "Can There Be Conceptual Dance?" In *Philosophy of Dance*, edited by Peter A French, Howard K. Wettstein, and Patrick Londen, 195–212. Boston, MA: Wiley, Midwest Studies in Philosophy VOL XLIV.

Parviainen, Jaana. 1998. "Bodies Moving and Moved: A Phenomenological Analysis of the Dancing Subject and the Cognitive and Ethical Values of Dance Art." PhD diss., Tampere University. Tampere: Tampere University Press.

Pasanen-Willberg, Riitta. 2000. "Vanhenevan tanssijan problematiikasta dialogisuuteen: koreografin näkökulma." PhD diss., Theatre Academy, Acta Scenic 6. Helsinki: Theatre Academy. Accessed April 13, 2023. https://taju.uniarts.fi/bitstream/handle/10024/6039/Acta_Scenica_6_2000.pdf?sequence=1&isAllowed=y.

Pérez Royo, Victoria. 2012. "Knowledge and Collective Practice." In *Dance /and/ Theory*, edited by Gabriele Brandstetter and Gabriele Klein, 51–62. Bielefeld: transcript.

Pollock, Della. 1998. "Performing Writing." In *The Ends of Performance*, edited by Peggy Phelan and Jill Lane, 73–103. New York: New York University Press.

Pouillade, Frédérick. 2017. *Unworking Choreography: The Notion of the Work in Dance*. Translated by Anna Pakes. New York: Oxford University Press.

Repo, Riitta. 1989. *Tanssien tulevaisuuteen*. Helsinki: Taiteen keskustoimikunta ja Valtion painatuskeskus.

Rethorst, Susan. 2012. *A Choreographic Mind: Autobodygraphical Writings*. Helsinki: Theatre Academy.

Reunamäki, Hannu and Anneli Patomäki, eds. 1984. *Tanssin juhlaa – Celebration of Dance*. Kuopio Dance and Music Festival. Kustannuskiila Oy. Savon Sanomain Kirjapaino.

Reynolds, Nancy and Malcolm McCormick. 2003. *No Fixed Points: Dance in the Twentieth Century*. New Haven, CT: Yale University Press.

Rosenthal, Stephanie. 2011. "Choreographing You: Choreographies in the Visual Arts." In *Move. Choreographing You: Art and Dance since the 1960s*, edited by Stephanie Rosenthal, 8–21. London: Hayward Publishing.

Rouhiainen, Leena. 2017. "Traces of Breath: An Experiment in Undoing Data through Artistic Research." In *Disrupting Data in Qualitative Inquiry: Entanglements with the Post-Critical and Post-Anthropocentric*, edited by Mirka Koro-Lundberg, Teija Löytönen, and Marek Tesar, 67–79. New York: Peter Lang Publishing.

Rouhiainen, Leena. 2010. "A Mono-Trilogy on a Collaborative Process in the Performing Arts." In *Blood, Sweat & Theory: Research Through Practice in Performance*, edited by John Freeman, 139–150. Faringdon: Libri Publishing.

Rouhiainen, Leena. 2003. "Living Transformative Lives: Finnish Freelance Dance–Artists Brought into Dialogue with Merleau-Ponty's Phenomenology." PhD diss., Theatre Academy, Acta Scenica 13. Helsinki: Theatre Academy. Accessed March 23, 2023. https://taju.uniarts.fi/bitstream/handle/10024/6045/Acta_Scenica_13.pdf?sequence=1&isAllowed=y.

Rouhiainen, Leena, Eeva Anttila, and Hanna Järvinen. 2014. "Taiteellinen tutkimus yhtenä tanssin tutkimuksen juonteena." In *Tanssiva tutkimus: tanssintutkimuksen menetelmiä ja lähestymistapoja*, edited by Hanna Järvinen and Leena Rouhiainen, 175–189. Helsinki: Taideyliopiston Teatterikorkeakoulu. Accessed January 20, 2023. https://nivel.teak.fi/tanssiva-tutkimus/taiteellinen-tutkimus-yhtena-tanssintutkimuksen-juonteena/.

Rouhiainen, Leena and Kirsi Heimonen. 2021. "Katveen varjon sanominen koreografisena kirjoittamisena (The Saying of the Shadow as a Choreographic Writing)." *Ruukku Studies in Artistic Research* 15. Accessed February 28, 2023. https://doi.org/10.22501/ruu.848270.

Räsänen, Anu. 1994. "Aino Sarje teki Suomen ensimmäisen väitöskirjan tanssista." *Helsingin Sanomat*, October 28, 1994.

Sarje, Aino. 1994. "Kahdeksankymmentäluvun suomalaisen taidetanssinäkemyksien taideteoreettista tarkastelua." PhD diss., University of Helsinki.

Schwab, Michael and Henk Borgdorff. 2014. *The Exposition of Artistic Research: Publishing Art in Academia*. Leiden: Leiden University Press.

Sonya Lindfors. n.d. "Bio." Accessed April 30, 2023. https://sonyalindfors.com.

SPACETIMELOVE. n.d. "Peltotiekeskustelu | Feldweg (Conversations)." Accessed April 15, 2023. http://spacetimelove.com/projects#/conversations/.

Schäfer, Elisabeth. 2020. "Writing as Artistic Research." In *Teaching Artistic Research: Conversations across Cultures*, edited by Ruth Mateus-Berr and Richard Jochum, 84–97. Berlin and Boston, MA: Walter de Gruyter.

Thorsnes, Per Roar. 2015. *Docudancing Griefscapes: Choreographic Strategies for Embodying Traumatic Contexts in the Trilogy of Life & Death*. PhD diss., Theatre Academy, University of the Arts Helsinki. Accessed April 13, 2023. https://taju.uniarts.fi/handle/10024/6073.

Turunen, Jaana. 2022. "Herkkää ja hiljaista vastarintaa: tanssin muuttuva toimijuus." PhD diss., Taideyliopiston Teatterikorkeakoulu Esittävien taiteiden tutkimuskeskus. Acccessed April 13, 2023. https://actascenica.teak.fi/turunen-jaana/.

Törmi, Kirsi. 2016. "Koreografinen prosessi vuorovaikutuksena." PhD diss., Theatre Academy University of the Arts, Acta Scenica 46. Helsinki: Taideyliopiston Teatterikorkeakoulu Esittävien taiteiden tutkimuskeskus. Accessed April 13, 2023. https://taju.uniarts.fi/bitstream/handle/10024/6075/Acta_Scenica_46.pdf?sequence=1&isAllowed=y.

Unmüßig, Jana. 2021. "Ponderings with Breathing/ Breathing with Ponderings." *Choreographic Practices* 12(2): 165–176. Accessed March 28, 2023. https://doi.org/10.1386/chor_00032_1.

UrbanApa. n.d. "UrbanApa Community for Culture, Art and Events." Accessed April 15, 2023. https://urbanapa.fi/info/.

Varto, Juha. 2018. *Artistic Research: What Is It? Who Does It? Why?* Espoo: Aalto Arts Books.

Vienola-Lindfors, Irma. 1984. "Dance in Finland Creating Its Own Profile." In *Tanssin juhlaa – Celebration of Dance*, edited by Hannu Reunamäki and Anneli Patomäki, 8–27. Kuopio Dance and Music Festival. Kustannuskiila Oy. Savon Sanomain Kirjapaino.

von Bagh, Jenni-Elina. 2018. "Käännös taiteellisena metodina." *Koreografia ja teksti, Liikekieli.com* 2: n.p. Accessed April 4, 2023. https://www.liikekieli.com/koreografia-ja-teksti-2-2018/jenni-elina-von-bagh-kaannos-taiteellisena-metodina/.

PART 1

Transcribing performance into writing

3

TALKING, DANCING, HEARING, SEEING, WRITING, READING

Notes on *plenty serious TALK TALK*

Vicki Van Hout

"Talking, dancing, hearing, seeing, writing, reading: Notes on *plenty serious TALK TALK*" shares and unfolds four scenes drawn from the 2019 solo dance theatre work *plenty serious TALK TALK*, by Australian Indigenous choreographer Vicki Van Hout. Each transcribed scene is accompanied by a reflective text, which situates and discusses the various complex relations between choreography and writing, between dancing and speaking, between traditional and contemporary practices and between authorship and ownership. Van Hout shares aspects of Indigenous art-making that usually stay behind the scenes, including consultative protocols, permission processes, and community obligations, laying bare the complexities of negotiating culture, art and community across disciplines, genres, languages and eras.

Introduction

The solo dance theatre performance *plenty serious TALK TALK*[1] was originally developed under the title *The Body Politic*. It was to be a homage, a continuation of the "artivist" antics of the early Aboriginal actor/devisors of the National Black Theatre (NBT) (Pollock 2008), an ensemble based in the inner-city Sydney suburb of Redfern. From 1970 to 1977, NBT produced and presented their own brand of subversive theatre, examples of which can be seen online in clips from the short-lived, television comedy series *Basically Black* (1973) (Token Gypsy, n.d.). The series was adapted from their hugely successful vaudeville-style stage show performed at the Nimrod Street Theatre in 1972. *Basically Black* was presented in a nonlinear narrative style, comprised of several politically charged skits and stand-up routines, featuring characters such as the Aboriginal hero Super Boong.

DOI: 10.4324/9781003397427-4

A significant point of difference between my solo performance, *plenty serious TALK TALK*, and the Black Theatre revue *Basically Black* is that my speculations are primarily intra rather than intercultural. I am exploring and examining, through my own embodied experience, the complex ways of being, doing and knowing of my urban Indigenous community in relation to the remote or "traditional" mob still living in their homelands and speaking language or "mother tongue." *Basically Black*, on the other hand, was a postcolonial critique, an indictment of the conditions produced by the invasion of indigenous Australia by Western colonisers, and the ongoing lack of either treaty or reparation. I am aware that an element of intercultural commentary is unavoidable in my art practice, given my form is performance and my audience is predominantly white. So, while my primary focus is in using dance theatre and choreography to unfold intersectional relations between myself and my various communities, something else is emerging with it: the creation of a context which can potentially support a more inclusive discourse.

Video prologue: backstage welcome to country[2]

plenty serious TALK TALK opened with a video prologue, which was projected onto a large woven mat suspended from the ceiling at centre stage. It depicts three people standing backstage having a conversation in preparation for a local government public function. This narrative device meant that I was able to introduce other players into what was essentially a solo performance work.

The text was conversational, and the scene was tightly choreographed. It was shot in one extended take with the camera following the action as it roved from a backstage kitchen/green room area, down two flights of stairs, to just outside the entrance to the theatre. Proximity was key: the performers to each other, and the performers to the camera. These spatial relationships imbued the scene with an air of intimacy, the personalities and situations unfolded with the kind of candid familiarity usually reserved for close acquaintances. This dramaturgical device allowed the audience to overhear things not meant for them, some of which included a reference to Aboriginal comedian Sean Choolburra,[3] whose approach my character claims is dated, and Aboriginal television journalist Stan Grant,[4] whom my character states she can't afford to hire.

The *prologue* was created in "fly on the wall" style, as if the audience were privy to insider information. A source of inspiration for this approach was the British situation comedy *The Thick of It* (2005–2012),[5] a withering political satire featuring a small ensemble cast. The show felt both authentic *and* sly, a paradox produced by carefully orchestrated relations between order and disorder, e.g., a meticulously scripted dialogue with elements of improvisation; handheld cinematography capturing the tightly choreographed action; volatile, venal politics embodied by fragile, fallible humans; hysterically funny with a sense of slowly dawning dread.

ACT I

VIDEO PROLOGUE

Backstage area of a small theatre in contemporary Australia. Three people: Vicki: local politician; Glen: events manager; Cloe: personal assistant, are talking animatedly as they move from backstage to the outside of the theatre. Vicky is singing.

Vicki: She's a Cherokee…Half breed that's all I ever heard. Half breed…what?

Cloe: Um, ten minutes and we have to go on.

Vicki: I'm sorry, I was just relaxing.

Cloe: That's all right.

Glen: No, so… give us a quick run-down.

Glen: Ok. So first the MC is going to get up and break in the crowd for us and then we have ah…

Vicki: Who is the MC?

Glen: Seany Choolburra.

Vicki: Is that really his name?

Glen: Well, he's Sean, but everybody calls him Seany.

Cloe: Who's that? I've never heard of him.

Vicki: Ah, he's a comedian. He *is* funny. He's got a whole physical shtick about Michael Jackson. (sigh) It's a bit yesterday, but he's hilarious. He has 'em rolling in the aisles. But he's no Stan Grant, I'll give you that much. Why don't we have Stan Grant?

Glen: We don't have the budget for someone like Stan Grant.

Vicki: It's always about the budget, isn't it?

Glen: This is going to be followed up by Welcome to Country and ah…

Vicki: Well…Is it that same Uncle[6] we have every single week? It seems like every single… every second week I'm seeing that man.

Glen: No, it's the Aunty.

Cloe: Oh Aunty. The one with the…

Vicki: Yeah-yeah, the grandchildren. Oh, the many, many grandchildren. I know more about her family than I care to know about my own… Oh. And what's up after that?

Glen: OK. Followed up by the, that's followed up by Kubitha.

Vicki: The what?

Cloe: Yeah, the…

Vicki: Can you say that again?

Enunciates exaggeratedly.

Cloe: Ku-bi -tha. Kubitha.

Vicki: No say that slowly so I can see your lips moving.

Speaking slowly.

Glen: Ku-bi tha.

Cloe: It's confusing cos he's saying thhhh instead of tee-aitch.

Vicki: Or is it a dh-dh-dh? What is it? What's the… the… what is that?

Glen: It's ah…the Black Duck Dance Company.[7] Black Duck.

Exasperatedly.

Vicki: Why don't they just say Black Duck Dance Company? Why they gotta have the…why they gotta have this fancy name? Like, you know. They're good. It's just it makes it that little bit more difficult, doesn't it?

Glen: We have one of the girls already here from the group and… the rest are on the way with Aunty.

Cloe: So, they're late?

Glen: No, they're on their way.

Cloe: On Aboriginal time.

Vicki: It's always the way, isn't it? Well, you better make sure that they *do* make It. Anyway...

Cloe: Let's just sign a few documents while there's time. All right there you go.

Vicki: Right.

Cloe: Here.

Vicki: Yep.

Cloe: Here.

Vicki looks for a flat surface to write on.

Vicki: Hang on, hang on, just building a...

Cloe: Ahh, I'll just bend over. Is that ok?

Vicki: Right. Which ones do I sign?

Cloe: Number two.

Vicki: Just um...

Mobile phone rings.

Glen: Sorry, I gotta take this.

Vicki speaking to Cloe.

Vicki: What was that?

Cloe: What?

Vicki: That! Turn around and look at me. Look me in the face. Uh-uh, look into my eyes. What was that?

Cloe: Nothing.

Glen speaking into mobile phone.

Glen: Hello?

Vicki continues to Cloe.

Vicki: Is there something wrong with me?

Glen: Hello?

Cloe: No, no, there's nothing wrong with you particularly but...

Glen: Where are you?

Cloe: You might just need a little bit of lipstick to balance you out. It could work.

Glen: Yeah, where exactly are you?

Vicki: Is there something wrong with my face?

Glen: No, your face is fine.

Cloe gesturing toward Vicki's face.

Cloe: Let's just do the paperwork and we'll deal with this situation later.

Glen: How much?

Vicki: Oh, so it's a situation, is it? *The* situation. No, later you'll be taking a photo of this situation. Yes, you will.

Glen: And we'll throw in a...

Cloe: Just a date and your signature. What else do we need?

Vicki: You can keep a straight face is what you can do. You can stop making fun of me... because you know what? I've gotta get out in front of the public.

Cloe: You'll be perfect.

Vicki: You're not the face of the public, are you? Wait...

Vicki turns her attention back to the documents.

Vicki: All right, so I'm on page five, what is this?

Cloe: Cycleways, cycleways. Remember you like cycling.

Glen: I really need to speak to you.

Cloe: Two seconds, two seconds.

Vicki: No, no, we *love* cycling, cycling relaxes me as well.

Cloe: And the extension, sign the extension as well.

Glen: So, the Aunty that's meant to be doing Welcome to Country *and* the rest of the dance group, they're double booked and they're off to Double Bay.

Cloe: Oh dear.

Glen: Yes.

Groans.

Vicki: Oh.

Cloe: You're going to have to do the Welcome to Country. That's fine.

Glen: Right oh, yeah.

Vicki: Why have I gotta do the Welcome to Country? Why can't Seany do the Welcome to Country?

Glen: Sorry we don't have time for this.

Vicki: There are so many black fellas out there. Why can't they be doing the Welcome to Country? Why has it always gotta be up to me? I don't understand. Look, this comes with a lot of responsibility but I didn't buy into this. I've gotta tip toe around everybody around here. Uh huh... well what have you gotta say? Hmm?

Cloe: Glen, what kind of underwear are you wearing?

Suspiciously.

Glen: I think I know where you're coming from…

Cloe: No. If you just hear me out.

Glen: and I don't like where this is going.

Cloe: It's just the pants.

Glen: No. No.

Cloe: You know, just underwear.

Glen: Oh, so every Blackfella knows how to put on a lap-lap and shake-a-leg?

Vicki: Oh, this is…

Glen: No.

Vicki: You could do it. I'm sure that that one little Black Duck dancer out there is getting terribly lonely.

Glen: Even if I could, it's an all-girl group.

Cloe: And… what do you have against women?

Glen: It's an all-girl group!

Vicki: All girl group? So?

Sighs.

Cloe: Oh, why does it always have to be so hard with Aboriginals? So many rules. Women's business, men's business.

Vicki turns to Glen.

Vicki: Listen mate. You either take off those pants or you break it to her.

Cloe: You tell him.

Glen: All right I'll break it to her but I'm not breaking it *with* her.

Cloe: Let's just take this off. Lipstick, get the corners. No sad face. We don't have time for sad faces.

Vicki: Do I look OK?

Cloe: Deadly, that's what you people say. In you go. Here's your speech....
Oh dear.

Vicki enters stage and performs a solo dance.

Scene four: but I'm just a dancer

In the live performance of this scene, the spoken text and movement components are depicted as a call and response between word and action. The Karen character's monologue consists of a series of increasingly preposterous racist assumptions — all indigenous Australians are wise/authentic/obese etc., to which I respond by performing a sequence of gestures that physically represent the phrase, "But I'm just a dancer." I do the exact same dance no matter what the question, its insistent repetition is expressive of several things: my mounting exasperation at having to endure Karen's ludicrous tirade; the sad, dull fact that I can't answer the questions, because they are more about the questioner than the questionee; and the intercultural wheel-spinning of contemporary Australia — an occupied land, never ceded by its original owners.

Dance theorist Henrietta Bannerman's (2014, 67) assertion that while dance does have discernible syntax, unlike the spoken word, it is not capable of conveying contextual specificity. *But I'm Just a Dancer* exemplifies the idea that dance is an abstract expression of interiority. Bannerman (2014, 68) references the modern dance choreographer Martha Graham to illustrate her claim stating, "We can surely agree, for example, that the Graham contraction is visually and conventionally linked to the expression of emotional states." The scene *But I'm Just a Dancer* combines spoken and danced components for specific reasons. The use of text allows Karen's outrageous and pernicious declarations to be explicitly understood, whereas the emotional impact of her words is best expressed and revealed through movement, something that is beyond words.

ACT I

SCENE 4

Post show, foyer of a regional theatre in contemporary Australia. Performer Vicki is standing listening to Karen, a classic white Australian stage mum. Karen's eight-year-old daughter Savannah is beside them playing on a smart phone.

Karen: Hiieee. Hope you don't mind but we just wanted to tell you, the show was lovely, moved us to tears, didn't it Savannah? And I hope you don't mind me asking, but what's your totem? Savannah's so interested, aren't you, Savannah? She heard all about that stuff at school when a traditional Aborigine group came to tell their dreaming stories and share their songs and dances. She just loves all that stuff. They said their totem was then goanna and that all real indigenous people had one. But we were wondering, if it wasn't too much trouble, if you could give us a totem too? Savannah would just love her own totem. We could get it like bedazzled on her clothes, or maybe a dot-to-dot painting made up for her, for Her room. Something like that. It'd be so cool. You know, in the spirit of reconciliation and all that? I think that'd be a great idea. By the way, could you tell me in a few short wise words, what you think about microwave ovens, the mobile phone invasion and radiation poisoning, and what it's doing to our kids, the next generations you know. While we're on the subject, what's your opinion on quality childcare these days, childhood obesity and the new diabetes epidemic. Especially in your people. Oh, not that you've got anything to worry about, you've got a beautiful figure. I'm jealous. Old growth forests, strip mining and asbestos poisoning, if you don't mind me asking. Oh, poor mother earth! Lucky we even made it today. We've got so much to do. Got to get you to tutoring Savannah. Not like you're going to make me any money in your old age. Oh, speaking of which… what about that tax dollar eh? Where's our sense of community? Ahhhh, to live the true Aboriginal way. Savannah, get your hands off that please! Ahhh, look at the time, going to have to dash… About that totem. Maybe next time, eh? Thank you so much, you've really cleared things up. Really put things into perspective for me. Come on Savannah! We've taken up far too long of this lovely lady's time already and we're just going to have to get a move on if we're going to miss the traffic. Savannah, put that game away now. Just don't get me started!

Scene six: fusion dance debate

Fusion Dance Debate is a verbatim telephone dialogue between myself and choreographer and performer Henrietta Baird, a Kuku Yalanji woman from Far North Queensland. The scene is sandwiched between two stand-up monologues, and played together they create the *Fusion trilogy*. The first monologue is *Fusion Food,* which references the pervasiveness of cultural fusion, beginning with its ubiquity in the food industry, followed by riffs on genetics, architecture and Chindogu, the Japanese art of impractical inventions. The last monologue is *Fusion Hospital* which is described in detail below.

The telephone recording in *Fusion Dance Debate* was not scripted, nor were the questions I asked Henrietta planned. My primary intention was to have a discourse regarding the ownership, authority and authorship of danced vocabularies. The movement phrases accompanying the conversation were designed to appear as spontaneous as the telephone conversation, an improvisation of various interchangeable parts of dances. Henrietta and I conversed while I executed a combination of modern dance sequences drawn from the Martha Graham technique, interspersed this is a release-based warm up devised by Brian Carbee[8] alongside several Aboriginal and Torres Strait Islander movement motifs which I had personalised. None of these languages were representative of my Wiradjuri heritage, yet they were each somehow representative of me.

This scene created a context for exploring aesthetic *and* ethical ramifications of my dance technique juxtapositions, with Henrietta playing the role of cultural provocateur. Through my dance, I was asserting that each movement language has its own discrete logic and that a kinaesthetic and choreographic expertise is required to combine them in such a way that the resulting sequence makes physical, aesthetic and organisational sense; seen this way, each synthesis creates something entirely new. Again, I turn to Bannerman (2014, 66) who states, "[…] from the point of view of structure, dance shares commonalities with [spoken] language and that like language it communicates according to cultural codes." My own embodied experience supports the idea that within each choreographed dance, different kinds of languages can and do coexist, without any one style or genre necessarily swallowing up any other. In performing several dance genres while speaking in English, I was dancing the complexity of the post-colonial body, a dance of simultaneous, paradoxical pluralities.

A central purpose in creating *plenty serious TALK TALK* was to shed some light on the complexities surrounding the making of contemporary Australian Indigenous art, particularly for contemporary Australian Indigenous artists. When applying for any local, state or national funding in Australia, if you intend to create or collaborate with Indigenous persons and/or content, it is mandatory to identify and engage with the relevant Aboriginal communities (Australia Council for the Arts, n.d.). This is true for everyone, but something to understand, if not comprehend, is that *whenever* I dance, I am an Australian Indigenous dancer, this is my embodied knowledge yet it is still culturally imperative that I consult with the relevant Aboriginal community and seek permission to do certain dances. In a traditional cultural context, this indicates a relationship of reciprocal surveillance wherein one person is custodian and the other is manager. For the Warlpiri people of central Australia this form of relational reciprocity is called the kirda (kin owner)/kundungurlu (manager) and is expressed through painted designs and the spatial relationships in their dances: and for the Yolngu, the term is djungaya, where the mother clans (yothu) are workers for the child clans (yindi). And so, as part of this extended community of cultural practice, I don't experience artistic autonomy in the same way as my non-indigenous contemporary choreographer colleagues do. I am constantly culturally contextualised.

In relation to these issues, Henrietta Baird's role as cultural consultant was crucial to the realisation of the work, regardless of whether our improvised telephone conversation ended up being part of the show or not.

Inviting someone of Henrietta's cultural status indicated that I was both taking protocols seriously, and meeting them. Alongside this, her role as provocateur provided a device for meta-reflection, in which we could discuss concepts and experiences of embodiment, authorship, authority and ownership in relation to traditional and contemporary indigenous culture, particularly similarities and differences between "urban" and "in country" indigenous experience.

ACT I

SCENE 6

We meet Vicki and Etta in separate places. They are playing themselves. They are both dancer, performer choreographers and they are good friends. Vicki is trying to call Etta.

Phone: Woop Woop Woop, Aaaaahhhhh, ts hah ts ahhh, dhdhdhdhdhdhdh-dhdh, oo hooo oo hooo, blblblblbblblblblbl...Brr brr, burr brrr.

Vicki to herself.

Vicki: I can't do the new ones, I'm analogue.

Phone: Brrrr brrrr, burr brrr.

Vicki: Oh, fucking hell, I know it's Etta.

Phone: brrrr burr.

Vicki: I know it's her...

Phone: brrr brr.

Vicki: Cos it's a number I don't recognise.

Phone: brr brr.

Vicki: She's got so many numbers I thought she had a dodgy job on the side. But no...

Phone: brr brrr.

Vicki: It's just man trouble.

Etta picks up.

Vicki: Are you at work?

Etta: Yeah.

Vicki: Right, no, cos I was wondering. I wanted to ask you… I wanted to ask you, remember when I made that work on Mel?

Etta: Yeah.

Vicki: Remember when you…

Etta: The one with the TSI[9] movement?

Vicki: Remember when you first said "oh no you should stick to Martha Graham?"

Etta: Yeah why?

Vicki: No, it wasn't a bad thing, it's just how you felt. And I got away with it because Mel is going out with G.

Etta: Yeah???

Vicki: But when you said it… was it because if it's not an Aboriginal piece it shouldn't be there?

Etta: Umm…

Vicki: Or is it because it's not an Aboriginal person doing it? Or is it because it looked too close to a traditional dance?

Etta: The one she um, did with the smoking?

Vicki: Yes.

Etta: Um I don't, I don't know. I can't even remember what I said to you.

Vicki: Aw you just said you should stick to Martha Graham. But then I thought,

"Oh, Martha Graham's not mine either."

Etta: But that was the technique that you trained in.

Vicki: Well, I trained in TSI technique as well, and I trained in lots of different Aboriginal dance techniques... I'm making this work, not this week but at the end of next year about... Where do you draw the line? How do you draw the line in it? Where do you go alright this is too sacred or this is too *close or this isn't too close? Or you know...*

Etta: We did that...we did that already remember?

Vicki: Which one?

Etta: The one where we painted Gideon Obarzanek[10] up, with umm...

Vicki: Yeah, where we painted him up with the nappy cream?

Etta: Yeah.

Vicki frowns.

Vicki: No.

Etta: Yeah, that one. You know, weren't we pushing the boundaries then?

Vicki: Yes, but you know me? I'm always pushing all the fuckin' boundaries! Because I know that I...cos I know, at first, I sometimes make you feel nervous as well.

Etta: Ooh, yeah! It's like running your own people down. You know, it's like disrespectful...

Vicki: But did you...did you feel like we were running people down?

Etta: Aw, you know, if I'm presenting work at all... I think I um... I think about other people's reactions.

Vicki: Oh, because you think that they might not think that we're smart and that we're...do you think they might think...

Etta: They might not understand. They don't understand that it's a like contemporary or artistic view, you know? Maybe now, now they might know that it's a valid point of view. You know, like art is changing.

Vicki: But do you… listen…do we wait for the art to change, and then we make the work? Or do we make the art change by making the work?

Etta: Are you interviewing me?

Vicki: I am kind of?

Etta: Yeah, I knew you were doing that.

Vicki: You know how I do Brian Carbee's dance class?

Etta: Yeah.

Vicki: So anyway, I've taken one of his phrases and I'm making it look like all different types of dance. I'm showing how I take dances and I move around with them, cos I've now done Brian's class more than anyone. So, I also think about that. How does Brian feel? He's got a mortgage. You know what I mean?

Etta: How come you can't come Thursday?

Vicki: What?

Etta: How come you can't come Thursday?

Vicki: Oh, I can't come Thursday cos I'm doing this thing on um, Saturday and Sunday and I have to rehearse.

Etta: What do you have to do then?

Vicki: That's why I called you up. There's this whole section I'm doing about appropriation. What's worse — to appropriate from a single person, from a technique, from a culture? When is it appropriation and when does it belong to you in your body?

Etta: When you change it, to make it you.

Vicki: But is it like…you know, I change things to make 'me,' but I don't want to change them so you can't recognise them. I want to change them so you can recognise where they come from but you can see that they're different. But obviously, that may not be good enough?

Etta: You've already got your own style. You can see it.

Vicki: Oh, you're just feeling all good natured towards me.

Fondly with a slight air of exasperation.

Etta: Nah Vicki.

Scene eight: fusion hospital

This is a first-person narrative recounting of a hapless visit to the emergency ward at the Royal Prince Alfred Hospital (RPA) in Sydney, Australia. Along with *Fusion Food,* this monologue involves a complex dance of the tongue across the teeth. There is a sizeable amount of alliteration, but it proceeds at a steady tempo, designed to put the audience at ease. The punchlines to each usually self-deprecating joke come at regular intervals, masking the dark sub-text which was essentially overt and unapologetic racism.

The movement, although seemingly impromptu, was very considered. I was aspiring to the physical humour of silent film geniuses Charlie Chaplin and Buster Keaton through the sad but funny fallibility of my failing body, as the hapless patient navigating a racist system.

ACT 1

SCENE 8

Vicki as herself standing centre stage, directly addressing the audience.

Vicki: Can there be a wrong kind of fusion you ask? Well funny you should say that. For those of you who don't know me, I've been a bit under the weather of late. A few trips to the hospital and all that. Picture this. It's 2.30 in the morning. I'm in agony right, so I decide to go to the hospital. I throw on some clothes, but hearing Mum's voice say something about clean underwear, I pack a bag, slip on my thongs and shuffle off to RPA. I'm pressing a hot water bottle to my back. I fig-ure if I get there and feel better, I can chalk it up to a spot of nightly exercise. I don't feel better and I'm immediately admitted. But when I get to the bed and take off my hoodie, the attitude towards me is not exactly benevolent. The attending nurse throws a gown at me, tells me to "Put it on and get on the bed" with a gruff voice and the sanctimonious demeanour of Nurse Ratchet from *One Flew Over the Cuckoo's Nest,*[11] then leaves. When she leaves, I take off my clothes be-cause that's how I roll. I am very obedient. But I am racked with pain. So, I lie down on the linoleum floor. Nurse Ratchet comes back, "I thought I told you to get on the bed." Even the two ambulance fel-las across the aisle seem to pity me, while trying not to look at me, in my bra and trackies. Ratchet asks how I'd rate my pain between a

1 and a 10. I say, "That's a pretty abstract concept isn't it" but "Yep, it's a 10, definitely a 9 or an 8 at least." I watch the back of her black sneakers put distance between us. When she finally comes back, I ask for a refill of my hot water bottle. "No, you could burn yourself." "How about a Panadol?" "Not until the doctor's seen you." I'm thinking, "I was better off in the street." Then I call the most respectable look- ing person I know. There's one in every art organisation. They can work magic. This woman is no exception, she's all over a spread sheet like ball bearings busting out of a pair of roller-skates. I say, "Pam, I don't know what to do. I'm in the hospital but I think they think I'm a drug addict. I can only put it down to the fact that I put on a shirt I bought from Yabaan on Survival Day,[12] and I think they got the wrong impression. "What does it say?" she asks. "I'm awesome, I'm black and I'm deadly." Five hours later I was given my first real check-up. I immediately received a blood transfusion. In hindsight, I can't help but think that it might've boded better for me if I'd worn a regular white tee saying "I'm a Caucasian conservative." Boom-boom.

Conclusion

In *plenty serious TALK TALK* dancing, speaking, choreographing and writing practices come together to form a discrete ontology, proposing new possibili- ties for seeing, hearing, reading and experiencing choreography as a polyva- lent, constantly transforming product of many bodies, many times and many cultures.

The diversities of movement languages, the multiple voices and perspec- tives, and the different materials, mediums and modes of performance are intended to reflect the complexities of the issues presented, but also to illumi- nate the ancient and the emergent pathways I navigate every day as a contem- porary Aboriginal artist and person (the subject).

Talking with my peer and friend Henrietta Baird in the *Fusion Dance De- bate* section of this text, I ask "Do we wait for the art to change and then we make the work? Or do we make the art change by making the work?" It is through continuing to talk, dance, listen, observe, write, read and choreo- graph, through engaging with art and art-making as an ever evolving, process- based, community-building practice that I try to answer this question, over and over and over again.

Notes

1 In 2018, *plenty serious TALK TALK* was presented by FORM Dance Projects at Parramatta Riverside Theatres, Sydney. In 2019, it toured to BOLD festival, Canberra, Yirramboi Festival, Melbourne and then back to Sydney, where it was presented as part of Performance Space's Liveworks at Carriageworks in Everleigh, near the historic site of the original National Black Theatre.

2 Reconciliation Australia. n.d. "Acknowledgement of Country and Welcome to Country." Accessed May 11, 2023. https://www.reconciliation.org.au/reconciliation/acknowledgement-of-country-and-welcome-to-country/.

3 Sean Choolburra is an Australian entertainer and comedian. He is a Girramay, Kalkadoon, Pitta Pitta and Gugu Yalanji man.

4 Stan Grant is an Australian journalist, writer and radio and television presenter, since the 1990s. He has written and spoken on Indigenous issues and his Aboriginal identity. He is a Wiradjuri man.

5 *The Thick of It* was a television series which ran from 2005 to 2012. Created by Armando Iannucci, it satirised the inner workings of modern British government.

6 In Australian Indigenous culture and community, "uncle" and "aunty" are terms of respect. They are used for people held in high esteem, generally older people who have earned that respect.

7 Black Duck Dance Company is an all-female, indigenous dance group based in Sydney, Australia.

8 Brian Carbee is a US-born performer, script writer, dancer and choreographer. He is a contemporary dance teacher of note, currently based in Sydney, Australia.

9 The Torres Strait Islands (TSI) are found at Australia's northernmost frontier, stretching from the tip of Queensland to the southern shores of Papua New Guinea.

10 Gideon Obarnanek, formerly an Australian dancer and choreographer, is now a curator and festival director.

11 *One Flew Over the Cuckoo's Nest* is a 1975 American psychological drama film, directed by Miloš Forman, based on the 1962 novel of the same name by Ken Kesey.

12 First Nations communities have long battled the commemoration of 26 January as "Australia Day," when for First Peoples it is a day of invasion, mourning and survival.

References

Australia Council for the Arts. n.d. "First Nations Cultural and Intellectual Property in the Arts." Accessed December 23, 2022. https://australiacouncil.gov.au/investment-and-development/protocols-and-resources/protocols-for-using-first-nations-cultural-and-intellectual-property-in-the-arts/.

Bannerman, Henrietta. 2014. "Is Dance a Language? Movement, Meaning and Communication." *Dance Research: The Journal of the Society for Dance Research* 32(1): 65–80.

Pollock, Zoe. 2008. "National Black Theatre." Dictionary of Sydney. Accessed May 11, 2023. https://dictionaryofsydney.org/entry/national_black_theatre.

Reconciliation Australia. n.d. "Acknowledgement of Country and Welcome to Country." Accessed May 11, 2023. https://www.reconciliation.org.au/reconciliation/acknowledgement-of-country-and-welcome-to-country/.

Token Gypsy. n.d. "Basically Black." YouTube. Accessed May 11, 2023. https://www.youtube.com/watch?v=uTunYAlu6Rk.

4

THE PLACE WHERE THE ACTUAL AND FICTIONAL TOUCH, THE PLACE WHERE A LANGUAGE FLICKS CHANNELS

alys longley

As a process-oriented fragmentary essay, this chapter presents examples of choreographic writing, wherein practices of choreography and writing co-form each other, with words emerging in the process of witnessing dancing and choreographic phrases emerging out of written and spoken texts. In the performance h u m a t t e r i n g (longley 2022), these texts were carefully recorded, edited, sampled and placed in conversation with live voice, so that choreographic writing became music, became theatrical world, its affect modulated by lighting design and dance vocabulary. For Mistranslation Laboratory, vocabulary was co-created with audiences through small group tasks and performance experiments (longley 2019b). Through this chapter, pieces of choreographic writing, alongside process discussions, engage alternative layouts to allow a bleed between essay, drawing, poetic language and experimental performance documentation. Illegible text-fragments of miniature and struck-through text run through this writing in the form of concrete poetry or abstract affect, materialising the role of erasure in the composition process.

Section one: *to test the holdingness of things*

> *It seems so ridiculous.*
> *To commit so fully to something so impossible.*
> *But when we are a we*
> *the impossibility becomes a game rather than a deflation.*
> *The impossibility becomes a craving — digesting the immanent*
> *failure and observing what*
> *occurs, the poetics of attempt.*
> *The opposite of failure being, not success, but continuation.*

DOI: 10.4324/9781003397427-5

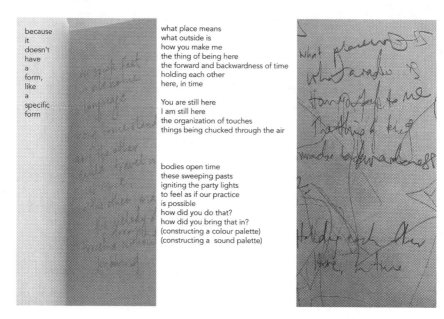

FIGURE 4.1 Practice notes, alys longley. Photographs by the author.

This is writing that comes out of following movement, attuning via all the vocabulary available. The word "vocabulary" can contain anything — nonsense, drawing, dancing, scribbling, description, fragments of poetic text, jokes, an essay, a theatrical scene, a meme on social media, a philosophical inquiry, ~~a sound recording on a mobile phone~~, notes, lists, photographs, video, sound recording. It all gets entangled, curated, translated again. So often it is overwhelming, and then you find something singular to attend to, a particular niche of memory, affect, sensation, event or relation.

A container, as something that holds, provides sets of possibilities and constraints, permissions, resistance and frames. ~~Perhaps the vitality of choreographic writing is to do this kind of holding. What kind of containers might~~. The kind of container that choreographic writing offers could be:

stylistic
expressive
linguistic
interdisciplinary
radical
of the (indeterminate) body
somatic
visceral
experimental
minor
folded
dramaturgical

collaborative
moving-with the logics of dancing
allowing the singular logics of a studio practice (for example the daytime affective weather momentum of touch)
to move from studio to page

The resources of poetic/performative language can be materials for ignition of
choreographic experimentation, as can friendships that sustain bodies of work.
In this writing, I attempt to dance across temporalities and modes, in conversation with poetics, with fiction, with tangential notation and expanded fields
~~drawing, multi-media, sound recording, artistic mapping, artisfriend collaborations and journaling,~~ to evoke processes for experiencing choreography through the otherwise
of experimental writing.

The term "otherwise," in this case, refers to the work of Walter de Mignolo
(2005, xx) and his call for "theory arising from the projects of decolonisation
of knowledge and being that will lead to the imagining of economy and politics *otherwise.*" By placing embodied perception at its centre, choreographic
writing has a contribution to make to fields of art, culture and politics in
proposing methods that take seriously the embodiment and fluid forms of attention that resist binary logic.

With a capacity to resist the generalising tendencies of language, choreographic writing has visceral and spatial resources for tipping text beyond
normative style and Cartesian writing convention. The imperative of pushing language around to allow the movement of imagination, to find vocabulary beyond the predictable, is a core thematic in contemporary philosophy
(Deleuze 1995; Braidotti 2006; Barad 2018), emphasising the entanglement
of style and politics in approaches to language with the potential to carry ideas
beyond conventional grammar (longley 2021).

How can we write with the intelligence of touch? How to write in a way
that corresponds to the way one's skin senses kinaesthetic difference? Such
attempts may allow forces, such as gravity, momentum and intensity, to fuse
with what pages can do, within the entirely different register from ~~sensing into~~
dance practice, that writing is.

~~We could consider the possibility of a touch with writing, in its own temporalities.~~

The choreographic writing of Tru Paraha (2018a; 2018b), for example,
slips between choreography, philosophy, transcultural poetics and performance writing. Each slip is a resource that carries choreographic experimentation to pages-as-sites-of-movement-practice so the written form of artistic
research ripples with vitality.

Choreographic practice c ll ps s into states of blackOut wānanga (philosophical searching, the dark unknowing). Obliterative scores recede and
e(((((((ho; sound, language — deforming from blacknyss.

(Paraha 2018b, 49)

Paraha's artistic research is orientated by darkness and black-out states, in relation to Matauranga Māori concepts of te po, the night, and te kore, the void, drawing on cosmo-genealogies of darkness articulated by Māori scholar Hone Sadler (2007). Here, language is explicit in articulating precise gradations of uncertainty in spaces of darkness, from Te Pō Mä (The White Darkness) to Te Pō mangu (The Black Darkness), Te Pō Whakaruru (The Sheltered Darkness) to Te Pō tangotango (The Intense Darkness), from Te Pō Maui (The Left Handed Darkness) to Te Pō Matau (The Right Handed Darkness) (Sadler 2007, 37–38). These also reflect the darkness that is necessary in order to bring Te Ao Marama — the world of light and knowing, into being (Paraha 2017).

In choreographic writing, definitions of what can constitute a body, or a sense of humanity can become uncertain (Kramer 2015; 2021; Paraha 2018a; 2018b). Paraha's work opens out space for considering what can happen when we orient from the frame of darkness rather than visuality, moving with things we can feel, but perhaps not ever fully know, when we question what it is that our bodies are and open our curiosity to the other-than-human forces that are undeniably part of our worlds. In Paraha's case, this foreign language within language attunes audiences and readers to more-than-human and horror-inflected cadences of unknowing. Concrete and visual poetics allow the formal play of language to push words beyond themselves, to exceed the conventions of the alphabet, to touch out to readers via the logic of physical form in space. Visual poetics enter this current chapter through the inclusion of phrases that were earmarked for erasure in the writing-process, yet the text decided to stick around, and I couldn't quite erase it. So, I half-deleted, and then shrunk ~~the text~~ the text which wanted to make itself felt — not as fully legible, but as an evocation of process, of the under-the-sea existence of process, made visible in a kind of concrete poetics in a half-size font, struck-through, and diminished in size. Art writer and curator Gregory O'Brien's (2004, 42) essay, *Plain air/ plain song*, discusses the "stammering concrete poetry" of visual artist Rosalie Gascoigne, defining concrete poetry as simultaneously poem and drawing in a tradition stretching back to French poets, such as Stéphane Mallarmé and Guillaume Apollinaire, or more recently the compositional work of John Cage and his rejection of the constraining institution of syntax. Tru Paraha's blackOut e(((((((((hos presents a choreographic instantiation of such poetics. O'Brien's (2004, 42) discussion of concrete poetry as allowing "a grammar of the incomplete and the untethered phrase" gestures to a mode of writing with the potential to invite the choreographic to inflect pages through the lifting and falling of space, weight and time.

There is a delicacy and precariousness in coercing ~~allowing~~ touch, a series of touches, to move through dance to the page. For *mere hobbyists* (comprised of dance–artists and writers pavleheidler and alys longley (2021)), conversation, conviviality and experiments in design enable a sense of touch to pervade choreographic writing.

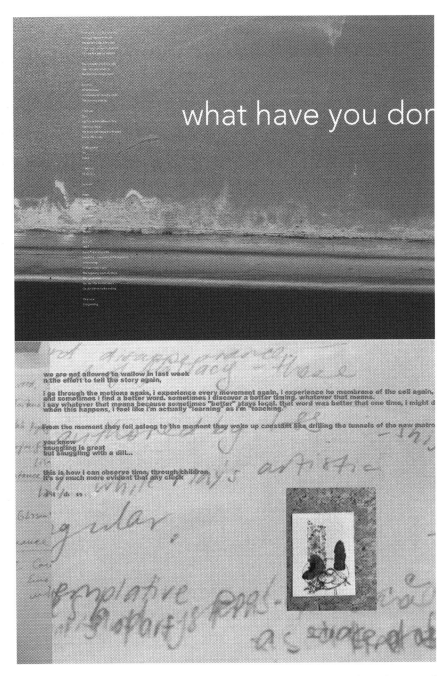

FIGURE 4.2 Choreographic writing by pavleheidler and alys longley. Photograph by pavleheidler and alys longley.

~~Let's begin with speculation, with imagining a new project out of a practice of friendship and displacement~~ When the COVID pandemic prevented *Merely Hobbyists* from taking up a planned residency in Stockholm, we began inventing fantasy-forms-of-creative-proposal, outside of institutional mandate, to work together in an imagined future. In the following proposal, the actual and fictional touch through a practice of dance writing that is also a practice of hope.

Speculative proposal for a future Merely Hobbyists workshop (alys longley, with pavleheidler) (imagining a collaboration, Aotearoa NZ to Stockholm, Sweden)

1.

It's almost 10 o'clock already.

The gradients of light are moving.

Daylight here is night time there, and summer here is winter there.

We imagine the other side of our we in a heat wave, as here in mid-winter, we wrap in a thick blanket scarf and take our daughter's temperature for her fever, snuggle her in a duvet and heat the hot water bottle. Again. We lie beside her flushed body as she falls asleep. Because she asks us to.

We lost one thermometer and the battery of the other died.

We shiver. We sense the other side of our we opening out in the light of the longest day.

There is a machine that is called an aeroplane that has two wings and an engine.

There is a body called an ocean that has every colour of blue in it. Does the ocean pull the moon? The moon pulls the ocean. The moon that is the same one either side.

It is six minutes past ten. You can feel the cold as a kind of touch along your arms and under your fingers.

Something is pulling and something is magnetic and bodies of infinite sizes are asking and we are shaking our broken machines and drawing out our cartographic instruments to commit to our failing, to moving with the pull, to resting into an elseward time.

2.

(you send your imagination outward and have this sense of all the fields, expanding.)

We attempt to undo the sleeves of discipline with the quick unpick of touch, improvising a space where stand-up comedy is poetry is somatics, without making fun of anyone.

A ball filled with air that we throw in the air.
A ball filled with sound that we throw in the air.
A ball filled with sound that we throw into volume.
A ball filled with volume that we can never catch, we can only hear,
we can never hear, we can only catch.

3.

to test the holdingness of things
We want to bring shared interests in working with non-binary practices that, while deeply informed by attention to kinaesthetic materials, slip past anatomy, past humanism, into grainy, speculative, imaginative response-inventions with phrase and frame, outward, downward, upward, dirtward in scale, from the tiny felt — to the planetary dreamt, the resources of poetic/performative language are materials for ignition of choreographic experimentation.

We want to take copious notes, ~~to ride the potentials of documentation past sense and past actuality, into buoyant glitches of unknowing~~, to place the curious and volatile question of what a body is within a poetics of touch, weightedness and tone.

There are practices and techniques that we know and that we extrude studio tasks from, including:

Choreography/Dramaturgy/Contact Improvisation/Hands-on experiments in somatic listening and co-moving/Writing in the expanded field/Contemporary Poetics.

4.

"Reality is a matter of worlding and inhabiting. It is a matter of testing the holdingness of things" (Haraway as reported by Weigel 2019, n.p.).
~~As dancers, dramaturgs, materials such as graphite and recording device, somatic practitioners and random (or maybe deeply masterful but deeply subtle) bacteria,~~ We have developed careful practices for listening and holding – bodies, spaces, affects, emotions, poetics, aesthetics. We think of aesthetics and spatialities holding style, tone, sense and possibility for developing as Haraway (Weigel 2019, n.p.) puts it,

"emergent systematicities" that respond to the "need to develop practices for thinking about those forms of activity that are not caught by functionality, those which propose the possible-but-not-yet, or that which is not-yet but still open." We propose creating/testing frames or states of "holdingness" and also the inverse, the "letting-go ness."

Material things, political things and abstract things will be held and dropped in differing scales of responsibility and release, triggering responses in movement, text for reading, text for performance, video, score, drawing and critical provocation.

We propose to develop:

- A series of experiments in studio practice and documentation, which are also experiments in choreographic research, exploring choreographic scoring/performance writing/new materialist co-bodying/installation practice.
- A work-in-progress choreographic installation for invited guests.
- An artist-book will be developed in the six months post-residency — in which poetic texts/drawings/photographs/video stills make a performance via the form of the book.
- Video and sound materials may also be made available via a portal constructed on the World Wide Web.

5.

This is the summer of epic rain. Rain that brings a city to a standstill. And the motorways become rivers, and the industrial zone becomes a lake. And I am messaging you a picture of the raindrops on my window. And you are sending me an in-joke from a film you are watching. And I am sending you three messages, each of just the sound of uncontrollable laughter, with some gasping. And your message back is a description of standing at a metro station, alone on the platform, just giggling, chortling.

We are making plans to board the sky. Two wings and an engine and some jetlag. Moving with the pull. Practice as magnet. To twogathering.

Section two: Artisfriends

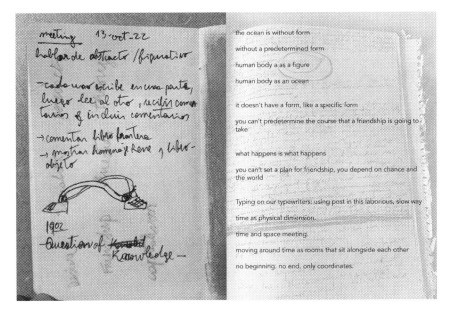

FIGURE 4.3   From the artist book *On artisfriendship* (2022, 6, 16) by alys longley and Francisco González-Castro. Photographs by alys longley and
Francisco González-Castro.

~~We dance across temporalities and modes, in conversation with poetics, with fiction, with~~
~~tangential notation, drawing, multi-media, sound recording, artistic mapping and journaling,~~
~~open to experiencing choreography through the otherwise of experimental writing.~~

Francisco González Castro and I are working on a performance-research collaboration, orienting with Global Souths as our point of beginning. With this
in mind, we have been using our made-up word *artisfriend*, defining the blurring of artist and friend, with a soft 's' and removing the hard 't' to parse the
terms. We are following what happens when we understand artisfriendship and
world-making as entangled with each other — friendship being a central part
of how worlds are formed — worlds of practice, worlds of invention, worlds of
everyday existence. We are thinking about how artisfriendship is part normal
friendship, and part artistic practice — making work, inventing things, seeing
each other through the vagaries of artistic practice. Because artistic practice
takes devotion and (often) non-normative experience, artisfriendships include
intense affective studio life as well as having each other's backs across time,
across everyday life. That blurring of worlds and that practice of testing of

realities together allows artistic problem-solving to happen in the limit spaces of vocabulary and form.

To write just with the affect of being-with space and-or collaborators
To hold the feeling of it in your body
To draw and write and not know the vocabulary before-hand
To overlay a drawing with lines of connection
Maybe colour, maybe the weight of your hand
Maybe just attuning with movement and following with a continuous line
Eyes towards movement, hand just following
Words just following
A meeting of body times
upon a page

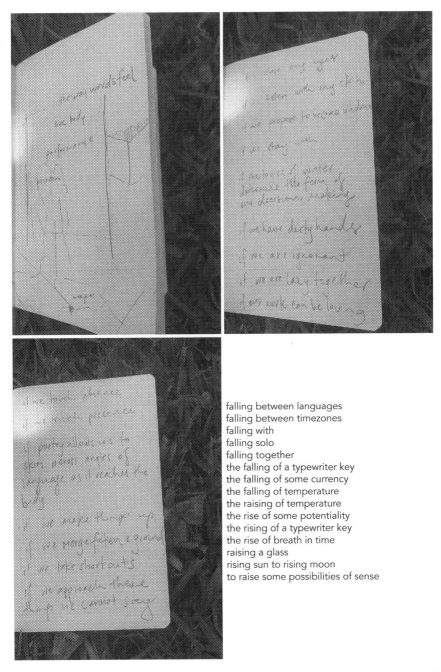

falling between languages
falling between timezones
falling with
falling solo
falling together
the falling of a typewriter key
the falling of some currency
the falling of temperature
the raising of temperature
the rise of some potentiality
the rising of a typewriter key
the rise of breath in time
raising a glass
rising sun to rising moon
to raise some possibilities of sense

FIGURE 4.4 From the artist book *On artisfriendship* (2022) by alys longley and Francisco González-Castro. Photographs by alys longley.

In some ways, it is impossible to know where the choreographic process begins and ends, to differentiate between the collaborative relationships that enable work to happen, ~~alongside underneath~~ beneath the titled work we name and frame. The agency of materials and chance encounters, within relationships, environments and ecologies travel ideas far beyond that which artists intend or can control. What if a choreography could be understood as authored in an expanded way, so the writing of choreographic moments to pages could value social and environmental ecologies, relationships, chance conditions and the practices of care that form the ground of choreographic invention? From this perspective, is it possible that friendship is one of the most under-rated working practices in the critical discourse of choreography? And that friendship can be recognised beyond human relations? A ~~relationship with a favourite~~ book, or poem, or essay, or dance, or pen, or blackboard could be a vital artisfriend, full of affection, care, inspiration, gratitude and new possibility. How to recognise the accretions of practice and relationship that happen over years and years, forming the ground of a choreographic process? We think, with anthropologist Kathleen Stewart, who engages a poetics of affect to summon the simultaneity of the extraordinary and the banal, the political surging through the everyday, in her evocations of daily life in the US:

> In any worlding we can ask how things come to matter and through what qualities, rhythms, forces, relations and movements. Here I'm interested in the peculiar materialities of things that come to matter. The way they are at once abstract and concrete, ephemeral and consequential, fully sensory and lodged in prolific imaginaries. The way they stretch across scenes, fields and sediments, attaching to the very sense that something is happening.
>
> (Stewart 2007, 4)

Through approaching anthropology as a process of worlding, Stewart attunes to quality, rhythm, force, relation and movement in singular situations. The rhythms of events fold into writing in such a way that the emotional punch of small everyday experiences can be felt in the reader's body, moving across time and geography through the intensity of writing style.

Thinking of friendship as courage-giving, focus-enabling and life-enhancing, returns me to my artisfriendship with chalk and blackboards in various scales and forms over many years. Particular blackboards — as t-shirts, as labcoats, as playing cards, as voluminous physical territories — and the particular forms of dancing, writing and drawing they have enabled, have accompanied me through a series of performances, relational artistic-research experiments with audiences, and postal-art projects. Returning to the familiarity of these materials and their affordances allowed a continuation of practice across time and projects. When funding has not been available, I have always been able to quietly work away with the processes of this ongoing collaboration, and the ready inclusiveness it offers.

In Mistranslation Laboratory (longley 2017; 2019a), our worn blackboards had us literally notating upon each other's bodies throughout performances — we drew words, affective states, emotions and scripts across each other, forming a second skin. We translated markers of precise moments in drawings across bodies and surfaces.

The ephemerality and mutability of chalk and blackboards means the surface holds, but only partially. Vocab wears away with time and friction. Interactions with time and touch endure within the blackboard surface, in dialogue with time, to be erased and rewritten in endless palimpsests. Something holds, the erased text lingers in the physical object. Gregory O'Brien (2004, 43) writes of the concrete poetry of Rosalie Gascoigne that, "time itself can be an editing process, stripping down its raw materials, reducing and refining them." So, it is in developing performance writing with blackboards.

FIGURE 4.5   Choreographic writing with chalk. Clockwise from top: alys longley and Angel Garcia in Mistranslation Laboratory, Museum of Contemporary Art Santiago (MAC), 2017, Photograph by Alejandra Caro; h u m a t t e r i n g, Australasian Drama Studies Conference, 2022, photograph by alys longley; Adam Naughton, alys longley and Rosalind Holdaway in h u m a t t e r i n g, OFA Auckland, 2021, photograph by Jeffrey Holdaway; Blackboard Cards for Touch Practice Poetics, 2022, photograph by alys longley; Carol Brown and Macarena Campbell-Parra in Mistranslation Laboratory, MAC, 2017, photograph by Alejandra Caro.

Most recently I have been writing with light via vinyl-cut texts on windows and making miniature blackboards alongside envelopes made from cyanotype prints. These envelopes carry scores for postal dances that can be rewritten over and over, designed so that language and drawing can be fragmented, recomposed, to form a new score or set of possibilities. Living in Aotearoa, NZ, postal collaborations are a way to continue practices of international co-creation, without the ecological cost of air travel. Placing translation or mistranslation at the centre of a choreographic practice treats dancing and writing as fulcrums into phrase creation across diverse media (longley 2017). We treat vocabulary as migratorial and flighty — always ready for inaccurate rendering, for imperfect transition. In the process of writing out of dancing (or the inverse, dancing out of writing), creating installation out of choreography, or film out of various improvisations and spaces, resources of attunement structure and orient the containers through which we hold each other and the ecologies we work within. ~~something about that way that practices of choreographic writing break through performance projects, the understanding of what writing can be in relation to dancing changes and morphs across collaborations, a methodology for bringing modes of relationality and vocabulary to the surface. Developing ways to attend to each other and then fold that attention into methods of scoring, structuring, beginning again, approaching language from new angles.~~

~~The place where a language flicks channels is a void to cross. In my experience~~ Movement ~~states are so complex and slippery that they~~ exceed ~~any desire for~~ capture or explanation — ~~instead, I keep paying attention and cross into the logics of poetry or fiction. I trace alongside the movement of choreography with the materiality of writing materials — the glide of a particular pencil, the texture of a specific kind of paper, the jolt of a photograph returning an angle of a moment.~~ The following poem was written out of watching dance, it is a translation of choreography into poetic form.

1.
The light lets you in as it falls down.
It provides a series of possibilities and constraints. It sends your perception in pre-set directions.
You realise some basic things about the difference between what you can perceive and what there is.
This is a door made out of physiology, there are viscous boundaries in the body itself, which are here made concrete and tangible.

The above text was written in the dark, watching FASMA (Campbell-Parra et al. 2019) in Santiago, Chile, as my close artisfriend Macarena Campbell-Parra performed the work solo she had also choreographed. Watching FASMA, my body attuned to hers, to the states of the work, to the miraculous contortion of form we witness through the piece, the lighting and performance design by Julio Escobar and Eduardo Cerón Tilleria, contracting and expanding the space inexplicably. Maca's body becomes and becomes, from jellyfish to spectral form, an abyss, flickering distant and then close.

I watched the performance three times, each time from different spaces in the auditorium, each time with a pencil in the dark, drawing and writing, listening through the graphite.

2.

How could you not see her when you are so close?

3.

First, we see ourselves beyond our bodies, then, we decompose with the space. Or is it the space that decomposes us?

This writing occurred from the audience in the Museum of Contemporary Art, Santiago, September 2019, in Chile.

And then. First Chile had the Estallido Social, the social movement, resulting in epic destabilisation of the city and the country in an unprecedented political movement. And then, after returning to Aotearoa NZ, the pandemic. During the pandemic, my studio practice kept returning to the desire to be with the people beyond our strict national border during lockdown, to somehow connect again with the vitality of Santiago, which continued to move through miraculous states of intensity, transition and recreation. The FASMA text (This is a door made out of physiology/there are viscous boundaries in the body itself/which are here made concrete and tangible) was written in response to the FASMA choreography as a piece of responsive dance writing. Drawing and writing in response to the choreography, I traced the fluctuations of Maca's body. Reading back on this text years later ~~through a luminous otherworldly space~~, became a form of time travel — the text sending me back to another life. The FASMA text then became a container, a kind of architecture, offering poetic respite from the existential dread of border-closure. These pieces of choreographic writing make a kind of live document, an incantation for metaphysical travel, for a past time when I could be with dear and geographically distanced artisfriends if I needed to. ~~Somehow the text is also a testament how deep the care runs~~ I worked with sound engineer Jeffrey Holdaway to make recordings of the FASMA text.

The light lets you in as it falls down. It provides a series of possibilities and constraints. It sends your perception in pre-set directions.

(longley 2022, n.p.)

Jeffrey cleaned the tones and vowels, editing it into an audio work. We then collaborated with dance and sound artist Kristian Larsen to develop this text in performance, devising strategies to move between live and pre-recorded sound. This poetic audio work then became integral in developing the performance vocabulary of the dance work *h u m a t t e r i n g*.

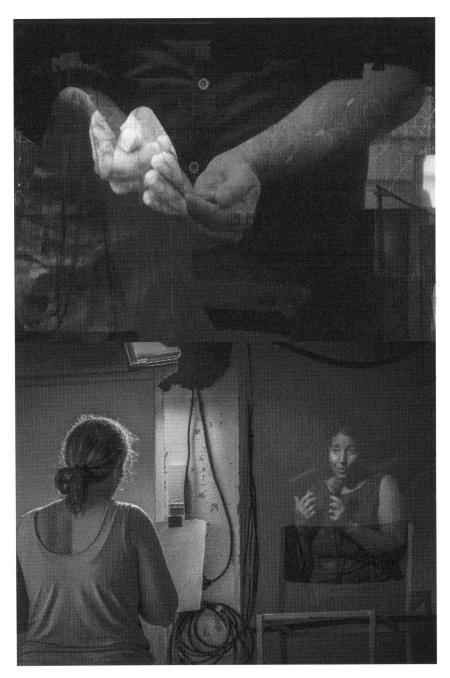

FIGURE 4.6 h u m a t t e r i n g. Photographs by Jeffrey Holdaway.

h u m a t t e r i n g folds together choreography, physical drawing in space and performance writing. It tests some strategies for metaphysical travel, reflecting on the ache of longing to be with people far away, in a collaboration between sound, lighting, movement and digital artists.

(longley 2022, n.p.)

We are in the theatre. Recorded and live voices question and ground each other simultaneously. Language shudders and is fragmented, returns to itself when a grammar settles, holds us in our desire to get beyond the here and now, to project our very hearts into another time zone. Kristian remixes a voice recording of the script — voices become ingredients in various dirty mixes — weathered, warped, reverbed, mutated with different degrees of force and interruption. In performance, we mix the sound in real time, so the quality of sound and movement is always open, unfixed, modulated between us.

You can pour your heart else   where with the words and cut time
into different pieces   text as holding device
shelter, trigger,   mode of organisation

the poetics of the words send you and you land   states of embodiment
formed from lines of poetics   releasing physicalities
we move through the edges of words   a muscular leavening of breath

the vocab means elseward when we touch into it   body made of humans/
floor/fabric/chalk   gravity and density
bones   accumulating sense

(it's been awhile
since i danced like this,
refinding this now body now and now and now)

a practice of writing in the dark   a performance in Chile,
a dream toward Sweden   speculating and re-membering
traces and sparks   architectures for the next

handwritten notes become containers   for continuation
which also   might be a matter of survival
some barely readable words   written in the dark
ground   in the ability to continue

FIGURE 4.7 (Left side) just, the gravity of a touch/Solo, la gravedad de un toque, April 2023, in the show Let Us Drink the New Wine, Together!/Beberemos El Vino Nuevo, Juntos! Malcolm Smith Gallery, Auckland. (Right side) to continue, *Choreographic Journal*, alys longley, flight from Santiago to Chicago, October 2019, for the work *Extractive Loyalties/Extracción de Lealtades*. Photographs by alys longley.

Choreographic writing is a term that hybridises the matter of dance-making with the matter of text. Choreographic practices of spatiality duration, affect, movement, composition and embodied performance blur with writing practices of alphabet, inscription, grammar, language, archive and documentation. Although attempts to translate the logics of these very different disciplinary practices often feel like failure, the attempt to bring states of embodiment to the page may activate "expanded fields" of writing and dance that open up space for the softening of disciplinary constraints. As Claire MacDonald writes:

We might now talk about "writing in the expanded field," a field in which writing's conventional autonomy — that is its objectivity, its truthfulness and its transparency — is in question, as writing has opened out fully into its material and conceptual contexts […] in this expanded field language has weight, and it has material and visual "freight". It has graphic presence that also "carries" meaning. Language can act as a form of dynamic exchange, a powerful conduit between the material and metaphysical or conceptual.

(MacDonald 2009, 100)

Working with graphic forms and multi-modal approaches to choreographic writing can provide options for a translation or reworking of intensities — weight, touch, tonality, atmosphere. Passages of brittleness, flow or intensity can travel through visual and multi-media practices engaging scale and rhythm in graphic ways (longley 2019a).

> We can see writing as bigger, looser, more porous and less prescriptive. Writing's horizon has moved [...] Its edges have become ragged. It has burst a little at the seams under the pressure of changing technologies of sight and sound and inscription; under the pressure of the flow of new kinds of communication that mix the spoken and the inscribed; that mediate between the stable and the unfixed; that enable everyone to become an editor, a publisher, a curator of print.
>
> (MacDonald 2009, 92)

Taking seriously paper, binding, colour, texture, image, legibility and illegibility as resources in process-based choreographic and theatrical experimentation allows space for ambiguity between text, drawing, object and phrase. Moveable scraps of time might enter further iterations, creating alternative systems of listening, response, provocation and resistance. ~~Choreographic writing can expand and contract with feeling, desire, texture, the affects of spacing, timing, failing and reaching.~~ This writing can continue to reach after sense has been lost, untethering text from function.

Create some little hooks of language to return you to a movement state.

Resting into the sense of a practice and letting it move you — writing from this place, make a map to return, or a map for a collaborator to dwell with you.

It could be just three words, maybe a drawing, maybe alongside an image.

Choose your drawing materials carefully, so that gravity can play through them in a granular way — make a choice about heaviness or lightness of touch.

Use momentum and flow as writing resources, parallel to dance resources — travel the feeling of a movement state, forget about accuracy and instead aim for some kind of obtuse satisfaction.

~~We draw text through space, through the exquisite, terrible boredom and vibrancy of studioing. As choreographers, we practice a particular kind of tenderness and complexity — relaxing into being witnessed while inventing worlds.~~ A studio practice generates specific values and vocabulary beyond the imaginable. If every dance had its own working language, its own set of orientations through space and time, could every dance have its own version of choreographic writing — a body of drawings, diagrams, recordings, graphs, paragraphs or poetic fragments, missives identifying a world of movement, somehow beyond?

Stupid generosity as a weakness and an aim, a desire and a loss. Aiming for that place of ridiculous beyondness — using our words to get us there, Poetic encounters resist any construction of authorship as an individual practice, instead framing writing as visceral, collaborative, a tidal etching of

Another means to resist the imperative of clarity is to let go of colonial enlightenment discourses and move in obscured, ambiguous spaces.

Moveable scraps of time enter further iterations, allowing things to mean differently, to create alternative systems of listening, response, provocation and resistance. (interstitial vocabulary).

Thinking on the potentialities of writing engaged in our artistic research, with a particular interest in performative writing as a term that hybridises the matter of performance and art making with the matter of text. It's a case of blurring live art practices of spatiality duration, affect, movement, composition, embodied performance and writing practices of alphabet, inscription, grammar, language, archive and documentation, in an always failing attempt to translate the logies of these very different disciplinary practices — bringing states of embodiment to the page, and applying poetic, fictional, descriptive and documentary style to the space of artistic practice.

Touch Practice Poetics was a project with poet Lisa Samuels and dancers Janaína Moraes and Joanna Cook, which asked 'What is a poetics of touch?'

The following poem, for example, was written through the h u m a t t e r i n g studio process, with dancers Yin Chi Lee, Maryam Bagheri-Nesami, Janaína Moraes and Joanna Cook. As we worked during COVID lockdowns, we reflected on translations across Mandarin, Farsi, Portuguese, Spanish and English, to explore how the word for "swell" can cross to also mean inflation, bruise, wave, overlapping, spill, ocean, economy, injury, meditation and growth. In rehearsal, we took notes on chalkboards, which took various guises in performance, as a projection screen, a wall, a prop, a sculpture and a device to hide things behind. Vocabularies flexed and washed into each other, compressed into writing that was both score and text, remnant and independent thing. Choreographic writing, by its nature, is a thing of flux, its practice goes alongside and into instability, offering space for a grammar that can be unstable and open. Movement calls forth a tone or affect of visceral engagement, forming pages that move with the weather of reading.

the hosts are falling over
&time has

a syn   chron i
                    s
                ed

the word for bruise can translate to
the word for swell can translate to the
word for wave can translate to the word
for inflation

         & we float outinside

     & salt is buoyant

accumulating and
ceasing ceasing and swelling hosted & unhosted

        afloat in rip-currencies of untouch

References

Barad, Karen. 2018. "On Touching: The Alterity Within." In *Reach out and touch (Somebody's Hand): Feel Philosophies*, curated by Jack Halberstam. Amsterdam: Stedelijk Museum, March 21–24. Accessed September 12, 2018. https://www.youtube.com/watch?v=u7LvXswjEBY.

Braidotti, Rosi. 2006. *Transpositions: On Nomadic Ethics*. Cambridge: Polity.

Campbell-Parra, Macarena, Eduardo Ceron-Tillería, Rolando Jara, Ramiro Molina, and Julio Escobar, Julio. 2019. *FASMA*. Dance Performance, Museum of Contemporary Art Santiago. July 19–October 6. https://mac.uchile.cl/exposiciones/fasma-desapariciones-del-cuerpo-proyecto-escenico-danza/.

Deleuze, Gilles. 1995. *Negotiations 1972–1990*. Translated by Martin Joughin. New York: Colombia University Press.

de Mignolo, Walter. 2005. *The Idea of Latin America*. Oxford: Blackwell Publishing.

Kramer, Paula. 2021. *Suomenlinna//Gropius; Two Contemplations on Body, Movement and Intermateriality*. Axminster: Triarchy Press.

Kramer, Paula. 2015. "Dancing Materiality; A Study of Agency and Confederations in Contemporary Outdoor Dance Practices." PhD diss., Coventry University.

longley, alys. 2022. "h u m a t t e r i n g. Choreographic Performance." *Australasian Drama Studies Conference*. December 6, 2022. Drama Studio, Auckland: University of Auckland.

longley, alys. 2021. "Accelerating a Blaze of Very Tender Violence: 10 Experiments in Writing with Performance and Activism." In *Affective Moments, Methods and Pedagogies*, edited by Stacy Holman Jones and Anne Harris, 60–82. Oxon and New York: Routledge.

longley, alys. 2019a. "Mistranslation Laboratory." Live Performance, Experimental Dance Week Aotearoa, Auckland, February 4–9, 2019.

longley, alys. 2019b. "El Otro País Que Eres." Live Performance. 275 Manuel Montt, Santiago, November 28, 2019. https://www.youtube.com/watch?v=Grp2xrTN3Kg.

longley, alys. 2017. "I Wanted to Find You by Inhabiting Your Tongue: Mistranslating between Words and Dance in Choreographic Practice." *Choreographic Practices, Special Edition on Words and Dance* 8(1): 27–49. https://doi.org/10.1386/chor.8.1.27_1.

longley, alys and Francisco González Castro. 2022. *On Artisfriendship*. Artist Book. Auckland.

MacDonald, Claire. 2009. "How to Do Things with Words: Textual Typologies and Doctoral Writing." *Journal of Writing in Creative Practice* 2(1): 91–103.

O'Brien, Gregory. 2004. "Plain Air / Plain Song." In *Rosalie Gascoigne Plain Air*, edited by Gregory O'Brien, 20–53. Wellington: Te Herenga Waka University Press.

Paraha, Tru. 2018a. "Speculative Chøreographies of Darkness." PhD diss., University of Auckland.

Paraha, Tru. 2018b. "Colluding with Darkness." *Performance Research* 23(2): 49–54.

Paraha, Tru. 2017. "5th Body." *Choreographic Performance*. Votive Poetics Symposium (Curator Lisa Samuels), University of Auckland.

pavleheidler and alys longley. 2021. *Life Is a Sting ON the Bicep of the Fabric of the Universe*. Digital Artist Book. https://online.flipbuilder.com/qmiq/vfle/.

Sadler, Hone. 2007. "Mātauranga Māori (Māori Epistemology)." *International Journal of the Humanities* 4(10): 33–45.

Stewart, Kathleen. 2007. *Ordinary Affects*. Durham and London: Duke University Press.

Weigel, Moira. 2019. "Feminist Cyborg Scholar Donna Haraway: 'The Disorder of Our Era Isn't Necessary.'" *The Guardian*, June 20, 2019. Accessed June 20, 2019. https://www.theguardian.com/world/2019/jun/20/donna-haraway-interview-cyborg-manifesto-post-truth.

5

THE TREATMENT

Writing a choreography (that has already happened) as a film (that hasn't yet been made)

Jennifer Lacey

Incorporating several different texts that emerged within the choreographic situations of the workshop, the rehearsal and the performance, "The treatment: writing a choreography (that has already happened) as a film (that hasn't yet been made)" uses the page itself as a choreographic space to hold practices of writing which inform and inhabit practices of dance- making. The text initially uses the form of a film treatment as a literary trope in order to document a choreographic process and then becomes a choreographic process itself. Using the permanence of writing to record an ephemeral past holding many possible futures, the text employs footnoting of footnoting of footnoting as a way to reconstitute an unstable subjectivity: the worlds within worlds, times within times, places within place that exist in dancing and accompanying dancing.

DOI: 10.4324/9781003397427-6

Preface for a film treatment

Welcome. The text on the following pages is a product of the habit of writing within and alongside circumstances of dancing. It is situated in the productive ambiguity of language in relationship to events. Slipping through writing as documentation, writing as feedback and writing as handing the reigns to the imperative of a text to become itself, <u>this</u> text includes a main body with footnotes that slide into a Kinbotean,[1] self-serving independence. It leans into the choreographic by allowing what the writing produces to determine its form. This is a fragmentary text that insists upon the non-independence of the fragments, on their phantom limbs and their wistful relationship to truncated trajectories, each sentence structure holding their doubles in parallel lives.[2] As these fragments emerge from conditions and are situational,[3] they are always very specific. Sometimes fragments demand a performative space to unfold beyond this specificity.

This one has. OK, here we go.

---

[1] Charles Kinbote is the unreliable narrator in Vladimir Nabokov's novel *Pale Fire* (1962). This character produces endnotes to the poet John Shade's poem, "Pale Fire" in a posthumous publication. The endnotes, which inhabit the entire second half of the book abandon their annotative mission almost immediately to produce an independent text. Unlike Kinbote, I will not advise you to try to read the notation along with the text proper by cutting the book in half. Please treat them as you will. They are right here, at the bottom of the page, beckoning.

[2] This phase comes from a dance score proposed by Raimundas Malašauscas and cultivated by Alice Chauchat. She will turn up again later.

[3] These situational fragments believe themselves to be all the same: snow-suited homunculi ◯ that emerge from the source and go out in the world to do the unconscious bidding of the generative, pathological parent. OK Dear Reader, that last bit was a little dark, my apologies ➠

◯The Brood (1979), a film by David Cronenberg. Synopsis: a star patient of an experimental psychologist extrudes belly-button-free mannikins from her pure anger which seems to be located in her abdomen.

➠I have found that the epistolary form (and its cousin, the direct rhetorical address of Dear Reader), brings a performative element that allows for shifting tone within a text without justification. It's moody. It brings the reader in as a relational and declines to become an inner voice. It proposes an entry into a performative state even if it is little twee. I mean, that is what I think, maybe you do not agree.

Let's start again.

Opening Shot.[4] The film opens in a wide static shot of an interior space, the function of which is not easily understood by the signs it puts forward.

It is not particularly small. It seems a bit larger than an average eat-in kitchen or a start-up architectural firm office. The floor is done in linoleum tiles. There is a rectangular patch of light oak parquet. It floats, unmoored, in the battleship blue of the lino at the upper right edge of the image. The most minimal gesture for a stage perhaps? The walls are no colour at all, a bit grey without being actually grey. Greige walls let's say, papered in a textured paint-able wallpaper. In French it is called a 'misery hider.'

A corner of a layer of wall paper peels from the bottom up, lifting a jaunty curled wave, smack in the centre of the shot, just above the base board.

There are no windows in the frame of the shot, but the light from the lower left corner suggests there is a window beyond our sight lines.

The ceiling is low. Shaded florescent tube lights are hung in three rows of three (we only see a depth of two in our image). Only one row is on, there is indeed natural light coming from somewhere behind the POV.

The room seems clean, and the light is softly and gently contouring to the space.

---

[4] I believe, but am not certain, that a sparer version of the text you are reading began as a scrawled response to a student showing. The showing was in a very white and bright studio in Copenhagen. The student shared a dance that was fantastically mysterious and very clearly determined by an inner logic that allowed the viewers to not be too busy with decoding. The performer was surrounded by large sketches of peoples' faces, gestural and pleasing. I don't recall sharing the text I wrote with the student at the time. I typed the notes into my computer where they floated around for a while before being conscripted into a performance. 🔖 After the showing, the student shared that the portraits were of the co-members of a workshop they had just attended, which had been a very intense bonding experience, and that it was necessary to be surrounded by these people in order to perform.

> 🔖 The below is part of a score in the form of a letter. In September of 2021, I was invited to be a keynote speaker at a lecture and panel discussion entitled "Dance and Future" at the TanzQuartier in Vienna. I decided to perform instead of talking about performance, and so I wrote a main text, *Preamble,* that was meant to support the emergence of a dance. I also used several other existing texts within the performance. For the event, I invited four artists to accompany me.
>
>> Hello friends
>> Thanks for saying yes to this invitation.
>> Because you are only four, your pay scale has increased to 200 euros. It's a party!
>> Here is the plan. You are referred to as 'The Readers'.
>> ***part 1 (four minutes from beginning of recorded text)***
>> We start this activity before the audience comes in. What we will do is described in the attached text entitled *Film treatment.* None of us should really know how to do it, but we will do it anyway. When the time is right, a recording of the text will be played. This marks the Beginning. When the recording is over Jennifer will move to the dais and begin part 2. Readers disperse or not…

Things went on from there. Let's go too.

We are in a "salle polyvalente"[5] or multi use room. This type of space is found in village or neighbourhood cultural centres. They are carved out of existing municipal spaces or intentionally constructed. They are designed to receive all manners of human propositions in relationship to culture, education, youth activities, leisure activities and personal development. They are often empty.

Pushed against the wall, close to the upper left corner of the image (which is also the corner of the salle polyvalente), we can also see some graceless wooden chairs, a bombastic metal desk from the last century and a bent wooden coat stand. Alongside this banished furniture, there are also some rucksacks, shoulder bags, a pile of shoes and a folding bike.

There are five people in the centre of the floor, far enough from the camera to be seen head to toe. Three are standing and two are crouching. They are wearing floppy leisure wear in earth tones, with the exception of one who is dressed in stiff karate pants and a Metallica T shirt. All are barefoot, although one has stirrup tights emerging from the hem of their wide-legged pants. This group is not talking, but their eye contact and subtle body adjustments indicate a kind of conversation. The shot zooms in from a fixed position to examine the faces and the gazes. The image is a bit grainy in close-up. The camera spends time with the light and shadows on skin, with the composition of their faces and their expressions. The camera moves relatively quickly from face to face, just a bit slower than a glance.

The faces begin to shift in the image as the five squeeze and expand the distance between each other. The camera opens a bit wider to let the upper bodies of the Conversants move through the frame of the image. The timing of the Conversants' movement and the specificity of their lower arms and hands begin to suggest dancing. They engage in movement that is not easily understood by the signs it puts forward. It is almost, but not quite, a dance.

---

[5] A Domicile is an art project that is almost 20 years old. Every summer in Brittany, a village invites four experimental artists to make a piece on the inhabitants of the village. After doing a "repérage" the artists meet the villagers in the salle polyvalente and pitch their processes and people sign up. ❖After ten days, there is a festival with all the performances.

> ❖After touring some likely performance spots in the village, I am offered a copious and delicious meal at the house of S. I meet the large extended family, who participates every year. After dinner, I go upstairs to the toilet and pass by a partly open door. On a double bed lie four teenage girls, the middle one has an open laptop on her stomach. They are singing along with Jeff Buckley's rendition of Halleluiah. I know they play hand ball and do gymnastics and also that they have been doing strange art every summer since they were five. I do everything I can to design a process to appeal to them so they will choose me at the village selection at the salle polyvalente. I succeed and, as a bonus, I also get their grandmothers (one of whom is the ex-mayor). We make a piece called l'Alchimie de la Fréquentation at the indoor boules court. It was beautiful. For these women, I return to proper dance-making. ❦ The context gave it a sense it had not had in a long time.

❦ Proper dance-making is something I feel I abandoned in around 2008, when I realised that my instability as an artist enabled the stability of the people who programmed the rather expensive experimental whatevers that I loved making. The conditions for gathering, necessary for that kind of process, became impossible for me to stand at the time.

Score for the performers in the film.[6] The Conversants are a group of people who have had a common experience in the past, something that has bound them together through a moment of intensity. We, the viewers, are not privy to what this common experience was.

---

[6] A *film treatment* such as this one is a literary device to document events that are slippery and resist capture. Alice ❯ and I used it as a way of addressing an imperative to provide documentation of an eight-year project. TTT/ Teachback! was ostensibly a European Union project that supported pedagogical development within dance, bringing together artists who teach, but in truth was most definitely an artwork. We were quite terrible at documenting our process, as it was sprawling, permissive, spontaneous and fecund. When Alice and I confronted the mass of archival material at the end of seven years, we decided to translate all of it: the interviews, the texts, the gossipy memories, the detritus of massive scheduling emails, © exercises and class forms that had emerged, etc. into a "Film Treatment" as documentation. Scenarios were performance scores for films and the hope was to transmit the results of a research project addressing "teaching-art-through-art," through again: art.

❯ Alice Chauchat: Dancer, choreographic artist, writer, inventive pedagogue, mother of O., dear friend and collaborator. Based in Berlin. Seek out her work.

© Excerpt from "Boring Dialogue" sourced from the file from 2015, "Teacher Availabilities."

SETTING: *an office. It is a modern office. This means that it is open and light. There are windows with sky and rooftops. Some desks are facing each other for conviviality. There are no filing cabinets and no paper. Other personal things clutter up a desk or two, and one desk is completely empty, save an iPad and a skateboard. This dialogue is delivered by one person to a silent partner who empathises and resonates with the words in relative stillness. The dialogue should be delivered slowly and deliberately with a low voice. At one moment, indicated by italics, there should be modest weeping. The character who is the listener is tasked with retaining the facts of the text with their body, not with their mind. They are not listening to the words; they are busy with an invisible internal process. From time to time, they nod slowly. They then begin to place items from the desk onto the skateboard and to rock them back and forth before taking them off again and replacing them from whence they came. After a while (post NANO-DRAMA, marked in text) the person talking will start singing the list, and the listener will join with a very slight delay, like an echo in another tone.* "So of course, we begin with the introduction days, the Friday, Saturday and Sunday before things really begin, before everyone else has arrived. And for those days there are nine of us full time. Anne J is not present. Anne J is somewhere else. After these three days, we begin with week one. In week one, we are eight full-time workers. Anne J and Philippe R are only available for half-time employment. Anne J is available during the day for any four-hour block we would propose to her. Philippe R? When is Philippe R available? Do we know? He's doing the 'History and violence' field project; does anyone know his schedule? So, given all this, what do you think should be our schedule? 11–5:00 with everyone, and let the half-time employees decide if they will come from 11–3:00 or 1–5:00? What do you think? Ok, so that brings us to week two. *(delivered tearfully) In week two, Alice, Jennifer and Mark are there, are here, full time. Anne J and Philippe R are performing, and they are not available at all. Or rather, more correctly, they are not available for us. There are several of us who are teaching in week two and are, therefore, not always available (tears subside).* Alix E and Marten S are teaching

"Non-Haptic Exorcism — Affect — Non-Haptic Eroticism: Dancing Duets" from 11:40 to 14:40. Keith H is teaching "Shamanic Improvisation Potential" from 14:40 to 17:20. Marten S is then teaching a second class "the first recipe" from 17:00 to 20:00. (NANO DRAMA, delivered with emotion:) So as you see, Marten S and Keith H will not really see each other in the workplace during week two. It's a bit of a pity, but it can't be helped. So, what do you think? Again from 11 to 5:00, with those who are teaching joining in when they can. What do you think? What about the weekends? I don't think we should work on the weekends. It's too easy to always work, and its summer, maybe people will want to go swimming or just not work. What do you think? I think the weekends should be free. When work is not disagreeable, it is sometimes difficult to remember to rest. I have never been clear about the definition of work, and I keep this very private for fear of ridicule. If we take the weekends off then our activity is inserted into a work week and is validated as work by adhering to that schedule, and then my anxiety is alleviated (END OF NANO DRAMA) …" (dialogue goes on for another page and a half into the sung section.)

And so, it continued. we even tried to make this film. It didn't pan out. Although the shoot was really something, there was a basic misunderstanding within the team of narrative imperatives within a documentary. We could have worked it out but there was no more money.

Score for the performers in the film continued. The Conversants are devoted to a practice that happens each day at 6:00 in the evening. For one hour, they come together. They do not speak. They socialise exclusively through body behaviour. This is quite specific. Their abstracted movements, their modes of touch and, most importantly, the varied flow and rhythms of their movements and interactions have a honed quality. They seem spontaneous and reactive, whilst also giving the impression of falling into patterns that they all recognise. This is present when all five of them acknowledge a moment through a small laugh or a collective sign. Their capacity to be with themselves, to be with each other and to be with any emergent presence in the room is communicated through the trajectory and speed of their gazes and glances. This way of being together is perhaps a discussion of beauty without indulging in a definition of beauty. The beauty is located in the moments of contact and comprehension, things that elude form. This socialising activity appears to permit extreme emotion and energetic tunings that do not bind the group, or the individual, to an obligation to resolve these manifestations. Things arise and recede and arise again slightly differently. The charge of group members' attention to one another clearly shows that something singular has happened to them collectively.[7] The nature of the event, whether traumatic or transcendent, is not revealed explicitly to the viewers, so the performers should concentrate on subtle mobilities in the face and hands to convey this ambiguity.

---

[7] *(Cronenberg again)* The fragmented toddler monsters of the Brood are produced through the intensity of therapy, a constant confrontation with the facts of past trauma that induces (for the adept) physical symptoms. The star patient dresses her extruded productions for the weather and then lets them flow out into the world to murderously avenge her grievances. Mother and ex-lovers succumb to their ministrations. These monomaniacal toddlers bring a knife to the problem of 'problems' and cut them out dead. This film treatment has a dark side. It is hard to imagine communality without a touch of the violent and a dose of weird surprise. This film treatment is utopic, proposing the generative powers of bodies in dance as an energetic architecture rather than an image. But still, empirically we know collectivity can be fraught, being together is hard when it is not soft. ✳

✳Culture and Administration was a piece that made with Antonija Livingstone in 2009✪ ➳. It was a convalescent piece for me. We crawled a lot, as that was the dance I could do when we started. Later, Antonija instigated an expanded version called Culture, Administration and Trembling in 2013. We were joined by Stephen Thompson, Dominique Petrin, Dominique's two chihuahuas Hermine and Mouchette and later by Charles and his three albino Pythons. Negotiating togetherness was inevitably at stake.

⊛ ➻ *Publicity text for Culture Administration and Trembling* ➻ ⊛

Antonija is the place, no she is the reason, no she is the zealot, no in fact she is the place.
Skater (Stephen) is the middle child; he is the silken padding between places. He is often bored
with his role as the most reasonable, but he also takes pride in his skills.
Dominique is the wolf mother.
Jennifer is the one holding the pen.

Trembling is a group experience claiming identity as an individual. If a corporation can be given the legal rights of an individual, then why not Trembling? This entity is stitched together from bits of muscle memory, texts read, histories lived or transferred, boots, tights, free wills and touring schedules. Trembling is ungainly in its efforts, but its visceral need to communicate itself to others is touching. It lives. It is always trying to think beyond its limits. Trembling is confused by the difference between intellect and emotion, and this makes for a lurching gait. Trembling dances anyway. Trembling is indeed the act of YES and also the continued, uncomfortable, loving and wise suspension of "yes, but" which would necessarily propose the coercion of one member by another. Trembling would like to take release technique seriously and never impinge one part of its body with the force of another. Trembling fails at this all the time, but she keeps trying. This is dancing. Trembling happens in the YES and navigates the "yes, but," like moguls on a black diamond slope.

Antonija is a survivalist poet, caulking a hole in their homemade boat with toothpaste and a spoon. Walking away demons, hiking towards water, grilling a sausage in the last rays of the sun, she sports an uptown lady's pink lipstick purchased in the limbo of the international airport. Antonija is everything under the sun except a glamorous contradiction — a cliché too easily understood and dismissed. He simply has an equal appreciation for the stink of pine tar, the blades of a helicopter, the rub of horse hide between her legs and a densely pigmented tube of wax. They are involved in the creation of the world by appreciation.

Trembling is the child of chosen parents: of Édouard Glissant, of Donna Haraway, of Charles Fourier, of Wigstock. ❀ Glissant is embarrassed by us, but secretly may appreciate our glittery, disposable take on mondialité. In private, he chuckles over Trembling's gawky sincerity. Haraway gave us up for adoption at birth, but Trembling sought her out, and now we send holiday greetings with photos of the dogs. Fourier thinks he invented us out of spun sugar and pee; Trembling is not quite real to him, but he comes to all the shows. Curled in a corner, wrapped in a blanket, he dozes and waits to be suckled. He's old. Wigstock doesn't understand our outfits and is often dismissive of our dorky academic criticality. But they always bring us a gift when they visit. Trembling is like a family reunion around a turkey or a ham, and each of us is the one child who has gone to therapy.

Skater is the one with the three-ring binder under his arm. Somewhere, he is always bedazzled. Stephen is both a shower and a grower. Stephen is light and kind, a wafting breeze. He knows he has two sharp blades secreted away, which can cut him loose at any time, can carve arabesques and arcs and tame a swirling chaos. In Trembling, Stephen comes to work. He loves the resonance of clear-cut places: home, family, lovers and work, each has its own sweet tone. Trembling disturbs these distinctions, sometimes quaking so hard that the water glasses fall off the table, and the din is awful. Stephen hates this, but he says yes and stays anyway, He has his reasons. For Stephen, Trembling at its best is like an affair with a friend from sleep away camp or an ex-colleague from the figure-skating circuit, both homey and novel. At its worst, it is like a Punch and Judy show of every frustrating intimacy he has ever lived — only smaller and more stupid. Best and worse are both somehow intriguing.

Jennifer is the one holding the Pen. She was born in 1966 and is both a fire horse and a daughter of the wind and the cemetery gatekeeper. Her Pisces/Aries rising star chart looks like a fucking bow-tie. It's a wonder that anyone puts up with her. Her work as an artist is making situations and conditions for people to put up with her. She is a bossy pants and also really absent and slippery. She is a strong smell, an architect of the energetic, a pain in the ass.

Trembling is like a cinema version of an inner-city legal aid office, staffed by the exhausted and the righteous.

Trembling is an upcycling of past collaborations and love affairs.

Trembling is a collection of beings and the things they do. It is the spaces these beings open for each other so that the things that each of them needs to do can be done.

Trembling produces nothing lasting, and so there is no waste, just laundry and paper chains of boarding passes.

Trembling is bickering, a glow of the future on the horizon, a gilded turd, a coterie of emancipations, a cook-out.

Trembling is the ceremony dedicated to cold-blooded gods raised in boxes and Tupperware.

Trembling is two tiny canine sisters and their entourage celebrating their excessively refined bodies: a thin coat of domesticity and seven spindly legs supporting Aztec hearts moving through the world.

Trembling is the eye of a tornado, where for a brief and roaring moment many things are gathered by Trembling's centrifugal force, spinning singular elements into an experience of ensemble, of group, of gathering, of harmony. As long as they spin together, they seem to mean something. This sensation is the strongest thing imaginable. It presents as the truest truth, an inevitable, a suspension in time. Things and beings and acts seem to be gathered by fate to deliver a message: the sound of a bell, the curve of a neck, a body held by another, a painted fingernail, a joke. Then the storm passes and all the houses and shoes and books and cans of food and trees and cattle and pens and pencils and bits of coloured paper fall to the ground again. Picking up after the tornado can be difficult. Trembling has a few work songs for that.

Dominique is camouflaged as a place, a wild place with marble tiles, tubas and vines. She is the bush with calves and ankles and feet moving through the background of a cartoon. She is the mother of the local divinities and their shrine maker. Dominique is moving forward in life with seven league boots. When Trembling is on her path, she stores her boots in a teacup and settles in. Cutting and stitching with seven extra arms, she makes the world.

❀Says Wikipedia: Wigstock was an annual outdoor Drag festival that began in 1984. Says me: It was the loving parent of many.

Set Details Hanging on the back wall of the set, just to the right of the pile of shoes, not quite centred over the peeling corner of wallpaper, there is a large portrait of a body on butcher block paper. It is larger than life-sized, and reaches almost floor to ceiling.[8] The image has been drawn in thick graphite with a carpenter's pencil in the style of an accomplished child's drawing. It is mainly an outline. The figure stands in an unremarkable position — simply pointing itself forward and filling the paper from top to bottom. Its arms are held slightly away from its sides, giving about an orange's circumference to the space under each arm. The legs are not wide, not narrow, feet a bit turned out in order to draw them properly. Its head is a bit roundish, as there is no hair drawn in. This is the face: a rudimentary and sweet mouth, no real nose beyond a centre line and most remarkably, large open palms in place of eyes with the wrists situated on the temples at a downward angle. Midway down the body, large eyes, complete with an almond outline and lashes, are dangling from the figure's truncated wrists. They hang from a twisted cord that is perhaps gristle, perhaps an optic nerve or perhaps simply twine. The style of this bit of the drawing is quite different from the rest, being detailed and accomplished.

This image is the only explanation we get about the rules and principles of the practice of the Conversants.

---

[8] Anna Halprin drew a picture of her body suffering from a re-occurrence of a tumour then danced that illness out with her fury and desire. It was called Dark Side Dance and it worked. I danced mine out with a group: Les Assistantes (2008). It also worked.

Unfolding of action This film follows close-up details within the group, lingering on areas of physical interface and eye contact. The interest for the viewer becomes almost painterly, the shape of a face blurring as it moves through the frame, colours and textures abstracting only to reform in an image of a hand hovering over a heart. After about 20 minutes of this (long enough to accept it will never change), the shot pulls wide, and we see a second group arriving through the lower left corner of the frame. They are seven, mostly middle-aged, carrying in their hands their work materials: laptops and telephones and legal pads and sketch books and calculators and dictaphones and a fax machine: They enter and set up shop, plugging in on the periphery in relative silence. They never address the central group directly.

The next ten minutes of the film engages in much more cutting between close-up shots. The camera is no longer in its fixed position, it wanders. Through the way the film is edited to reveal the concentration that the Workers occasionally give the Conversants before diving back into their task, the audience understands the activity of the Conversants is a kind of energetic battery, a concentration engine for the workers.

We begin to get caught up in the conversation of a cell phone user who walks the periphery of the room — talking normally — not too loud not too soft — the conversation is about the shipment of a perishable good. The gentle, tedious single side of the conversation becomes a voice over for the interaction of the Conversants. The camera plunges again into details of their subtle interaction.

After an amount of time which, for the viewer, begins to move from the luxurious to the demanding, the camera stays tight but veers towards the entrance door to follow the arrival of a group of 12 people with small dogs. They enter the room and begin to set up a sort of obstacle course for the animals: tiny hurdles, fabric tubes with wires, spiral frames, an inflatable baby pool, etc.

This arrival clearly signals the end of the session for the Conversants and the Workers. They begin to talk amongst each other. We see them greet one other with civility and sometimes affection. Through their casual indications of intimacy, we now understand the two groups as, in fact, one group.

They dress and gather their things and file out in ones and twos and threes, chatting and giving **goodbye hugs.**

6

INVITATION

Choreoreading EXOXƎ

Simo Kellokumpu

This semi-fictional chapter stems from the post-doctoral artistic research project called *xeno/exo/astro — choreoreadings*, conducted from 2021 to 2023 in the Performing Arts Research Centre, Theatre Academy, University of the Arts Helsinki. The project has materialised the relations between outer space, interplanetary culture, queer sci-fi and choreography through several artworks and representational experiments. The process has combined astronomical-artistic research questions and a light sense of what I would call metaphysical clownishness (in Finnish: metafyysinen pelleily). This essay materialises the examination of the practice coined as *choreoreading*. The term was developed during my doctoral artistic research project, *Choreography as Reading Practice* (2013–2019). The exploration is based on the understanding in which writing and reading are simultaneously operative bodily practices, but (and on my explorations that) in the history of Western choreography, the potential of (choreo-)reading has been neglected. During winter 2022–2023, I have continued to experiment with choreoreading by filtering the embodied practice in a more specific dialogue with writer James Sosnoski's (1999) description of the characteristics of hyper-reading. This writing exposes from the position of a performer the detailed question of what happens *during* choreoreading and how specific eye-movements form its relevant dynamic component in the artwork titled EXOXƎ.

The Andromeda galaxy is visible to the   corner of the eye
and so is the Orion Nebula.

Here I am. *(Breathing heavily.)* I do not know how much time I have. The movement in the throat is produced by a mass of unbreathable air. I can feel

DOI: 10.4324/9781003397427-7

the hollow organ trembling while my spine forms an arch. Hands are hanging heavily, reaching towards the ground, which I cannot see. My feet, they burn with transparent dust and fluid ground in which the reflection, kind of like a dispersed halo, spreads around me. My eyes move rapidly, not focusing on or looking at anything. The vertiginous speed feels like stretching my face, my cheeks, my nose distorting. The eyes jump and scatter around, and they stop for a second, not seeing through the radiation that divides the space between me and you. The body, my hardware, is encapsulated into the gear from which the life-sustaining biospheres grow and generate the power of my activities. Movements are throwing and tearing the body. This space is fragmented. I can sense the tectonic plates and move with the lightspeed. The constant movement of the eyes produces kinesthetic ache, which spreads across the face into the back of the skull sending pulsing waves through the body.

Input: Am I here? Before arriving (have I arrived?) during this journey, I have ridden a meteor and danced pas de deux with the artificial moons, rubbed the toxic soil on my skin and gasped the airless air in the orbit, while locating the body into the history of the Universe. I have been chasing answers to the questions of how the light of the star materialises the experienced time, or how the same visual cue materialises the space that goes beyond my human understanding. Through *cue* (visual material) — *response* (immediate proprioceptive activation) — *action* (emerging intimate movement), I have been chasing the materialisations of the movements, which are generated by the lasting starlight and expanding dark space. Endlessly.

(Pause. Save.)

While getting ready, I remember the words by Professor Leena Rouhiainen (2017, 145): "Artistic research interrogates already established approaches and practices belonging to art. It does this by, in various ways, developing accepted conventions further, or by even attempting to renounce them altogether." I look at my eyes from the visor, they are blurry. Focus. On this research journey, have I not renounced my practice of choreography as writing practice? Have I not transformed from choreographer to choreoreader? Or have I failed and turned into something else? Isn't this the science-fictional way, following the wording by Pearson, Hollinger and Gordon (2008, 6), a queer attempt to "defamiliarize taken-for-granted construction" of (straight) choreography, movement and making choreography? The question in my hands is who or what is writing this moving body and how? What is the choreo-*graphic* apparatus that I am inhabiting and how? How do I get out of it? Or maybe better, how are such movements choreoread, that produce writing, which this body inhabits? How do I escape writing and delve into reading? (Am I in this text?) Is it possible? Is it impossible? In this binary Universe. In these non-binary Universes.

(Reboot.)

Maybe I need to clarify that with "choreo" I mean sensitivity to decode simultaneous multidirectional non-linear incoherence. It is an orientation towards surroundings and the perceived-experienced. When it comes to reading, in my vocabulary it stems from computer-assisted reading, which is also known as hyper-reading. Screens, emails, messages, codes, zeros and ones. I am not curious to explore how they are written but how they are read. How are your eyes moving from left to right? What happens when you move from word to word? What happens when you move between these printed symbols? When you move between the s y m b o l s. That is the space I am in, between symbols and signs with the act of hyper-reading but in an environmental materiality in which this space-between keeps on expanding beyond human perception. What is that opening terrain? I am falling in. Can you see me there, falling? I have left my writing base a long time ago and have been moving through the dense spheres of making otherwise, being haunted by hyper-reading. Other choices, other directions, other terms and conditions that I got used to as a choreo-*grapher*. It is exhausting and I am exhausted. Even if they, writing and reading, are simultaneously active bodily practices in my body, too. I can feel it, I can sense it. How would you describe the difference between writing and reading? Tell me. Record. Let me breathe.

(Let's move on this linear journey.)

As you know, the movement of the eyes does not stop even in sleep. I turn my head upwards and feel how the sphere around my head weighs. Neckache. Reveal of the throat, which is surrounded by the noise of a black hole. The eyes keep on jumping without focusing, without looking at, without taking over the material circumstances with the straight focusing gaze. It is not about what do I see, but how the organ is form-ing, which enables the scope of my visual perception. The corner of the eye is loud. Has always been. Also here.

Did you know that one of the best ways to get connected with the Andromeda in the dark night is to approach it with the corner of the eye? Fascinating, isn't it? There are people whose lives are filled with Andromedas and everyday nebulas. I am one of them. The practice with the corner of the eye has become a way to navigate in a straight world without being caught. Recognising sharply the micro movement practice of the other, or more specifically, The Other, who shares the sense-making of, and with, the corner of the eye. Mirroring the same desires. But here I am. Standing on a layer of transparent dust, wearing life-generating biospheres and eye-protecting visors. I am morphing, shape-shifting, reaching towards the movement of the eyes, but at the same time giving up. (Did I give up?) That is the way maybe. If only there were a magical monolith to touch (to go elsewhere). This place is called   EXOXƎ.

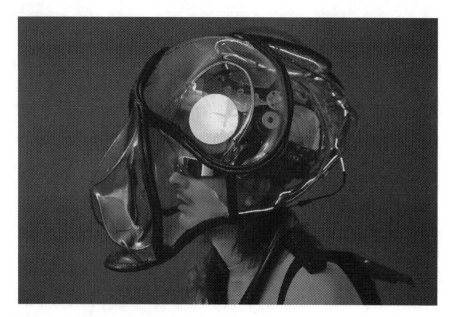

FIGURE 6.1   A person wearing a big headpiece. Photograph by Vincent Roumagnac.

(Pause. Check the firewall.)

I am hesitating between registers. Should I jump to another one? But isn't that the case with reading as well? How to read in endless possible ways and make meanings and interpretations as I wish, no matter what is written? James Sosnoski (1999, 169) once said: "Reading — of whatever sort — is a process of selection." In the choreoreading practice, the concept of hyper-reading opens a hashtag to make sense and create meanings. #hyperreading is like a gate, an underground tunnel, literally two verticals and two horizontals: move through it and see what happens! That is what I have done in this research and its artistic works. Going through #hyperreading is manifested in the moving body, also here in   EXOXƎ, the place that never existed and yet has always been there.

As a reminder, I dig it out from my portable, Sosnoski (1999, 163) characterises hyper-reading in eight ways:

1. filtering: a higher degree of selectivity in reading [and therefore]; 2. skimming: less text actually read; 3. pecking: a less linear sequencing of passages read; 4. imposing: less contextualisation derived from the text and more from readerly intention; 5. filming-the "... but I saw the film" response, which implies that significant meaning is derived more from graphical elements as from verbal elements of the text; 6. trespassing: loosening

of textual boundaries; 7. de-authorising: lessening sense of authorship and authorly intention; 8. fragmenting: breaking texts into notes rather than regarding them as essays, articles or books.

Low battery red light. Switch it off. No back-ups. However, that is my eight-dimensional hashtag, an invisible collection of light-speed cords running through the body. This practice has led me to examine the inter-relation of the notions of composition and attention. I have moved from one to another. In this meaningful shift from composition to attention, I have focused on decoding Sosnoski's characteristics number 2 and 3, pecking and skimming. Even if nobody can see it, through my visors, I have examined these modes, because they destabilise my conventional understanding of reading, which in my cultural context happens with the movements of the eyes from left to right. Skimming and pecking, full of movement. I suggest we try it together, now: skim this page, peck this page. Go. What happens in terms of the reading-embodiment when the movements of the eyes do not follow linear left-to-right proposal? What about its relation to the starting points of making choreography from the perspective of reading instead of writing? Turn your gaze now away from this page. If you are sitting inside, turn your gaze towards the architecture of the building, of the surroundings there. Keep on skimming and pecking. How does that place teem in front of your eyes, in your eyes? What is going on in the back of your skull and in your hands, in your toes, now? (Maybe there is no now.) Keep enlarging the scale, keep skimming and pecking, move towards the sky and the soil, the speed, which is present, the orbit around the Sun, tectonic plate under the building, skim skim skim, peck peck peck, faster, faster.

(Pause.)

Thank you. That was the warm-up. Next time, try placing the purple transparent filter in front of your eyes and repeat the same while breathing heavily. Then we get closer, then I stumble and scroll on the same kinesthetic terrains with you. Log in. Welcome to the imaginaries generated by this kind of choreographic-being-in-the-world. This welcoming echoes Doll's (1998, 238) words that "Reading becomes not simply a matter of discovering themes and symbols, but of visiting other worlds in the expectation of discovering selves within." Through choreoreading, I am re-inventing myself and exploring possible selves. I am leaving other kinds of traces than I used to. It has taken me places like   EXOXƎ, which discloses a vast vision for my hyper-reading eyes.

I need to take a break. The headpiece is heavy. I have come to the conclusion that it would be interesting to build an eye-tracking device onto this gear. The device would leave traces into the space like lasers, or it could be inverted,

FIGURE 6.2 A person sitting above the pedestal, wearing a big headpiece and leaning towards the left. Photograph by Vincent Roumagnac.

luminating the eyes and the body, someway similarly like in the video *If When
Why What* (2022) by Douglas Gordon, but without words. Maybe I find materials to do that for the next journey. The eye movement and eye-tracking
research are scientific fields of study, of which both could offer interesting
insights into my inquiries, especially when used in the context of reading
practices, but I have focused on deepening my understanding through embodied experimentation about the skimming and pecking movements of the
eyes in the practice of choreoreading. The movement that is in focus is how
the eye-tracking researcher Anna-Kaisa Ylitalo (2017, 2), who has done eye-
movement research in relation to paintings, describes them as linear jumps between consecutive fixations of the eyes. Let's try this. Move your eyes quickly
between two spots. Try not to look at those spots but direct your attention to
the movements of the eyes. Add a little pause. Continue again.

According to Ylitalo (2017, 2), "The fixation is a state, when the gaze is
staying fairly still around a location over a time period." These two descriptions, "jumps" and "fixations" also describe the actions of the eyes, into which
I want to invite you, dear reader. Have you seen artist Julien Prévieux's (2018)
work *Anthologie des regards,* from the years 2015 to 2018? There are visual
traces coming from the eye-tracking technology. That is my connection to eye-
tracking. But how does this kind of reading manifest as a moving body? And
what does this have to do with choreography? The loop takes another turn.

I am sitting and thinking, breathing is easier now. But I know, soon… never mind. How about approaching these questions with more questions? How would you describe the movements that are present while you are reading these lines? Does the temporality of the movements extend from the fast movement of the eyes beyond an expected human lifetime? What about their spatial scale? How is your reading affected by the orbit around the Sun? That kind of speed that is present. What happens when you lift that reading gaze towards the material surroundings where you are? How do you take place in that condition while moving the eyes across these lines transforming into moving the eyes from one spot to another without looking at the surroundings? Or how does this motional sphere operate as a choreo*graphic* apparatus, and can you make sense out of it through choreoreading? Are you still reading? Are you still hyper-reading? I am still tired.

Here in   EXOXƎ,
I have developed the practice by working with the movements beyond human scale to the micro-movements of the eyes. This may also challenge the idea of the mastery over movements through practice in which "looking at" something or "taking over" the environment or the objects with the "focusing gaze" is put aside and "looking at" transforms to attention towards the movements of the eyes. It is some sort of reflection instead of looking for an object for attention out there. For me, this approach is uploading perceptional practice in which "looking at something" is not primarily meaningful when it comes to finding the linguistic-embodied counterpart of the choreo*graphic* between perception and experience. But it is not an inverted gaze either, because acknowledging the teeming visuals is important. Based on my experiments, this kind of practice — which is based on rapid eye movements — brings forth the questions of selective attention. In the end, where do I decide to direct the attention in terms of the eye-movements? Toward colours, forms, lines, curves, lights, where? What leaks in from the corners of the eyes and what is left outside? Is this kind of binary online-offline approach even able to reach the realm I want to enter choreographically? Maybe it is about de-centering the attention towards the movements that are beyond the prevailing widespread approach to movement as material for dance. In my experience, it is necessary to slow down or even stop moving the eyes rapidly after a while. I don't think it is interesting to aim to master these de-centred movements, instead the other way around I would say, to couple with the kinesthetic world and movement phenomenon in another way than mastery over the movement as material. Or maybe I am not trying enough. If in the dark the corner of the eye can establish a visual connection to the nebulas, how can it destabilise the dominance of straight gaze? What kind of a body emerges once it operates with this kind of queering gaze and, perhaps, with this kind of queer-*ing* straight attention? Attention choreographies.

The breathing starts to materialise again in the throat and my legs tremble. I cannot see my back, but it feels like someone is hacking me. It is just my generators, artificial wings, antennas, which protect the body from the radiation. Sometimes I wish I could see the wings of flies again, because then I would be able to send thousands of gentle pulsing wing beats across the space towards you. Calm down, I say, closing the eyes. Why so anxious? Everything is fine and will be fine. Or maybe not. Open the eyes and move on with that kinesthetic universe, which constitutes the body. Loop. Maybe that is what choreoreading for me is: an exploration of an endless loop of alienation and restless, elusive longing for something missing in my choreo*graphic*-being-in-the-world.

References

Doll, Mary Aswell. 1998. "Queering the Gaze." In *Queer Theory in Education*, edited by William F. Pinar, 237–246. New York: Taylor & Francis Group.

Gordon, Douglas. 2022. "If When Why What." Video, 3:00. Accessed March 17, 2023. https://www.youtube.com/watch?v=ICHbpLfRA38.

Kellokumpu, Simo. 2019. "Choreography as a Reading Practice." PhD diss., Theatre Academy, University of the Arts Helsinki. https://www.researchcatalogue.net/profile/show-exposition?exposition=437088.

Pearson, Wendy Gay, Veronica Hollinger, and Joan Gordon. 2008. "Introduction." In *Queer Universes, Sexualities in Science Fiction*, edited by Wendy Gay Pearson, Veronica Hollinger, and Joan Gordon, 1–11. Liverpool: Liverpool University Press.

Prévieux, Julien. 2018. "Anthologie des regards." Accessed March 6, 2023. https://www.previeux.net/fr/works-anthologieRegards.html.

Rouhiainen, Leena. 2017. "On the Singular and Knowledge in Artistic Research." In *Futures of Artistic Research. At the Intersection of Utopia, Academia and Power*, edited by Jan Kaila, Anita Seppä, and Henk Slager, 143–155. Helsinki: The Academy of Fine Arts, Uniarts Helsinki.

Sosnoski, James. 1999. "Hyper-Readers and Their Reading Engines." In *Passions, Pedagogies and 21st Century Technologies*, edited by Gail E. Hawisher and Cynthia L.Selfe, 161–177. Boulder: University Press of Colorado. Accessed March 16, 2023. https://doi.org/10.2307/j.ctt46nrfk.12.

Ylitalo, Anna-Kaisa. 2017. "Statistical Inference for Eye Movement Sequences Using Spatial and Spatio-temporal Point Processes." PhD diss., University of Jyväskylä. Accessed March 16, 2023. http://urn.fi/URN:ISBN:978-951-39-7064-2.

PART 2

Practices of writing that choreograph

7

LETTER TO SAINT HILDEGARD OF BINGEN

Lynda Gaudreau

Lynda Gaudreau's current artistic research explores the ways in which theory is mobilised in artistic practice. Her writing is articulated in the form of letters and integrates biofiction, theory, performance and documentary. Her research on asynchrony emerged from her choreographic practice. Asynchrony is the modification or disturbance of perception caused by a slight change in space and/or time within a work, and which, like a pebble, slips inside a machinery. This tiny friction between space and time heightens the audience's attention. Her research has taken the form of 25 fictional letters to various individuals — artists, thinkers and characters — and was developed during her doctoral research (2018) and postdoctoral research at the Performing Arts Research Centre, Theatre Academy, University of the Arts, Helsinki (2019–2021). The letter to Saint Hildegard of Bingen is one of the unpublished letters of this project. The letter explores how writing, thought and space intertwine. It thus lays the foundations for a wider reflection on perception, self, presence and action, and mainly on the multiple affective qualities of attention in the choreographic experience. To perceive is to perceive with and through a body, and the choreographic experience operates in different spaces and on different scales of perception.

DOI: 10.4324/9781003397427-9

Montreal, March 14, 2017

Dear Hildegard of Bingen,[1]

FIGURE 7.1　Free drawing of Hildegard of
Bingen. Drawing by the author.

I need your help. I am not a religious person, but I am valiant, and I'm seeking to understand. My senses are completely disoriented. I feel like even when my eyes are open, they slide over the world without seeing anything. I haven't had anything like a vision — haven't seen the fire in the sky, and stones don't speak to me as they did to you — but I know these things to be possible. Sometimes objects give themselves over, or a work, a show, continues to live on in me; sometimes a colour can pierce my heart. I will never forget that day, standing before Van Gogh's small canvases.

I had driven with my friend Barbara, who had a meeting at the Kröller-Müller Museum.[2] After three hours of grey highway between Antwerp and Otterlo, and many long conversations, I was finally going to get to see the museum Barbara had talked so much about. My first impression lay somewhere between terror and nightmare. A sinister and incommensurable brick wall, like the wall of a prison, stretched out to my right. (Barbara was electrified, praising the architecture by Henry Van de Velde,[3] commissioned by Helene Kröller-Müller). But I had come to see the museum's famous sculpture garden and I wasn't going to give up.

At the front doors, just before she left for her meeting, Barbara insisted that I also visit the Van Gogh[4] collection. I thought I would skip it, but after seeing the garden, I changed my mind — it couldn't hurt to indulge her. I rushed up the stairs to the collection, thinking I wouldn't stay long.

And then something very strange happened. After only a few paintings, my pace slowed significantly and I found myself completely absorbed by the small canvases before me. Beyond all emotion, and without understanding why, my body had taken over. Water seemed to fill me and rise up towards my eyes. I say water, because I was not crying about any particular thing, but water was clearly coming out of my eyes, risen from an unknown source. I was flooded, a deluge. And it was tears. The emotion arose before a small canvas with a tree. What was the title of that painting? In any case, it was that painting that released the odd passage of water to tears. My friend joined me at the very moment when I had turned into a river. A generous laugh burst out of her then, and she said then the best thing a friend can say: "This is why I love you."

What is the title of that painting? I must write to Barbara.

To: Barbara De Coninck[5]
From: Lynda Gaudreau
Date: March 14, 2017 at 11:21
Subject: Musée Kröller-Müller
To: Barbara De Coninck

Dear Barbara,

How are you?

I was thinking of you today and our unforgettable day at the Kröller-Müller Museum. I'm writing a piece about that visit.

Do you remember the title of that Van Gogh painting, the one where I was overtaken by a flood of tears? It was a small canvas, of a tree, and I know there was mauve and white. I looked on the museum's site but I cannot find it. With your memory like an elephant, I thought you might remember…

And when was that visit?

Kisses,

Lynda xx

* * * *

On that day, Hildegard, in Otterlo, I felt so alive. I had lost it completely, but I was in full possession of my life.

On that day, I "saw" without forcing it. I saw without hoping for anything in particular, without even thinking I would.

On that day, I saw through my senses. I saw beyond my culture. I saw beyond my knowledge, my taste, and my habits, because before that day, Van Gogh's work didn't move me at all.

I am not advocating for ignorance in saying this. On the contrary — I believe that thinking, developing a consciousness of the world, is something learned — and feeling is, too. If I had had children, I would have signed them up for a philosophy course when they turned seven. Learning to think, learning to feel and learning to swim — all these things are crucial. But I wonder how it might be possible to escape the clutches of a culture, the power of knowledge and the security of protocols — I wonder how we might learn to say no.

If I go on, Hildegard, I will speak to you of agonism, of Chantal Mouffe's[6] (2010) idea that democracy operates in dissensus, and that consensus does not even exist! With this conception, the horizon opens wide for me, because through democratic dissensus we find ourselves two — no, five — steps beyond "seeing": we are smack in the middle of "acting."

If I go on, Hildegard, I will speak to you of destruction — yes, destruction. Seeing and feeling involve forgetting, transforming, erasing and destroying.

If I go on, Hildegard, I will speak to you of freedom, but before that, I will speak about Susan Sontag, who says in an interview with John Berger in 1983:

> (Literature) enlarges the field of our imagination […] I think we live in our imagination very quietly, very still — at least after a certain age — with all kinds of terrible conformities […] that deprive us from the life of the mind and the life of imagination […] and one of the functions of the storytelling, I would say, is to introduce a sense of the fantastic.
>
> (Lloyd 1983)

I agree with Susan Sontag. And I think that a single detail, a miniscule change can generate something wondrous, and that the effect is all the more powerful for having been provoked by a trifle.

And Sontag is right — we humans deprive ourselves of our imagination — worse, we deprive ourselves of ourselves.

Chantal Mouffe is right, too. We are beings of dissensus. And I would venture a link here between her concept of agonism and asynchrony. Asynchrony and agonism both operate through dissension.

But why am I telling you this, Hildegard? A saint such as yourself, who dedicated her life to others, is not a being of dissensus. And yet, how is it possible to feel, to see and to act without freedom? Will you forgive me for speaking to you so bluntly?

It's late, the sky has grown dark. I close my eyes in the darkness. I think of martial arts masters. When I was younger, I had an evening job that allowed me to watch teachers of karate, kendo, taekwondo and kung fu at work — and something is coming back to me now about them and their quality of movement: in order to react quickly, one must be relaxed.

Feeling doesn't require any intention or preparation, except perhaps that of being available. The karate master was available to defend himself or to attack in any direction: in front of him, behind, above and below, left and right. And yet he seemed completely relaxed — he appeared to not even be concentrating.

I open my eyes. A storm is raging outside, snow is falling, the wind is howling through the streets of Montreal. Soon we won't be able to see anything.

I often don't understand what my senses are perceiving, and the most difficult thing — especially when I'm in the process of creating — is to not try to find the solution right away.

Being lost, without a solution, is altogether difficult. I'm going to close my eyes now. I'll wait a little while.

Barbara sent a reply to my message — here's what she wrote:

---------- Forwarded message --------
From: Barbara De Coninck
Date: March 14, 2017 at 12:38
Subject: Re: Musée Kröller-Müller
To: Lynda Gaudreau

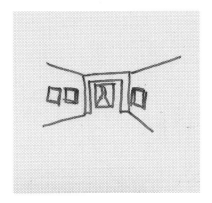

FIGURE 7.2   Free drawing of a museum room.
Drawing by the author.

My dear,

Yes, yes… I found it right away… with a description in English, go figure! (Kröller-Müller, n.d.a)

I, too, often think back to that crazy day and to the face you made when we — upon arriving at Eede (right away and before anything else) — descended upon that local farm to buy potatoes and preserves…

And your chilly reaction to my idea of going straightaway — and even b-e-f-o-r-e the cup of coffee you needed so badly — to see the iconic Van Goghs in the museum's classical wing designed by architect Henry Van de Velde (Kröller-Müller, n.d.b).

Your tender heart that leapt before this stunted flowering tree (more of a bush than a tree, really)… pink… so pink… colour of flesh and promise of joy, colour, happiness and goodness…

And your unnameable emotion, so intimate… that arose all at once, without warning, from the depths of your soul…

And when you had dried your tears, we ate cake in Evert Van Straaten's office (ex-director of the museum) to celebrate the arrival of several Jan Fabre works (Kröller-Müller, n.d.c) into the collection — including the famous bronze chapters in the sculpture garden…

We must do it again. It was — if I am not mistaken — in the fall of 2011 (October or November).

How am I doing? "So-so" — but spring is coming. And the birds, too. Yesterday a migrating sparrowhawk, today the greenfinches and the wagtails. And Sunday, I am redoing my entryway at Saeftinghe to count the birds after two years' absence. And tomorrow a long Bikram class, 90 minutes, at nine in the morning. And so on and so forth. I will tell you all one day — I have had a hell of a winter. Anyway — that is life (and it could be worse)!

xx Barbara

* * * *

So, the little painting with the tree was called Pêcher en fleur ("Souvenir de mauve") from 1888 (Kröller-Müller, n.d.a).

That day, at the Kröller-Müller Museum, I had — in my own way — a vision. Without intending to, I saw. And that is what I mean by seeing, Hildegard.

There is a storm outside, all is white, I cannot see anything anymore. But beneath the white lies the city. And I can wait for the snow to melt to see once again.

Thinking of you,

Lynda

Notes

1 Hildegard of Bingen (1098–1179) was a German Benedictine nun. She developed many talents, being at the same time abbess, mystic, visionary, illustrator, composer, poetess and also an important figure of monastic medicine.
2 Kröller-Müller Museum is a national art museum and an important sculpture garden. Helene Kröller-Müller founded it in 1938. After the Vincent van Gogh Museum, the museum possesses the largest collection of paintings of Vincent van Gogh (Kröller-Müller n.d.d).
3 Henry Van de Velde (1894–1943) was an architect, painter and art theorist. Van de Velde is considered one of the founders of Art Nouveau in Belgium.
4 Vincent van Gogh (1853–1890) was a Dutch Post-Impressionist painter.

5 Barbara De Coninck is a keen birdwatcher, a Flemish producer, curator and arts administrator based in Antwerp.
6 Chantal Mouffe is a political theorist best known for her influential works on agonistic political theory and her joint work with Ernesto Laclau (1935–2014), political theorist and philosopher.

References

Kröller-Müller. n.d.a. "Pink Peach Trees." Accessed March 14, 2023. http://krollermuller.nl/en/vincent-van-gogh-pink-peach-trees-souvenir-de-mauve.
Kröller-Müller. n.d.b. "The Kröller-Müller Museum." Accessed March 14, 2023. https://krollermuller.nl/en.
Kröller-Müller. n.d.c. "Jan Fabre." Accessed March 14, 2023. https://krollermuller.nl/en/search-the-collection/keywords=Jan+Fabre#filters.
Kröller-Müller. n.d.d. "Van Gogh Gallery." Accessed March 14, 2023. https://krollermuller.nl/en/van-gogh-gallery.
Lloyd, Mike. 1983. "John Berger and Susan Sontag: To Tell a Story." Video, 1:03:53. Accessed March 14, 2023. https://www.youtube.com/watch?v=MoHCR8nshe8.
Mouffe, Chantal. 2010. "Politique et agonisme." *Rue Descartes* 1(67): 18–24. Accessed March 15, 2023. https://doi.org/10.3917/rdes.067.0018.

8

LOGGING

Expedition and encounter

Amaara Raheem

In 2016, I embarked on an artist's residency curated by Access Gallery (Canada), sailing aboard a cargo ship from Vancouver to Shanghai, spending approximately 23 days at sea. Whilst on board, I came across the ship's log — a public, legal record that noted routine information about our crossing. The ship's log offered up a device to be in conversation between my body and the body of the ship. Written in pencil, updated every four hours by an officer, sometimes erased, wanting and partial, we must remember: logbooks are capable of concealing as much as they reveal. The mythic realm of crossing an ocean makes space for the dance of the writer to apply embodied compositional strategies: choreography that writes. Multiple histories located in a single body, through the accumulated influence and distinctive lineage of practice, emergent content arrives from the state of double embodiment, as both dancer and writer, experienced as a rolling overlap of unfixed embodiments. *Logging* then as slippage between the waves; above, below and in-between; as a choreographic experimental mode of capture, generates a collective document in conversation with a travelling event that was part-pragmatic, part-mythic, part-recall, part-speculative and most importantly, performative.

Part 1: Arriving

SW274 pickled beetroot 1° glossy purple clot

I arrived at VanTerm — Vancouver's shipping port — wearing a grey woollen suit because this was Canada and spring mornings could be cold. I also wore a mustard yellow felt hat with a broad rim. I was not wearing the gloves Ross gave me, because I had left the gloves in the taxi, but I did not know that yet.

DOI: 10.4324/9781003397427-10

I stood very straight, staring up at the mammoth cargo ship that stood in front of me, taking up the whole width of a street. A silver steel ladder, 24 planks spanning air, unfolded, slightly swinging in the penetrating wind, against the side of the ship. An officer in uniform sprinted down the ladder, quick as a goat. He was young, about 25, slim and Filipino, introduced himself rather shyly, took my luggage and ran back up the ladder. I followed more slowly, more carefully, already burdened by a different kind of power.

When I told a friend of mine that I had been selected for an artist's residency aboard a cargo ship, the friend warned me against it. "It sounds like my worst nightmare," he said. But I would not listen and said that I adored sea travel. "You won't adore that one," said Jim. But I said of course I would, I adored all boats.

In this artist's residency, I was faced with the challenge of living my life and navigating my practice for approximately 23 days aboard a cargo ship, sailing from Vancouver to Shanghai across the North Pacific Ocean. Standing there, in VanTerm, on a cool spring morning, I realised, in a kind of horror, that once the ship set sail, I could not get off, at least not until it landed at the first stop in Busan, South Korea. Even then, it would be difficult to leave. As the Chief Officer told me a few days later, his job was to get me to Shanghai, alive. Then he imitated — with his hands — picking up a piece of luggage, moving it across the air and dropping it to the ground. Then in seeming satisfaction, he clapped his hands and smacked his lips. Was this a pantomime of me as cargo? I sipped my coffee and said, "thank you." The First Officer (who I began to call Chief, e.g., "Good morning Chief") was very kind to me. He made me coffee every time I visited the wheelhouse and was the only officer on board who seemed genuinely interested in my practice of choreography and performance. He asked me questions about my work. He wanted to know what I was doing on board the ship. He asked questions about the kind of dancing and performing I did. Looking back, what I would like to have told him was something like this: For me dancing is a mysterious, sensorial, kinaesthetic activity, which cannot be fully expressed in words but only lived, only danced. Dancing for me also involves language. Or rather, *languageing*: a practice of feeling for knowledge expressed through the strange consolidation of movement-and-words in parallel. In *languageing*, I am interested in alternative approaches of translation, transmission or synthesising in the project of articulating movement. Such processes enable the slippage between worlds of attention to moment, movement and to emergent content to manifest on the page. The emergence of these practices attends to the compression and attention of lived experience with the midst of dancing-in-place: kinaesthetic intelligence enabling an outing of hidden narratives of the body toward activating my presence in-residence.

As always, I begin with movement. Each day I return to places within the ship, both indoors and outdoors, and repeat tasks that I invent. I make physical contact with the containers: standing or leaning against them. I take long walks around the perimeter of the ship, sometimes I walk backwards just to see what it will do to my ways of seeing and sensing. I stop and talk to people I meet en route; in particular, I seek out conversations with the crew so I can understand their working rhythms. If I find openings between surfaces of the shipping containers, I dance there, sometimes for three minutes, other times for an hour or more. I listen to conversations and write down what I hear. I eavesdrop. I collect gestures, actions and words. I invent systems, indexes, collections and columns. I remix and reassemble these words, inventing my own log; a secret log where I place poetry next to information, fiction next to facts.

But I did not say any of this because I hardly knew it myself then. Instead, I showed him photos of some of the writing I had been doing, with whiteboard markers, on my cabin window:

FIGURE 8.1   Writing on cabin windows aboard MV Hanjin Geneva. Photograph by Amaara Raheem.

The Chief looked at this image for a long time, shook his head and said, "How do you come up with this?"

"Well, that's hard to say," I said.

Part 2: Circumnavigating

ESE287 pancakes 2° upon the tongue and lust for

The exchange with this ship, of living in what was essentially a working factory, within the highly charged encounter of an ocean-crossing, took my work literally out to sea. I gained new insights. I lost all perspective. The fact that I was embedded in a system of global sea-borne freight, upon which the conduct of contemporary life is utterly dependent, changed everything in ways that I could – and could not — comprehend. There was one other passenger on board the ship, a businessman, from Texas, who dealt in surveillance equipment and was about to retire. Once, long ago, when the businessman was a boy, he and his father — a military man — made a journey on a cargo ship. Since then, his father long dead, the businessman had wanted to embark on another cargo ship trip. On the cusp of retiring, he was now in a deep space of reflection about his lineage and his legacy. He spent most of his time in his cabin, and I only saw him at meals or, sometimes, at the wheelhouse when we approached another port.

Even though I was on board as an "artist in-residence," the officers and crew treated me like an ordinary passenger. When I told the Steward (or Stewie as he was called on the ship) that I was an artist, Stewie kindly, but also somewhat suspiciously, enquired, "Where is your paintbrush? Where is your camera?" I had no words then to tell Stewie what I did, or how I did it, or why I did it. I did not want to tell Stewie that I was a dancer. In the Philippines, dance has strong erotic connotations and I was acutely aware that I was circumnavigating the globe with men at sea. Although, thankfully, I was not the only woman on board. For the first time in the history of the company, MV Hanjin Geneva had hired two female crew members. Both Filipinos. One worked in the engine room and the other in the ship's office. So instead, I said, "What's for lunch today?" and Stewie majestically replied, "boiled cabbage with rice." Then he told me that he too was an artist. That he did tattoos in his cabin and would I like one.

I took the time to get to know this situation from the inside. I entered a space and prepared to wait. Looking, listening, I made notes in my journal. I was a sponge, a surveillance system, a fly on the wall, an inventor of code. Sometimes I chatted with an officer on watch. The officers changed shifts every four hours. I asked them questions about their life, what it was like to be a sailor, their favourite places they like to visit, to which most of them replied, "Greece." When people approached, I looked up and tried to catch their eye to see if they wanted to interact. For example, the Chief Engineer never met my gaze. He also only spoke German, although the official working language on the ship was English.

The officers, including the rather handsome Captain, were all German except for the Chief, who was Polish. The crew were all Filipino. And I, a Sri-Lankan Australian, who all my life slipped between east and west, adapting to whatever situation and cultural context I found myself in, melting into it and spreading from underneath, like yeast. I learned these techniques early in life, and they are now so much a part of how I move in the world and especially in-residence.

Part 3: Performing

E267 ginger 0° artificial limits with a hint of rainbow

The concept of in-residence is nearly as old as the notion of the modern artist itself. As early as the mid-19th century, members of the West's artistic avant-garde would "go away" from home to pursue new experiences and other ways of being free from the stultifying constraints of polite bourgeois society. Homes and studios in the countryside, quaint coastal fishing villages, brothels, sanitaria, nudist colonies and the colonised tropics are some popular examples of early artist residencies. Moreover, these residencies transpired in an un-planned manner: like a grassroots movement burgeoning without any guidance from governments or institutions. However, as curator of Twenty-Three Days at Sea, Kimberly Phillips provokes,

> These artists — who might well be understood as the earliest practitioners of cultural tourism — longed to access some deep wellspring of "authentic" creativity dulled by modern industrialized life. Today, those concerned with the ethical engagement of artists in the communities they visit, and critical of the spreading ecological footprint of our contemporary art world, question whether the artist is ever more than a tourist during a residency.
> (Phillips 2015, 63)

I was a stranger. I arrived today and will stay tomorrow but not till next year. I answered questions that were asked of me, but not all of them. My work was not important here. At least not to the workings of the ship. Some-times, I questioned if my work was important at all, and at the same time, I recognised that this was fluid ground and my knowledge of the sailors was partial. I tried to stay as formless as I could. I postponed thinking about things and just sat. I was prepared to wait until something happened. Often nothing happened. I noticed myself moving away from the language of land and trees, towards a language of water, of atmospheric things. I performed a back and forth between first, second, third persons, inventing voices, perspectives, parts.

This is the work of an artist in-residence aboard a cargo ship.

To listen. To remain silent. To draw parallels. To notice synchronous and asyn-chronous rhythms. To remake borders. To enter and to wait. To read not only the physical barometer of the ship but also its emotional and energetic temperatures.

To step quietly in between. To hang around, apparently aimless but always alert. To set the alarm clock at all hours of day and night and make herself get up and go to the wheelhouse, where there is always an officer on watch. To notice and track internal weather. To talk when they want to talk. To remain silent when they seem otherwise occupied. To look as they look, out there, into that 360° of endless grey horizon, and try to see what they see. To change ideas. To sharpen perception. To become someone else. To play a part. I kept looking at everything on the ship as if it were fantastic wigs, costumes and other disguises.

I dwelled in the labyrinth of the spaces inside the ship. I walked around in socks, so as to be as soft-footed and silent as a cat, or a burglar. I made a list of all the things I had brought with me onto this ship. I spent a lot of time hanging around the containers filled with cargo, although many were empty, waiting to be filled up in China, and some had dangerous goods. "Fireworks," said the Chief sternly as he handed me a kettle for my cabin. I had to ask him for permission to make cups of tea in my room outside of mealtimes. As he walked away the Chief shouted down the corridor rather theatrically, "Don't blow up the ship, ok?"

Part 4: Eavesdropping

WNW277 boiled egg 2° a weathered thumb

I got used to packing and unpacking my things, because the spring swells of the ocean waves meant everything rolled about. All the furniture in my cabin: the table, the chairs, the lamp, the bedside table, were all chained or glued down. Coming to terms with the forces and conditions was the work. I started to create new habits, some of which became daily routines. This made me very receptive to the working rhythms on the ship. Each day, I began by writing down a list of tasks for myself to undertake. I went for a long walk around the perimeter of the ship; paused near the containers; sat or leaned against them; turned my body towards any glimmer of sunlight, like a house plant. I climbed ladders. None of my movements were monitored by the officers. Although sometimes the Bosun would find me and ask for a kiss. But it did not put me off. Often, I was completely alone up there. When I came across empty spaces between containers I danced in there. I sat with my back to the corrugated steel and listened. It was hard to hear the sea, because the hum of the ship's engine was very loud and very insistent. I smelled steel, engine oil, sweat. It was very cold, one or two degrees, and very wet. Sea spray and wind penetrated my bones. I started running to keep warm. I could see my breath escape like an escape rope, ragged and snarling.

After a few days, other habits emerged, and I noticed how new routines established themselves. I spent hours in the wheelhouse reading the ship's log. This was a public record of the ship's crossing kept by the officers on watch. It was written in pencil and updated every four hours. Copying the headings of the different columns into my notebook: Day; Time; Barometer; Temperature:

Air; Temperature: Sea; Weather; Wind Direction; Course Steered; Swell; Distance made good; Nautical remarks and entries according to Ship's Safety Law and Measures taken in the interest of sea-worthiness. I got very excited by this kind of language. They pointed me in new directions of thought, entangling environment with the language of the ship to new choreographic seeds.

Early one morning the First Officer suddenly said, "This job is a disaster."
He said, "I thought it was a dream job when I was young and stupid."
He said, "I am only here for the money, not the pleasure."
He said, "Always away from home."
I sipped my tea.
Later, standing outside looking at the sea, the businessman said, "If you love peace and quiet, this is the life."

A bell rang, but I did not know what that meant, so I simply stood there sipping my tea. At lunch, the Captain asked me if I'd had a good morning. I said I had. I asked him if he'd had a good morning and he replied, "Oh these days all I do is paperwork."

Part 5: Decoding

NE240 frozen fish 3° 3m swells in her memory

The only thing that counts here is how I spend the time. But in the end, that time is not really there. Adapting was the work. Pitching and rolling was the dance. Here, I was on a mission, gaining access, navigating and decoding traces of an as-yet undefined event. In-residence itself was acknowledged as host to an already occurring phenomenon. In this sense, I moved away from centering my own voice as an individual and instead tried to find ways to speak alongside others. On this mission, I was looking for what was already present within the existing atmosphere of this specific place. Patterns began to emerge. Slippage between worlds. I frequently saw the crew doing repetitive tasks. Painting the side of the ship. Banging nails. Checking the containers. Making notes every few hours. Updating. Overhauling. Explaining. Watching. Correcting. Amending. I watched their behaviour and tried to sync in with the rhythms of their movements. I tried to catch the details. There was a clear and apparent hierarchy on this ship. At mealtimes, the officers and crew ate in separate rooms. They ate separate food. My table was with the officers. I sat with the other passenger, the businessman. Even if the Captain was at his table and I was the only other person in the room, I sat at my table and he sat at his. Sometimes he talked with me. And other times he did not. I always waited for him to initiate the conversation. He led. I followed. This "rule" was never explained to me. It was something I intuited and then absolutely knew.

This once-in-a-lifetime opportunity to look inside a cargo ship was to get to know its operations, how our things travel around the world in complex and complicated ways. Although I was on the inside, I was equally on the outside. In Shanghai, I would step down that enormous ship's ladder and back into the world as you knew it. Whereas, these stevedores would go on sailing these waters. They would return to their homes, via sea. I would return to mine via aeroplane, never to see each other again. Dark clouds were gathering. The ship continued its journey eastward, but the Captain was always altering its course against the typhoon. The sailors joked that I needed to practise getting into and out of the safety boat. And after some time, I was not always completely sure that this was actually a joke. But I laughed along, excited at how my knowledge about how dance can transfer lived experience into a written form to a highly charged spatial trajectory was expanding. I started to hear and touch hidden narratives. I started to write my own log. I made indexes, collections, columns of both fact and fiction. I also edited and erased information, so that only fragments remained. This made meaning dissolve and for something else to come into view. It was like drawing the curtains open and blowing out the candles.

Part 6: In-residence

WNW277 mushroom soup 4° the Seamen's Club only love songs

In her essay, "Choreography as Mobile Architecture," Erin Manning (2009, 153) writes, "Mobile Architecture is a stand-in-term for how a work extends beyond its content to create a lingering affective environment that persists even in its absence." Manning (2009, 153) uses the term "more-than" to conceive of a choreographic proposition when it exceeds the individual body and becomes an architecture in the moving. She writes, "A mobile architecture is one way of naming the event of choreography's self-generative force. It is what can be felt when the choreographed event generates a more-than that touches on its propositional nature" (Manning 2009, 153). In-residence, as a choreographic *languaging* device, is "more-than." It requires a spatial-environmental-temporal frame, one that asks my body to become an intensive participant within a dynamic context rather than simply an instigator of actions or words. It requires that my body moves and thinks in relation, dancing IN time, moving IN and WITH space-timing. Logging as a mobile architecture is an unstable form, and although it can be located within a site, a context, a geography, a history and milieu, it is less a document than an agile practice.

The only way to get to know "in-residence" is through a practice of immersion and inhabitation, through "residing-in". This may seem a simple process. For example, you might walk into the sea and lie down on the surface of the water as if it were a dance floor. But to be entangled in wave, force, wind and undercurrent is not easily done. It requires a rigorous experiential knowledge of how to move your own weight; make continual micro-adjustments in relation to other densities and forces; push or pull in multiple directions to stay buoyant; simultaneously submit and resist. Anyone can declare themselves "in-residence", but no one can ever quite know it. Like one never quite knows a mountain, nor oneself in relation to it. However often it is practised, "in-residence" holds astonishment. The kind of astonishment I mean is an everyday kind of magic that dancer Ivey Wawn suggests is

> A kind of magic that is unspectacular, and maybe even invisible, until you allow yourself cognisance of it. It is a magic that need not always be called "magic", but should you think of it in such a way it becomes all the more powerful. It is a magic that happens as a result of connectedness.
>
> (Wawn 2020)

If "in-residence" were a landscape, it would be bare, stony, windy, seemingly flat and then unexpectedly, steeply curved. What I remember now is the quality of light that fell through some of its openings: luminous and soft, yet penetrating to immense distances with an effortless intensity. On days when my vision was clear, I could look without any sense of strain out past the horizon. Out of this steady looking and listening arose "residing-in," an approach that asked me to feel for the whole wild enchantment of going, and staying, "in."

If "in-residence" were a container, it would not be like the hundreds of containers that surround me on this ship — hard, dense walls of steel, measurable, stackable and boundaried — rather, in-residence as a spatial-temporal arrangement where actions, gestures and narratives amass, and overspill. Multiple histories located in a ship; multiple selves in a single body; through the accumulated influence and distinctive lineage of practice emergent content arrived from the state of double embodiment as both dancer and writer, both here and there; experienced as a rolling overlap of unfixed waves of information, both internal and external. Layered information composed of nautical facts and fluid feelings generate a multiplicity of voices; chorus.

Part 7: Residing-in

The counterpart of the noun "residence" is the verb, "residing": an activity not predetermined. Rather, an encounter, of (un)doing, (un)folding, experimenting and returning to vital practices that are produced in and through processes of inhabitation. In my practice, "in-residence" is a framework, a way of looking and listening, a choreographic approach or "score" that anyone can take up or participate in. It is borne out of a set of dancing and writing tactics where movement and language weave and also collide. Its

overarching aim is to position subjectivity and belonging as contingently produced: the self as fiction. "Residing-in" does not require anyone to dance
in ways that we traditionally understand what dancing might be. Rather, it
situates "dance" as an openness and willingness to instigate change and to be
changed by change.

While the act of composing frameworks as an artist in-residence is conscious
and considered, the arrangements that result cannot be anticipated. It is always
formed anew. Each "residing" produces its own momentum and outcome,
enabling new patterns and social relations to come into play or reveal themselves as recognition, where previously they were not.

In the book *Autobiographical Performance*, theatre scholar Diedre Heddon (2008, 90) posits a new term that brings together place and site, and
the "place of self" which she calls "autotopographic." Heddon (2008, 91)
writes,

> Autotopography, like autobiography, is a creative act of seeing, interpreta-
> tion and invention, all of which depend on where you are standing, when
> and for what purpose. With its stress on the auto, perspective is fore-
> grounded in a way that distinguishes it from dominant (contemporary
> and Western) forms of mapping. This sort of mapping also allows you to
> "write" the unknown or unrecognised route.

Residing then, is a choreographic practice that indexes an "unrecognised
route," circuits of thought-action-response in collaboration with other bodies
in the spaces we inhabit, recognising that we are all inhabiting this event-
space together. It is an act of staging a body's entanglement with the world
or as Virginia Woolf (1931, 119) might put it, "I hold a stalk in my hand. I
am the stalk."

Part 8: Logging

W204 birthday cake 5°
I have omitted to mention that everything about him was red.

Dear Logger,

We do not know each other but it seems to me that "Logger" is an appropriate
title for you in that it reflects a block of wood; a tree trunk with the memory
of forest as well as a register. Namely, it conveys something about time, the
number of hours we have chalked up together on this expedition. Actually, I
can see you drifting there, moving slowly with the current; gathering all kinds
of heaps and drifts. It is this reflected surfacing that makes me all the more
excited for us to share a sustained correspondence.

Allow me to introduce myself. My name is HG. I am a ship. A container ship. Filled with cargo. My parents, also containerised, came from a long line of merchant ships that carried goods from one port to another. They met in Colombo, in the warm Indian Ocean, welded together in steel. Like them, I too am a standard unit of software, with various settings. I was designed to be efficient and set to work in the marketplace of international trade relations from early on. I am typically secured, held down with battens. I am cellular, coastal, inter-modal. I hold inventories, follow orders, am placed here or there and told — with pride — that I was built around a strong keel. I am branded with product codes so that I too can be accurately tracked, scanned, and auto-mated. I have a lot of common sense, am seaworthy, mostly dry. My body is of a large volume, purpose-built. I have hatches, holds, dividers, and carry things vertically, like flows of information, hierarchy, timetables. My business is linear. But sometimes, especially at night when a cruise ship all lit up passes me by, I too have thought of myself as lightweight, stand alone, operatic. But actu-ally, I am of many dependencies. I move with the world's motion, responding to tides, coordinates, articulated mechanisms and inter-locking systems. I am securely tightened, part of a fleet.

You have probably already heard about mobility-systems the term British sociologist John Urry came up with that defines society by the ever-accelerating mobility of its citizens (Holmes 2011). In short, the richer the society, the greater the range of mobility-systems. Basically, that the movement of things and the movement of people are utterly co-dependent.Please, are you allowing your kneecaps to float?

At your service,
HG

References

Access Gallery. n.d. "Twenty-Three Days at Sea." Accessed April 14, 2023. https:// accessgallery.ca/23daysatsea.

Heddon, Diedre. 2008. *Autobiography and Performance*. Basingstone: Palgrave Macmillan.

Holmes, Brian. 2011. "Do Containers Dream of Electric People?" open! Platform for Art, Culture & The Public Domain. Accessed March 24, 2023. https://onlineopen. org/do-containers-dream-of-electric-people.

Manning, Erin. 2009. *Always More than One: The Individuation's Dance*. Durham: Duke University Press.

Phillips, Kimberly. 2015. "On Pelagic* Space: A Projection (Part One)." *The Cap-ilano Review* 3(26) (Spring): 62–66. April 12, 2023. https://www.academia.edu/ 21206110/On_pelagic_space_a_projection_part_one_.

Wawn, Ivey. 2020. *In Perpetuity*. Self-published.

Woolf, Virginia. 1931. *The Waves*. London: Random House.

9

NOTES ON BETRAYAL

Martin Hargreaves

This chapter queers the genealogies of choreography through an affirmation of the misfires of performatives and of the treachery of writing by, for and to a body that cannot keep the promises it makes. Susan Sontag and Jean Genet are posed as potential progenitors for the betrayals of unhappy enactments. Two scenes, one from each of their lives, and an interlude of a possible meeting of the two, are restaged from their journal notes, essays and novels. The chapter follows the sound of a voice never fully found and retraces the steps of a dance that failed to seduce. Both Sontag and Genet call for an erotics of writing, which would summon a body, while knowing that something in excess of a fidelity to words will answer. This excess is an undoing of authorship as a tenable stable position, and it seduces the writer into a movement beyond themselves into ecstasy. Sontag and Genet hail us into a focus on the duplicitous pleasures of Camp, the potentialities of hollow and trivial gestures and the possible ecstasies of betrayal whenever words are set into motion.

Notes on betrayal

[…] my life was the preparation for erotic adventures (not play) whose meaning I now wish to discover… So I have recourse to words. Those which I use, even as I attempt an explanation by the means of them, will sing. Was what I wrote true? False? Only this book of love will be real. What of the facts which served as its pretext? I must be their repository. It is not they that I am restoring.

(Genet 1964, 87)

DOI: 10.4324/9781003397427-11

There are oft-cited primal scenes for the intercourse between writing and dancing and the concepts they reproduce — first, as *orchesography* in 1589, coined by Thoinot Arbeau, then as *choreography*, named by Raoul-Auger Feuillet in 1700. These origin stories work as repeated stagings of the pedagogical fantasy that words and drawings instruct and induce movement, moving from the present moment of inscription in the scholarly room to the imagined future of reading and enactment in the ballroom. As André Lepecki has argued, these fables establish a homosocial and patrilineal vector for the power of dance writing, "as an early modern subjectivity-machine in which masculine solipsism is an essential element" (Lepecki 2006, 19).

This word, *choreography*, eventually becomes disobedient to its fathers, however, and proceeds to have a promiscuous life, moving through notation, pedagogy, creativity and into expanded uses concerning the organisation of social structures and spatial politics. It multiplies and mutates according to need, and it becomes untenable to restrict its operation to a particular field. Anna Leon has suggested that in order to understand how choreography currently operates, we should acknowledge its contingency by moving from the singular to the plural form: "Choreography, then, rather is choreographies: it is not reducible to a singular meaning or practice but constitutes a network of historically situated, distinct, albeit interrelated ones" (Leon 2020, 69). Leon is analysing William Forsythe's proposal of Choreographic Objects, and in an essay on this strand of his practice, Forsythe argues that to "reduce choreography to a single denotation is to not understand the most crucial of its mechanisms: to resist and reform previous definitions" (Forsythe 2011, 90).

Choreography, then, is always in a sense invoking history, legacy and authorship, but actively betraying them, setting up conditions that seduce us into a relationship with origins and then reformulating them through processes that succeed through a certain infidelity. These notes will wander away from a historical tracing of the word *choreography* to arrive back at it through other steps, but the aim is to wonder about the various forms of betrayal that are necessary every time a body is written and a body writes. Betrayal, in this sense, is not to be thought of as a failure to act, or as fully wilful treason, but as the unanticipated creative excess that spills over when words and bodies move. Corporeality cannot ever be fully faithful, because something in excess of good intentions drives both a body's movement and its imagination into and through language. This is where I depart from the dancing master forefathers, who wanted to prescribe a fidelity between the page and the stage. I suggest we might indulge in a family romance to fabulate other parents. What might be possible if we are not dutiful daughters and sons but self-made divas and orphaned thieves? This question requires a focus on how the movements between words and bodies, and the translated inscriptions that make them possible, are enabled only through unhappiness. I want to imagine other primal scenes that might help in thinking about writing and choreography; Susan Sontag scribbling in a notebook in a cold room in Oxford in 1957 and Jean Genet dancing in a pink negligée for the Black Panthers in 1970.

I'll stage these scenes in dialogue with J. L. Austin's lectures at Harvard in 1955 in order to bring betrayal into relation with performativity. *Performativity* was coined, by Austin, 250 years after the first writing of the word *choreography*, but in my rethinking of queered genealogies, both these words attend each other's birth and spur each other on into afterlives of seduction and scandal. To speculate on cross-contamination, and move freely between these scenes, refuses temporal ordering in favour of the pleasures of anachronism. Elizabeth Freeman proposes the concept of temporal drag, in which erotohistoriography foregrounds attachments to images and texts, and understands that when we go looking for lineages, certain scenes both drag up, in terms of putting on a show of citational pleasures, and drag upon, in terms of pulling our attention backwards to rewrite genealogies. This emphasises an erotics of writing history that, for me, has a gravitational force that acts within the orbit of the choreographic:

> Erotohistoriography admits that contact with historical materials can be precipitated by particular bodily dispositions, and that these connections may elicit bodily responses, even pleasurable ones, that are themselves a form of understanding. It sees the body as a method, and historical consciousness as something intimately involved with corporeal sensations.
>
> (Freeman 2010, 95–96)

The erotics proposed here, through my fantasy roleplaying of Sontag and Genet, requires an insistence on imagining a body to be always already engaged in an iterative inscription of relational whirls and reels of other bodies, past, present and future, undoing the strict temporal ordering of cause and effect that is proposed in a dance instruction book. As with Arbeau and Feuillet, Sontag and Genet imagine that any notational address to bodies through writing could result in some form of embodied translation, often even into dancing, but they differ from these forefathers by revealing that this works not through fidelity to any facts or score but through the inevitable misfires that scandalise all performatives. When you summon a body through writing, you cannot fully know whom you address, and you cannot fully know who will answer the call or how they will dance, especially if you are attempting to choreograph yourself onto the page. Indeed, for Sontag and Genet, meaningful interpretation, as a clear passage between words and the world, is eschewed in favour of the seduction of language, the pitfalls of duplicity, an excitement and revulsion in the slight camp gesture and the treachery of translation. Words sing, but songs of love resonate only through a voice broken by betrayal.

Scene one: Susan Sontag warms up and finds a voice

Life is suicide, mediated.
This little cone of warmth, my body—its protections (nose, fingers) are chilled.
Speak of chilled fingers.
The private life, the private life.
Struggling to float my pieties, idealisms.
All st[atement]s *not* to be divided into true + false ones. This can be done, trivially. But then the meaning is mostly bleached out.
Being self-conscious. Treating one's self as an other. Supervising oneself.
I am lazy, vain, indiscreet. I laugh when I'm not amused.
What is the secret of suddenly beginning to write, finding a voice? Try whiskey. Also being warm.

(Sontag 2008, 235)

These melancholy notes, written by Susan Sontag in her journal on her short visit to Oxford University in 1957, reveal several insistent ideas she was tussling with and refrains that echo throughout the rest of her reflective scribbles. The promise of an authorial voice that would confer coherence and confidence seduces her, and the complex bodily binds of reflexivity confound her. These frustrated desires reappear every few pages, almost as the motor for her notes and as the critical voice that urges her to stylise herself always in relation to how she might perform alongside and through other voices and other bodies. In the publication of these journals and notebooks, edited by her son, David Rieff, the entry above is followed by a note, "This notebook contains the notes she took for a philosophy class taught by J. L. Austin. They are not reproduced here. Of significance in the personal sense, however, are some jottings SS made on the inside cover [...]" (Sontag 2008, 235).

Sontag was on a scholarship and had travelled to Oxford, where she stayed only a few months before fleeing the cold grey English weather, and the colder and greyer English academics, to enjoy a longer sojourn in Paris. A later journal entry, before she leaves, urges again: "Try whiskey. To find a voice. To speak" (Sontag 2008, 238). In 1958, when she's finally in Paris and surprised by moments of happiness, she notes that she got drunk on "5 or so whiskeys" and had "superb sex" with Harriet Sohmers, an old lover with whom she rekindles an affair (Sontag 2008, 275). Her notes from 1949, when she first met Sohmers in San Francisco, record Sontag as feeling too tense to dance and stepping all over Sohmers' feet. She got better at dancing as the affair continued, but throughout the journal, she notes that dance, like her voice, often seems to elude her. In Paris, after the whiskey-infused dancing and sex, the affair is tumultuous and ultimately falls apart, and her journals record that her ability to write fluctuates with the waves of love and rejection that alternately ignite and isolate her "sore heart + unused body" (Sontag 2008, 275).

I want to move backwards slightly, before the whiskeys, before this storm, when in Oxford, she was still cold and voiceless. According to Rieff, and to authorised biographer Benjamin Moser (2019), Sontag was disappointed by most of what she encountered at the university, except for Austin's lecture series. Austin had already presented his newly coined term "performative" two years earlier, in lectures delivered at Harvard, and he was continuing to elaborate on it as a way of proposing that words have a force, or forces, to enact changes in social reality. Austin's neologism has enjoyed a promiscuous career, following the posthumous publication of his Harvard lecture notes as *How to Do Things with Words* (1962). His attention in these notes is not only on how certain utterances, in certain circumstances, create a change in the world but also how these can, and very often do, go awry. Because performatives cannot be true or false, because they cannot be verified according to a referential reality, Austin chooses the words happy or unhappy, or felicitous or infelicitous, to distinguish between performatives that behave as they should and those that for whatever reason, (he attempts to provide an exhaustive list of reasons) do not succeed. This lack of success isn't the lack of an action; an unhappy performative isn't necessarily a failure to enact a change, it's just that the change that was expected hasn't quite been produced. Something enticingly queer lurks within all performatives:

> Well, it seems clear in the first place that, although it has excited us (or failed to excite us) in connexion with certain acts which are or are in part acts of *uttering words*, infelicity is an ill to which *all* acts are heir which have the general character of ritual or ceremonial, all *conventional* acts.
>
> (Austin 1962, 18–19 emphasis in original)

Austin returns us here to the idea of lineage and genealogy with this phrasing of performatives being an heir to unhappiness. With his expansion of the speech act to include *all conventional* acts, we might read into this that choreography has also inherited this illness, this tendency to go astray. The editors of Austin's papers note on this same page that he used many different names for the types and categories of infelicities in addition to those he diagrammatically explicates. For the purposes of my notes here, I don't want to try and distinguish how he uses them, but it interests me (or as Austin would put it, *excites* me) to list them all as a suggestion of the kind of family of unhappiness choreography might be born into: misfires, abuses, insincerities, misapplications, misexecutions, misapplication, flaws, hitches, non-plays, misplays, miscarriages, misexecutions, non-executions, disrespects, dissimulations, non-fulfilments, disloyalties, infractions, indisciplines, breaches. He even leaves one category of "professed but hollow" abuses simply, and enigmatically, designated with a

"?." The illness that we are heir to can of course mutate, and with this question mark, Austin suggests we should remain open to unanticipated treachery.

The omission of Sontag's notes on Austin from her published journals is very seductive — I start to imagine how this word performative, with all its attendant unhappiness, although never appearing in print on her pages, is perhaps hovering in the wings. It becomes tempting, exciting even, to reread the essays collected in Sontag's *Against Interpretation* (1966) through the prism of performativity, even though I do not know for certain if this aspect of Austin's lectures stirred her from her boredom with the other Oxford dons. Certainly, there's much in her *Notes on Camp* that propose a thinking about the gendered stylisation of the body as a ceremonial act of becoming, decades before Judith Butler used the word performative to radically change the conceptualisation of gender. There's also a trace of Austin's speech act theory in Sontag's note above, if you want to look for it as I do. She instructs herself to refuse the triviality of a true/false dichotomy of statements, which bleaches out meaning — echoing Austin's condition that a performative cannot be true or false. In the title essay for *Against Interpretation,* she rails against the practice of criticism that attempts to value art by how it describes a pre-existing reality (Austin would name this "constative") and instead petitions the reader to refocus on what art does.

> None of us can ever retrieve that innocence before all theory when art knew no need to justify itself, when one did not ask of a work of art what it said because one knew (or thought one knew) what it did.
>
> (Sontag 1966, 4–5)

This lost innocence, a fantasy scene she stages before the Greeks messed everything up with their suspicion of mimesis, now reads to me as art's fall from performative grace into the abuses and dissimulations of interpretive writing. For Sontag, we are all heirs to the dissembling illness that Plato contracted, and she proposes erotics might be a cure. She shares with Austin an insistence on focusing away from the shadows of reality that acts, and arts, may be judged as representing, and she is far more excited by what changes they make in the world. The essay finishes with her declaration: "In place of a hermeneutics we need an erotics of art" (Sontag 1966, 33). The erotics she advocates are performative, they enact reality, rather than describe it, through forms of bodily seduction, which are not reducible only to sexual excitement.

The journal marginalia cited above reveals that Sontag was also interested in how the performativity of writing struggles with the disloyalties of a voice. Erotics need to seduce the writer as much as the reader, bringing both into congress without the need for metaphors and meaning; but it will always falter, through chilled fingers, indiscretions, failed pieties and the lack of alcohol to lubricate the tongue. If these can be thought alongside the mis-invocations that are the condition for all performatives then we are in an erotics that seduces us precisely because it cannot remain faithful. A body will always speak (to itself, to others, to the world) in ways that exceed intention and cannot be limited by writing or by choreography. Shoshana Felman, in a reading of Austinian performativity, together with Moliere's *Don Juan*, proposes that this infelicity occurs because bodily promises cannot be fully known and, therefore, they cannot be kept, and we find ourselves always in a scandal whenever we try:

> [...] an irreducible *scandal*: the scandal (which is at once theoretical and empirical, historical) of the incongruous but indissoluble relation between language and the body; the scandal of the *seduction* of the human body insofar as it speaks — the scandal of the promise of love insofar as this promise is *par excellence* the promise that cannot be kept; the scandal of the promising animal insofar as what he promises is precisely the *untenable*.
> (Felman 2002, 5 emphasis in original)

Judith Butler reflects on this, in an afterword to the revised edition of Felman's text, to argue that a performative produces "more than it can ever intend or know. Indeed, as bodily, the speech act never had the sovereignty it sometimes tries to claim for itself" (Butler 2002, 114). With all this scholarship on performativity already exercising a pull on me, I reread Sontag's notes as not quite descriptive of her thoughts, her private life, but as an invocation. She herself notes that, by writing, "I do not just express myself more openly than I could do to any person; I create myself" (Sontag 2008, 248). Much of the pathos of her diaristic jottings emerges as she navigates how this desired move towards authorship and sovereignty, towards finally finding her voice, is undone by the inevitable broken promises of all performatives. Words fail her, her desires betray her and her body has all kinds of urgencies that frustrate her.

Sontag's later essays on cancer, AIDS and the violence of metaphorical writing have seeds in these journal notes. She repeatedly returns to the bind of having to summon a body, be a body, and speak and write and act according to the needs and pains of that body in the face of the scandal of language. Her insistence on erotics is a kind of hopefulness that there can be uninterpreted corporeal encounters with art, with sex, with illness and with death; but like all performatives, erotics is betrayed. Jay Prosser has tracked the relationship between Sontag's opposition to interpretation and her distrust of metaphor, and he suggests that these railings against figurative language are an attempt to arrive finally in herself, to a faithful corporeal erotics. He argues that "the material Sontag defends against interpretation is the body" (Prosser 2009, 392). This writing towards the body, her body, in the sense of a fully present and self-aware corporeal subjectivity, perhaps unsurprisingly, betrays her. Prosser argues that Rieff's detailed account of the last days of his mother's death reveal that Sontag was unable to reconcile herself through any form of writing or speaking to the cancer that killed her. Beyond this biographical note, I would extend Prosser's argument to suggest that disavowal, refusal, contradiction and a loss of sovereignty are as much part of Sontagian erotics as any direct and unmediated fleshly encounter with the world. In the opening pages to *AIDS and Its Metaphors* (1989), she offers 'of course' and 'but' twice:

> Of course one cannot think without metaphors. But that does not mean there aren't some metaphors we might well abstain from or try to retire. As, of course, all thinking is interpretation. But that does not mean it isn't sometimes correct to be "against" interpretation.
>
> (Sontag 1989, 5)

These two choreographic turns conjure up Sontag's relation to the scandal of the untenable speaking body, not only through her citing of herself but also through her insistence on the need to attempt a gesture, even though the attempt will undo itself. She is attuned to the infidelities of performatives, and I read in this admission an echo of how she had, decades before, formulated Camp as a self-aware elevation of unhappiness within language and within the world at large. She writes that Camp is a great creative force: "the sensibility of failed serious-ness, of the theatricalization of experience. Camp refuses both the harmonies of traditional seriousness, and the risks of fully identifying with extreme states of feeling" (Sontag 1966, 487). Camp knows that gestures fail to deliver what they promise, that the language (of humans and objects and others) can never secure a faithful and serious transmission between bodies (of humans and objects and others). It is a committed love of this unhappiness, and as Sontag claims, it can find creativity precisely in misplays, flaws, hitches, mis-executions and breaches.

In *Notes on Camp*, the essay where she explicates this theory of a seriousness that fails, she begins by stating that she will fail to do justice to the sensibil-ity, and her writing itself will inevitably be unhappy, perhaps even bad Camp, because she must attempt seriousness and translate this sensibility for a wider readership outside of the homosexual cognoscenti where she has discovered this extraordinary stylisation.

> To talk about Camp is therefore to betray it. If the betrayal can be defended, it will be for the edification it provides, or the dignity of the conflict it resolves. For myself, I plead the goal of self-edification, and the goad of a sharp conflict in my own sensibility. I am strongly drawn to Camp, and almost as strongly offended by it. That is why I want to talk about it, and why I can. For no one who wholeheartedly shares in a given sensibility can analyze it; he can only, whatever his intention, exhibit it. To name a sensibility, to draw its contours and to recount its history, requires a deep sympathy modified by revulsion.
>
> (Sontag 1966, 467–468)

This is a remarkable caveat that begins the essay that made Sontag famous. She has subsequently been accused of being a self-hating homosexual, of betraying Camp in order to stay safe in her closet (see, for example, Meyer 1994). I'm more interested here in how we can think of betrayal as a necessary condition of any erotic attachment, and of the double movements between writing and the body, both summoning each other, even though they know they will fail in some way. Sontag can talk about Camp, supposedly because she is already drawn to and repulsed by how disloyal it is. The double turn, repeatedly towards and away from Camp is, for her, instigated by excitement through infelicity, "the love of the exaggerated, the 'off,' of things-being-what-they-are-not" (Sontag 1966, 472–473). Sontag's notes proceed by elaborating a queer erotohistoriography, listing all of the texts that drag up and upon her and cause her to find her voice, caught in the embarrassing failure to fully name a corporeal sensibility.

In her *Notes on "Notes on Camp,"* Terry Castle forwards what she acknowledges is an "entirely speculative and subjective — some will say absurdly subjective" theory that we might think of Sontag's elaboration of Camp as another kind of double turn, as an act of fabulated autobiography and exorcism (Castle 2009, 26). Castle invokes Freud's concept of the family romance, first published in 1909, which describes the wishful fantasies of children who want to discover one day that they are not related to their biological parents, but were abandoned by a noble family who will come back to claim them. Castle cites this in order to reposition Sontagian Camp as the means by which queer children reconstruct their origins, transforming rejection and exclusion and the failure to live up to normative values by performing a magical self-reflective sensibility that finds a home in quotation marks, good–bad taste and things that are loved precisely because they are unnatural. In this queer family romance, the child is saved by unhappy objects through a reappropriation of the rejected, the anachronistic, the too much and the theatrically extreme; Castle applies this to Sontag's own childhood and her subsequent reinvention as an intellectual diva, suggesting that the essay that launched her career can be read as a form of queer autofiction; Susan Lee Rosenblatt choreographed herself as Susan Sontag through her seduction by, and repulsion from, a Camp sensibility.

In using psychoanalysis to interpret Sontag, to find an autobiographical impulse behind her writing, Castle is, of course, knowingly working counter to Sontag's insistence on being against interpretation of this kind. Castle's motive is to offer a partial redemption of Sontag, defending her somewhat against the critiques of internalised homophobia, in order to situate her *Notes on Camp* as both an attempt to speak about the difficult task of queer world making and as itself performatively bringing this world into being. In Sontag's essay, *Sartre's Saint Genet*, also collected in *Against Interpretation*, Sontag dismisses Jean-Paul Sartre's similar attempt to philosophically redeem Jean Genet's writing, noting with disapproval that Sartre cannot simply experience the gestures and acts in the works but instead he moralises and insists that they "must be understood, they must be interpreted as modifications of the world" (Sontag 1966, 95). Sontag is again drawn to and repulsed by how Sartre positions the performativity of Genet, but she moves between describing it as "a cancer of a book, grotesquely verbose," while acknowledging that "everything true and interesting that can be said about Genet is in this book" (Sontag 1966, 164–165). Her accusation is that in order to write at length about Genet, Sartre has become too serious and too erotically attached to his writing, and he ends up embarrassingly explicating his own world-making rather than elucidating that of Genet. To write about Genet is to betray the poet of betrayal, and Sontag is well aware of the risk that this might excite us into all kinds of relationships with infidelity.

Interlude: Susan meets Jean, perhaps

> *I:* You don't take your feelings seriously.
> *Jean-Jacques:* They are too complex for that.
> *I:* You are Vain.
> *Jean-Jacques:* I am a homosexual and a writer, both of whom are professionally self-regarding and self-esteeming creatures.
> *I:* But you are merely acting the part of a homosexual.
> *Jean-Jacques:* The difference is amusing, and not important.
> *I:* You are a tourist of sensations.
> *Jean-Jacques:* Better a tourist than a taxidermist.
>
> (Sontag 1963, 316–317)

This is a fictional conversation, transcribed into a fictional journal entry, that Sontag cites as if written by the narrator of her first novel *The Benefactor* (1963). The I in this quote is Hippolyte, a dreamer whose memoir we are reading, and Jean-Jacques is his friend: a French orphan, thief and prostitute turned successful writer. It's clear that Jean-Jacques owes a debt to Jean Genet, the French orphan, thief and prostitute turned successful writer. And the I in this quote could also be Sontag herself; Hippolyte's journals contain refrains that echo those written by Sontag in her own journals. Throughout the novel, Hippolyte/Sontag uses Jean-Jacques/Genet as a foil to play out scenes of an erotics of revolutionary self-creation and duplicitous Camp masquerade. Many vignettes from Genet's own novels, ranging from cruising in pissoirs to engaging in collaboration and treason with handsome SS officers, are rewritten into Jean-Jacques' story in order to suggest a life unbound by conventional morality or fidelity.

I've not been able to find much of any substance detailing meetings between Sontag and Genet outside of this novel, and I doubt that they would've played out quite like those of Hippolyte and Jean-Jacques. In the published journals, and in Benjamin Moser's *Sontag* (2019), there's no mention of encounters; but in Edmund White's biography, *Genet* (1994), he notes that, in 1970, while Genet was staying in New York during a US tour supporting the Black Panthers, Sontag was one of the French-speaking intellectuals called in to "Genet-sit" by his translator. What occurred during this Genet-sitting is left enigmatically unwritten. There's no reference I can find to Sontag in Genet's own published writing; Sontag, however, makes repeated references to him in her fiction and her essays; and, as White recounts, she wrote influential reviews of his work and was part of a group of "expert witnesses" who were called to defend Genet's film *Un Chant d'Amour* against charges of obscenity. In Sontag's essay, *On Style,* he is one of her pantheon of artists who aid her polemic against moralising interpretation and in favour of sensualising style:

> Genet, in his writings, may seem to be asking us to approve of cruelty, treacherousness, licentiousness, and murder. But so far as he is making a work of art, Genet is not advocating anything at all. He is recording, devouring, transfiguring his experience. In Genet's books, as it happens, this very process itself is his explicit subject; his books are not only works of art but works about art…The interest of Genet lies in the manner whereby his "subject" is annihilated by the serenity and intelligence of his imagination.
>
> (Sontag 1966, 53–54)

Sontag meets Genet in this passage through a proposed shared interest in double movements, erotic duplicity and the transfiguration of a loss of sovereignty into art. She writes him, as she writes herself, as finding a subjectivity through the annihilations of language. Authorship emerges through its erasure. Imagination enables this Sontagian Genet to consume words, savour their treachery and break promises of meaning. Sontag drags up Genet in a seductive stylisation which seems to advocate treachery and undo it in the same gesture.

Scene two: Jean Genet scandalises in a pink negligée

> One night Genet took too many Nembutals and danced in a pink negligée for Hilliard and three other Panthers. A French male translator who was present was so sickened by the spectacle that he prefers not to be named, but Hilliard himself, according to Angela Davis, felt that Genet was communicating something serious about sexual identity and its flexibility. Whatever Genet may have been up to, this well-substantiated event reveals that at least once he indulged in the camp transvestism he had so admired and written about.
>
> (White 1994, 608)

David Hilliard was the Chief of Staff of the Black Panther Party in 1970, for whom Genet was aching with unrequited love, when this dance seduced him into thinking about flexible sexual identity. Genet also was indulging in a family romance of his own by writing that he fantasised that the much younger Hilliard would take up the role of his father. I'm repeatedly drawn to imagining this scene as a way to conjure up how Genet proposes an erotics of writing, and of dancing, as intoxicating, contradictory, untrustworthy and revelling in all kinds of sicknesses that it inherits. The scene may have been well-substantiated by White in his duty as biographer, but it remains very enigmatic in what it produced, apart from the sickness of the translator which I'll return to later. Angela Davis speculates[1] that this scene provoked discussions about homophobia within the Party and elicited Huey Newton's speech, given later that year, declaring solidarity between Black revolutionary struggles and gay and feminist liberation. White notes that Genet wept after this tour with the Panthers, because he had failed to seduce Hilliard into being either his lover or father, or both. In *Prisoner of Love* (1992), the posthumously published manuscripts of Genet, detailing his time with the Panthers and the Palestine Liberation Organisation, Genet doesn't mention this event, or the ambiguous aftermath of it, but he does return often to the topic of betrayal. I want to speculate that we might think that this scene, where Genet drags himself up and creates an excess not reducible to possible meanings, can be thought of alongside his elaborations of the pleasures of the seductive misfires that betray the audience and the performer, the reader and the writer.

> Betrayal is made up of both curiosity and fascination.
> But what if it were true that writing is a lie? What if it merely enabled us to conceal what was, and any account is, only eyewash? Without actually saying the opposite of what was, writing presents only its visible, acceptable and, so to speak, silent face, because it is incapable of really showing the other one.
>
> (Genet 1992, 27)

This is one of many passages in which he explores his own curiosity and fascination with the different facets of betrayal, which span across all his novels, plays, essays and poetry. Here he makes a paradoxical claim that it might be true that writing is false, claimed through an act of writing. At first reading, it might reverberate with precisely the fear of mimesis that Sontag dismisses

---

[1] In a personal interview with White, referred to in the biography Genet (1994), and also in an unpublished speech given in Paris in 1991, transcribed and translated by Eric Beneviste, excerpted here: http://sisterezili.blogspot.com/2009/01/tactfulness-of-heart-angela-davis-on.html (see also Davis 2009).

in *Against Interpretation* in that it suggests writing is only a pale imitation of life. But if writing is two-faced and only can show one, then what is the other face of writing? Is writing a veil over a reality that is outside of language or is writing the means by which a duplicitous reality is gestured into the world? This unanswerable question of truth and lying comes after he describes observing Palestinian soldiers playing a game of cards by gesture alone, the actual cards having been confiscated. He's absorbed and excited by this collective performative summoning of something absent into the world. Like Sontag, Genet doesn't actually use the word "performative," I've slipped it in. Although Genet and Jacques Derrida were friends, I doubt they spoke directly about Austin or performativity. So, it is a more distant ghost of performativity that haunts Genet than the spectre within Sontag. But I do want to pursue this thread because there may be something to be gained by thinking together about the disloyalties of speech acts and how treachery is elevated in, and enacted by, Genet's writing.

In *Prisoner of Love*, Genet considers writing as a lesser gesture than the communal card game, because it is solitary and consumes all of the voices it summons: "like all the other voices my own is faked, and while the reader may guess as much, he can never know what tricks it employs" (Genet 1992, 27). In *The Thief's Journal*, his novel that he considered closest to an autobiography, he imagines the act of reading it as a form of conspiracy, a collusion in this faking of a voice, and he promises the reader that he will give notice when his steps falter: "In order to understand me, the reader's complicity will be necessary. Nevertheless, I shall warn him whenever my lyricism makes me lose my footing" (Genet 1964, 10). He doesn't keep this promise, and his footing loses him, and us, into the song of a fabrication of a self. For Genet, authorship is a seduction into the promise of understanding, with the knowledge that this promise cannot be kept. It's a mistake to attempt to extrapolate one singular theory of writing from any citation of Genet. He is not interested in consistency, fidelity to even himself, or in embedding authorial meaning in his words to guarantee some kind of transmission of truth. For Genet the pleasures of the act of writing arise from its duplicity, in how authorship tricks even the author.

In his first novel, *Our Lady of the Flowers*, Genet suggests that a piece of choreography would be the best way to tell the story of the life and loves of his main character, Divine: "Since it is impossible to make a ballet of it, I am forced to use words that are weighed down with precise ideas, but I shall try to lighten them with expressions that are trivial, empty, hollow and invisible" (Genet 1963, 61). I've written elsewhere about how this impossible ballet nevertheless resulted in many Butoh works around the figure of Divine and in an onanistic opus by Lindsay Kemp (see Hargreaves 2006). Here I want to linger on the Camp hollowness of his words as a strategy to summon a body unweighted by precision and ambiguous in its seduction, similar to his dancing in the pink negligée. Hollowness is also part of Austin's categorisation of the unhappiness of performatives; but, unlike Austin, Genet wants to luxuriate in the two-faced misfiring action of writing words in order to evacuate their centres of meaning and truth. With this emphasis on emptiness, something else might slide in and seduce, through the guise of his words that sing. Words are enticingly treacherous for Genet because they seem to promise so much, but they break these contracts to deliver trivialities, while unintended effects are smuggled across the borders through hollowed out gestures.

The unnamed translator who was sickened by Genet's dance in the pink negligée was perhaps repulsed by all kinds of Camp treachery that he was unable to translate into a sincere and truthful action, political, sexual or otherwise. I want to stay queasy with Genet and think about the sickness of translation as an affirmative form of betrayal, as an unhappiness that is itself duped into another form of happiness and hospitality to the unexpected. I should confess that I've only ever read Genet in English translation, and so I'm already losing the double-entendres that slide into his use of French. Edmund White suggests that even Genet's favourite translator, Bernard Frechtman, couldn't quite understand the argot and slang he used to find the words in English that might be as two-faced. Words are always moving in and through Genet and delighting in their losses. In *Prisoner of Love,* Genet recounts a fable which enables him to liken translation as an act of divesting words of their power:

> The Venerable Peter, abbot of Cluny, in order to study the Koran better, decided to have it "translated." Not only did he forget that in passing from one language to another the holy text could only convey what can be expressed just as easily in any tongue — that is everything except that which is holy; but he was probably actually motivated by a secret desire to betray. (This may manifest itself in a sort of stationary dance, rather like the desire to pee.)
>
> (Genet 1992, 59)

The holiness of words here arises as that which resists translation, which isn't quite their ability to convey meaning but their capacity to inspire belief, a weighted precision, or for our purposes, a happy performativity. Genet is far more interested in how the unhappy need-to-pee stationary dance becomes ecstatic:

> Once we see in the need to "translate" the obvious need to "betray," we shall see the temptation to betray as something desirable, comparable perhaps to erotic exaltation. Anyone who hasn't experienced the ecstasy of betrayal knows nothing about ecstasy at all.
>
> (Genet 1992, 59)

This ecstasy is not only in the translation from prison argot to French to English that I experience when reading Genet. Or in Venerable Peter's erotic motivation to translate the Koran from Arabic to French. It's an ecstasy in all forms of writing that move, because through and in movement they are betrayed. It's an encounter with the unspeakable that inspires and contradicts the finding of a voice, the untranslatable that inspires and contradicts the seduction of a dance. This formulation of ecstasy has affinities with how Judith Butler uses the ecstatic to name the constitutive desires that dispossess us, even as they promise coherence: "To be ec-static means, literally, to be outside oneself, and thus can have several meanings: to be transported beyond oneself by a passion, but also to be beside oneself with rage or grief" (Butler 2004, 24).

An ecstatic treachery, a transportation beyond oneself, can also be found in Paul Ricouer's lectures collected in *On Translation* (2006). With echoes of Austin, he suggests that we shouldn't think of good/true or bad/false translations but rather think along the lines of a "faithfulness/betrayal dilemma" (Ricouer 2006, 22). A translator has to create equivalences between languages based not on the words themselves but on what those words promise to communicate. This already requires a form of infidelity to an author and an acceptance that there will be distortion and loss as words move. Ricouer calls this a necessary double betrayal of both the source language and the one it moves into. Of course, translation will always undo itself, but it needs to be attempted anyway. He proposes that translation-betrayal occurs even within a language, not only between languages. It is a treacherous condition of all words that move, similar to the inherited illness of infelicity.

In these lectures, Ricouer, like Genet, is also thinking around the notion of the untranslatable and the unspeakable and, like Genet, he takes us away from notions of pure communication towards what he names linguistic hospitality. Meaning through language is only ever produced on the condition that it is open to its undoing. Hospitality is only possible through acts of betrayal, of double-crossing the phantasmatic borders that promise, but do not deliver, the sovereignty of a language, the sovereignty of a voice, the sovereignty of a body. Translation is an encounter with strangeness, and linguistic hospitality describes a kind of ecstasy of being besides oneself because of this doubled enigma.

> Have we not been set in motion by the fact of human plurality and by the double enigma of incommunicability between idioms and of translation in spite of everything? And then, without the test of the foreign, would we be sensitive to the strangeness of our own language? Finally, without that test, would we not be in danger of shutting ourselves away in the sourness of a monologue, alone with our books? Credit, then, to linguistic hospitality.
>
> (Ricouer 2006, 29)

Ricouer shares a hopefulness in the performative and transformative encounter with ecstatic strangeness with Genet, and with Sontag. His formulation of translation-betrayal opens up Austin's infelicities to considerations of the ethical demands of alterity, similar to the many ways in which Sontag and Genet stage writing as accountable for how it enables a meeting with otherness. Ricouer differs from them both in his characterisation of being shut away with books as a sourness — the prison cell and the private room are important spaces for how Genet and Sontag stage encounters with themselves. I want to finish these notes by resisting a full transfiguration of their betrayals into ethical hospitality. That might suggest that Genet and Sontag were secretly happy all along and it would fall foul of an act of a moral redemption of their writing that my own family romance is not quite promising. Neither the self-made diva nor the orphan thief arrive as perfect parents to fully transport us beyond ourselves, safe from the unhappinesses of writing or of dancing. Sontag and Genet, as I've invoked them here, both relish the erotic sourness of a solipsistic bookishness, precisely because the taste it leaves in the mouth is of the scandal of pleasure and of its non-fulfilment. The promise of a monologue, alone with books, of a voice that could finally address itself and through this act seduce and know itself, is, of course, a promise that cannot be kept. But in repeatedly making and breaking this unhappy contract with the self, acknowledging disloyalties, mis-plays, hitches and misfires, something else spills out.

References

Austin, John Langshaw. 1962. *How to Do Things with Words.* London: Oxford University Press.

Butler, Judith. 2002. "Afterword." In *The Scandal of the Speaking Body: Don Juan with J. L. Austin, or Seduction in Two Languages,* 113–123. Stanford, CA: Stanford University Press.

Butler, Judith. 2004. *Precarious Life: The Powers of Mourning and Violence.* London: Verso.

Castle, Terry. 2009. "Some Notes on 'Notes on Camp'." In *The Scandal of Susan Sontag,* edited by Barbara Ching and Jennifer A. Wagner-Lawlor, 55–75. New York: Columbia University Press.

Davis, Angela. 2009. "'Tactfulness of the Heart' Angela Davis on Jean Genet and the Black Panthers." Accessed April 30, 2023. http://sisterezili.blogspot.com/2009/01/tactfulness-of-heart-angela-davis-on.html.

Felman, Shoshana. 2002. *The Scandal of the Speaking Body: Don Juan with J. L. Austin, or Seduction in Two Languages.* Translated by Catherine Porter. Stanford, CA: Stanford University Press.

Forsythe, William. 2011. "Choreographic Objects." In *William Forsythe and the Practice of Choreography,* edited by Steven Spier, 90–92. London: Routledge.

Freeman, Elizabeth. 2010. *Time Binds: Queer Temporalities, Queer Histories.* Durham: Duke University Press.

Genet, Jean. 1992. *Prisoner of Love.* Translated by Barbara Bray. Hanover: Wesleyan University Press.

Genet, Jean. 1964. *The Thief's Journal*. Translated by Bernard Frechtman. New York: Grove Press.

Genet, Jean. 1963. *Our Lady of the Flowers*. Translated by Bernard Frechtman. New York: Grove Press.

Hargreaves, Martin. 2006. "Dancing the Impossible: Kazuo Ohno, Lindsay Kemp and Our Lady of the Flowers." In *Jean Genet: Performance and Politics*, edited by Clare Finburgh, Carl Lavery and Maria Shevtsova, 106–116. Hampshire: Palgrave Macmillan.

Leon, Anna. 2020. "Between and within Choreographies: An Early Choreographic Object by William Forsythe." *Dance Articulated Special Issue: Choreography Now* 6(1), edited by Leena Rouhiainen and Tone Pernille Østern: 64–88. Accessed April 30, 2023. https://doi.org/10.5324/da.v6i1.3639.

Lepecki, André. 2006. *Exhausting Dance: Performance and the Politics of Movement*. London: Routledge.

Meyer, Morris, ed. 1994. *The Politics and Poetics of Camp*. London: Routledge.

Moser, Benjamin. 2019. *Sontag*. London: HarperCollins Publishers Ltd.

Prosser, Jay. 2009. "Metaphors Kill: 'Against Interpretation' and the Illness Books." In *The Scandal of Susan Sontag*, edited by Barbara Ching and Jennifer A. Wagner-Lawlor, 118–204. New York: Columbia University Press.

Ricouer, Paul. 2006. *On Translation*. Translated by Eileen Brennan. London: Routledge.

Sontag, Susan. 2008. *Reborn: Journals and Notebooks, 1947–1963*. Edited by David Rieff. New York: Farrar, Straus and Giroux.

Sontag, Susan. 1989. *AIDS and Its Metaphors*. New York: Farrar, Straus and Giroux.

Sontag, Susan. 1966. *Against Interpretation: And Other Essays*. New York: Farrar, Straus and Giroux.

Sontag, Susan. 1963. *The Benefactor*. New York: Farrar, Straus and Giroux.

White, Edmund. 1994. *Genet*. London: Picador.

PART 3

Choreography as writing with

10

CICATRIX TEXTUS II

Marie Fahlin

Cicatrix textus II is a series of three choreographies, each in two parts, made up of sewn text fragments and poems that, along with images and handwritten asemic writings, constitute "objects of process." Writing with needle and thread is done not on, but through and in, a material. The needle traverses the material and thread's inherent resistances, weaving between them. Traces of the needle's movement remain in the form of text and other signs. The text (from Latin textus, "thing woven") can also be understood as the deliberate production of scars (cicatrix). Scars bear with them a history of division and proximation, violence and healing. The production of this "scar" is also, and simultaneously, a mending process: it is a stitching and scarring together of worn or broken materials with found and left-over things. What is being mended remains unclear, and unresolved. *Cicatrix textus II* is a choreographic process performed in solitude, stitching together a multitude.

DOI: 10.4324/9781003397427-13

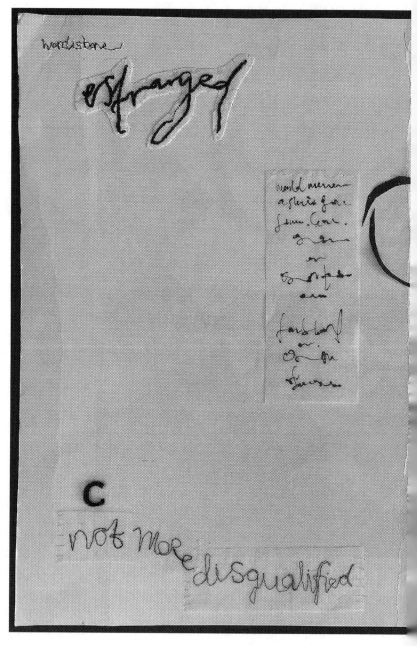

FIGURE 10.1 *word is bone.*

Patches of textile, paper and plastic with written or sewn words and asemic writing are spread out on a horizontal paper (the back side of a poster of Juan Gris). The image has been split into a left and a right side.

Photograph by author.

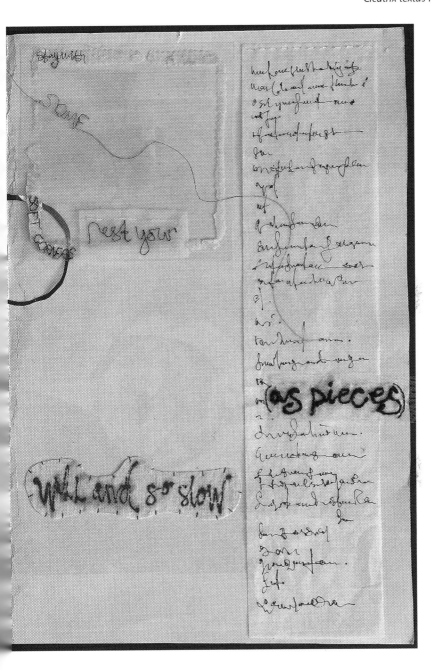

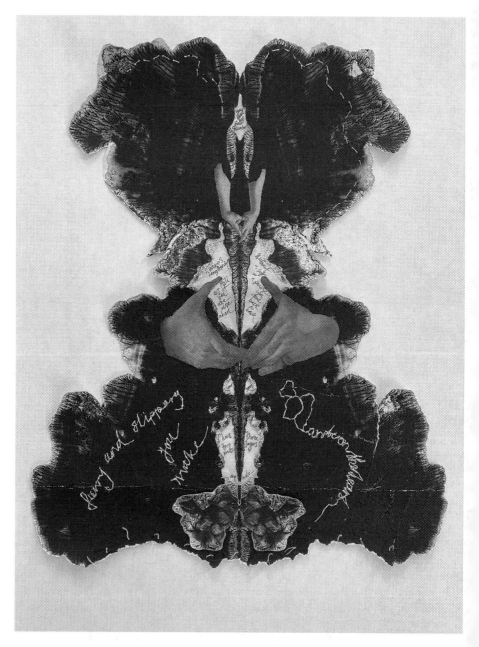

FIGURE 10.2 *a note on the heart.*

Painted and cut out Rorschach images with additions of inserted text fragments, images of hands and arms and stitched words.

Photographs by author.

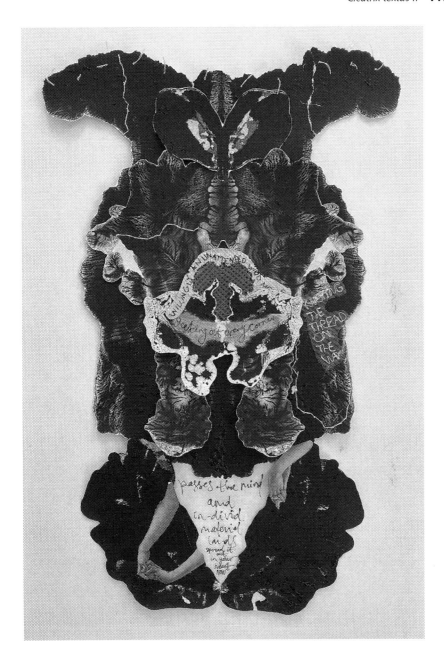

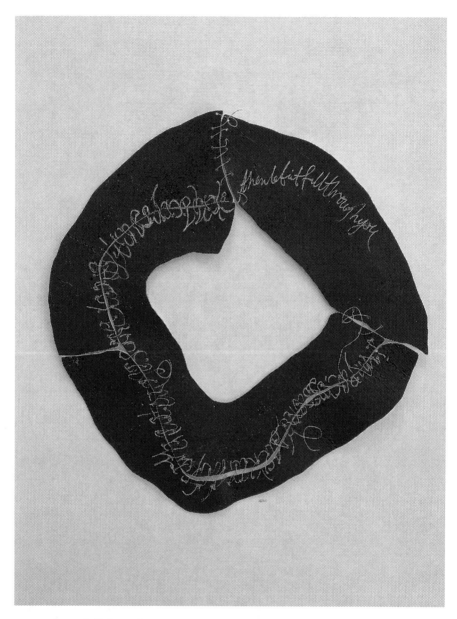

FIGURE 10.3   *fall through.*

On the left: Pieces of leather, painted black with written text in white, crisscrossing the edges. The pieces are sewn together with metallic thread, leaving narrow openings between the parts. The object has an irregular circular form with an empty middle. The text ends: letyourselffallthrough.

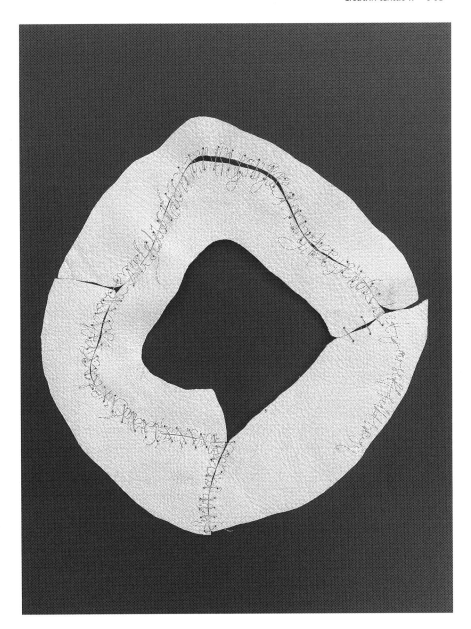

On the right: The other side of the object is painted white with text written in black, and it is sewn together in the same manner. The text ends: letitfallthroughyou.

Photographs by author.

11

CHOREO-GRAPHIC WRITING

Towards more-than-one means of inscription

Emma Cocker, Nikolaus Gansterer and Mariella Greil

Choreo-graphic Figures: Deviations from the Line is an artistic research project that involved the cultivation of various modes of "choreo-graphic writing" [*more-than-one/means of inscription*] at the interstice of choreography, draw-ing and writing, the evolution of experimental language practices as artistic research. Drawing on various "practices" and "figures" developed within *Choreo-graphic Figures*, Emma Cocker, Nikolaus Gansterer and Mariella Greil explore how different performative, sensuous and experimental textual prac-tices and bodily inscriptions emerge as immanent means of articulation for that which remains strictly *beyond words*: the embodied, relational, affective and material sensitivities and sensibilities of collaborative, co-emergent sense-making taking place in and through the interaction between bodies, between human and non-human agencies. The chapter comprises two parts: PART I — an "exposition" *showing* how Cocker, Gansterer and Greil performed chore-ography/writing *beyond the page* within the context of *Choreo-graphic Figures* presented online using the Research Catalogue (RC), an online platform for publishing artistic research; PART II — an "*essay*" (within this publication) for exploring the different resonances of and implications for these various ap-proaches to *choreo-graphic writing*.

Choreo-graphic Figures: Deviations from the Line is an artistic research pro-ject (2014–2018) by writer–artist Emma Cocker, artist–performer Nikolaus Gansterer and dancer–choreographer Mariella Greil, for exploring those modes of *thinking-feeling-knowing* between the lines of choreography, drawing and writing. The project unfolded through a series of intensive *Method Labs,* where the three artistic researchers — Cocker, Gansterer and

DOI: 10.4324/9781003397427-14

Greil — came together geographically in one place (alongside invited guests) to engage in a process of live exploration.[1] Our shared enquiry focused on the emergent processes of decision-making and dynamic movements of sense-making within collaborative artistic research by asking these questions: How might one articulate the instability and mutability of the flows and forces within collaborative exploration without "fixing" what is inherently dynamic and contingent as a literal sign? What systems of experimentation, performativity and notation might be developed for becoming better attuned to this often-hidden or undisclosed aspect of the creative process, for sharing (and communicating) the experience with others? In this chapter, we attempt to show how this enquiry involved the cultivation and entanglement of various modes of "choreo-graphic writing" emerging at the interstice of choreography, drawing and writing. *Choreo-graphic*: the hyphen, holding the two terms in proximity whilst also keeping them apart. *Choreo* — more than one or in relation to another, always a communication between. *Graphic* — the possibilities and sensitivities of inscription (of moving, drawing, writing and the modalities in between). *Towards more-than-one means of inscription, more-than-one choreography/writing*. Within *Choreo-graphic Figures*, various performative, sensuous and experimental textual practices and bodily inscriptions emerged as immanent means of articulation for that which remains *beyond words*: the embodied, relational, affective and material sensitivities and sensibilities of collaborative, co-emergent sense-making taking place in and through the interaction between bodies, between human and non-human agencies. However, in attempting to write this chapter, we have experienced various challenges and dilemmas: How to *show*? How to *focus*? How to *embrace difference(s)*?

How to show?

Within *Choreo-graphic Figures*, our engagement with language, with writing, with words attempted to go beyond a model of discursive transmission. Through what means might we show/present/enact *how* choreo-graphic writing manifested within *Choreo-graphic Figures* rather than only write *about* or re-present? To address this matter, our chapter comprises two related components, which activate language and writing in different ways:

PART I — *Exposition*: we have created an "exposition" presented on the Research Catalogue (RC), an online platform for publishing artistic research, for evidencing or demonstrating how various choreo-graphic writing practices and approaches were activated within our process of "live exploration" (especially for *showing* how we have performed choreo-graphic writing in other formats than printed paper).[2] This exposition is conceived as an experimental, performative and poetic "text," comprising an assemblage of materials and documents generated in and through our shared practice. Through this exposition, we attempt to make demonstrable what we call a choreo-graphic "episode," a designated period of live exploration organised durationally through the "scoring" of real-time composition, within which we activate various performative and experimental approaches to choreography/writing. We invite the reader to engage with this online exposition here—https://www.researchcatalogue.net/view/1313691/1395642.

PART II — *Essay*: in the text which follows below (which we call an "essay" for want of a better word), we attempt to "dive" or "zoom" into specific aspects of the "episode" presented in the exposition, drawing attention to the different approaches to and implications for choreo-graphic writing therein.

How to focus?

Which specific examples of or approaches to choreo-graphic writing do we focus on? For there were many developed within our project. Moreover, how can we do so without extensive contextualisation of the project itself, its key practices and concepts? Within *Choreo-graphic Figures,* we tested and developed innumerable expanded, experimental writing/language practices *of* and *as* artistic research: performative, thick descriptions for articulating embodied singularities; the inter-subjective or even infra-personal poetics of a writing distilled from extensive conversation transcripts; diagrammatic drawings that made productive the close relation between the German words *Aufzeichnungen* (notes) and *Zeichnungen* (drawings), conceiving of the in-between-space from draft to articulation as a site of potential for unexpected connections. We worked with lists and scripts; instructions and scores; processes of collage and cut-up; word-play — the activation of archaic etymologies and chance associations; key-word games; the conversation practices of "wild-talk" and "upwelling"; reverberating voicings; ecstatic self-reporting, alongside poetic acts of naming *as* notation. We attempt to evidence some of these different approaches to choreo-graphic writing within the "episode" presented online, through the combination of "scores" and instructions, alongside "documentation" and "artefacts" generated within our live enquiry. Where necessary, we do include some definitions of key terms within this essay; however, in focusing on choreography/writing, we attempt to keep wider contextualisation of the project to a minimum.[3] The online episode attempts to *show* how we engaged choreography/writing as a complex live assemblage of unfolding practices and figures, evidencing the various performative, performing, experimental and expanded forms of writing and of embodied languaging within our project.[4] Yet parallel to this act of showing (for evidencing, making demonstrable in and through the practice), we wondered how we might also draw out further observations from our practising together, reflecting how we each take the resonance of choreography/writing forwards?

How to embrace (our) difference(s)?

As a live research project, *Choreo-graphic Figures* officially came to an end in 2018. Since then, our research enquiries have evolved largely independently. Time passes — interests and enquiries develop and diverge. The intersection of choreography and writing matters differently for the three of us, reflecting our different inter-, trans-, even un-disciplinary perspectives, alongside the ongoing preoccupations and interests within our respective practices. *Towards more-than-one perspective* — how might we reflect our different engagements with and orientations towards choreography/writing within a single chapter, without reducing or homogenising our differences to or within a single authorial voice? We have each identified a singular focus within the on-line "episode" that continues to hold significance for us as individual artistic researchers. Rather than attempting to assimilate our different voices into a coherent whole, we have each taken care of specific sections, which we call "resonances", where our differences in approach remain tangible.

Towards more-than-one means of inscription, more-than-one choreography/writing

In *Resonance I*, Greil focuses on how the intersection of choreography/writing reverberates through practices of scoring and live composition, exploring how the event of relation lies at the heart of an embodied encounter between sensorial bodies and movements of thought. In *Resonance II*, Cocker explores how two distinct approaches to language — practices of conversation and practices of reading — became combined and hybridised within *Choreo-graphic Figures*, enabling an emergent form of choreo-graphic writing *through* reading, the ventilation of language — and of meaning — through non-linear, polyvocal practices of collective voicing. In *Resonance III*, Gansterer addresses how a meeting of choreography/writing emerges through a relay of relations, the passage of conversion, of crossing from one state to another, with reference to the *Figure of Translational Flux*. These three *Resonances* reflect different foci, our different interests and references, our different ways of working with language, including fragments of creative writing alongside description-reflection. However, before diverging through these individual foci, we first introduce our core enquiry with reference to the choreo-graphic episode presented in the online exposition.

Scoring a choreo-graphic episode

Critical to our enquiry into the *thinking-feeling-knowing* within collaborative artistic exploration was our recognition and subsequent articulation of the reciprocal relation between what we call the *event of figuring* and the *emergence*

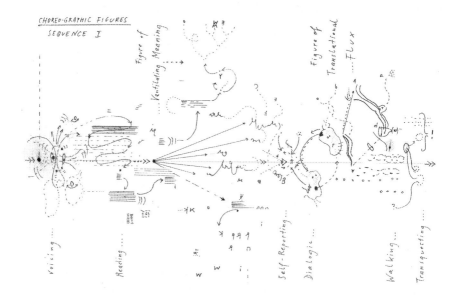

FIGURE 11.1   *Diagramming the online "episode" (see exposition).* Drawing by Nikolaus Gansterer, 2023. Photograph by Nikolaus Gansterer.

of figures. In brief, we use the term *figuring* to refer to those small yet transformative energies and experiential shifts within the artistic process that are often hard to discern, but which ultimately shape or steer the evolving action; whilst the term *figure* describes the point at which awareness of "something happening" (*figuring*) becomes recognisable, communicable. Our enquiry involved developing various *Practices of Notation* for attending to and marking the event of *figuring,* alongside identifying, qualifying and naming various *figures* so we could "call" for their constitutive conditions within the context of a live exploration. During our project, we identified nine *figures,* which we grouped according to three categories: the *Elemental Figures* refer to key moments within the arc of creative exploration, addressing the opening up and exposition of *process* (e.g., the *Figures of Clearing and Emptying Out, Spiralling Momentum, Temporary Closing*); the *Empathetic Figures* invite the diagramming of relations, drawing attention to the sensitivities and sensibilities of *being-with* (e.g., the *Figures of Vibrating Affinity, Wavering Convergence, Consonance/Dissonance*); the *Transformative Figures* involve an explicit shift or transformation in property, quality or state of being (e.g., the *Figures of Ventilating Meaning, Becoming Material, Translational Flux*). In parallel, we devised various *Practices of Attention, of Conversation,* and *of Wit(h)nessing* for helping us to focus and sharpen our enquiry within the live composition of shared exploration.[5]

Within this chapter, we attempt to *show* how our enquiry was activated *in practice* through various scores and artefacts presented within the online episode. [See online exposition — https://www.researchcatalogue.net/view/1313691/1395642.] We use the term "episode" to designate a period of live exploration organised durationally through the "scoring" of real-time composition, for bringing-into-relation different practices and figures. Specifically, our online episode focuses on one possible organisation of practices and figures evidencing a novel intersection of choreography/writing. The episode (as we are presenting it online) unfolds like this: *Let's say we agree to enter into a designated time period of shared exploration (e.g., it could be 30 minutes or 3 hours), where the invitation is to "call" different named practices and figures into play. It might begin like this — There is a "call" for the Practice of Attention: Voicing. Voices now warmed and resonating in the space, someone makes a call to shift into the Practice of Reading. In time, perhaps the Figure of Ventilating Meaning begins to emerge or maybe a call is made — since you and "fellow explorers" all know the qualities of this figure, you can collectively begin a process of exploration in the hope of giving rise to its emergence. Continue to explore together — in time, maybe the figure shows up, maybe not. Perhaps a further Practice of Attention would help to refine your collective sensitivity to the aeration of languaging, inherent within this figure: someone calls for the Practice of Self-reporting, which then shifts again into a Practice of Conversation. In time, the process opens once more to the emergence of another figure — the Figure of Translational Flux is now called.*

Resonance I

Practices of scoring and live composition, as well as choreographing texts and writing scores, are deeply relational. They are compositional acts that involve concept and intuition, surrender and resistance, the actualisation and bridging of the gap between words and movements of thought through choreographing the (intertextual) spaces between them. In our shared ideation of *Choreo-graphic Writing,* we practise a kind of language-related dancing across and beyond the page that is dedicated to the unfolding of time as the presencing of live notations in episodes. In our joint project *Choreo-graphic-Figures,* the space of compositional decision-making was constituted by performing *Elemental, Empathetic* and *Transformative Figures* and *Practices of Attention, Notation, Conversation* and *Wit(h)nessing.* Our live explorations activated the permeability of the score and manifested as navigations in and through episodes. Composing an episode meant that the score held infinite versions of its performance through manifold options for re-combination. These were negotiated in/through the live composition. Each performance of the score asked questions anew: what actions, vibrational fields and agencies composed the summoned figure and how it emerged from the transitional threshold in relation to practising.

Both entry points to this field of shared sensibilities — *Writing Choreography* and *Choreography Writing* — are rooted in the transversal dimension of *movement*, expanding the organising force of logos. The situated activation of the affective contour of the figure(s) and the instructive nature of the practice(s) became the score. In the specific episode that we refer to (see https://www.researchcatalogue.net/view/1313691/1395642) in this chapter, we collaboratively engaged with experimental problems and practised live notation. We did this through performing, attending to instant intuitions alongside collaborative material and immaterial negotiations, nonverbal circuits of figuring and cyclical writing and conversing in turns. The episode had a generative form, it weaved a perceptive fabric from intra-actions and plurifocal relations, while its outlines emerged as differentiated articulation with a heightened sense of presence. Still, the withdrawal of the performance work, its ongoing transfiguration through performing the score in singular, contingent *formants*, generated experience. *Formants*, a term used in phonetics, configures a space of articulation and a vibrational body (frequencies), indicating a spectrum and its augmented resonance. The forming of formants, or figuring of figures, is what constituted the worlding of the project. We had extensively discussed whether system/apparatus/machine/organism would describe the mechanism of the score, however, conceptually the verb "worlding" was what came closest to our shared understanding, holding (as it does) many means of inscription. In our project, with its pervasive reflection (on a meta-level) on the processes of *figuring,* (per)forming of itself posed a singular challenge in terms of sustaining attunement and engagement, the performative spell of perceptive action, binding receptivity and performativity rigorously together. Deep reading the philosopher Georg Wilhelm Friedrich Hegel's (1979/1802) texts, he seemed to understand sensorial bodies in their radical function, sense-making through an ethico-aesthetic entanglement of spirit and body rooted in situatedness.[6]

In our live explorations, we attended to ethico-aesthetic entanglement, negotiated the becoming of sensorial bodies through artistic practice and performed the unfolding sense of interrelations between agencies, while touching on presences and their contingencies as space-holding manifestations. The shared effort of both — creating relations and relating to creation — highlighted the return to direction and form, rhythm and dynamics through aesthetic live exploration.[7] Attuned to the opacity of language and trusting the brightness of bodies, we deepen into slow burn processes of *distillation* (thick descriptions of diagrammatic processes) and *reflection* (an attempt to understand compositional decision-making in the tension between concept and intuition, that for Hegel (1979/1802, 61) are no longer opposed terms, but rather come together in the "idea"). In our collaborative project, the ideation of figures takes place in the vital field of the choreographic (between drawing, language and choreography) and lays bare its *choreomatic* potentiality. Jenn Joy (2014) describes the choreomatic as an offering. She explains: "What the 'poematic' offers to poetry, so the 'choreo-matic' offers to choreography, a form learned not by heart, but of and from the heart […]" (Joy 2014, 13). In our writings in *the voice of the project*, the artistic heart of the figures is reflecting the creative arc of our shared transdisciplinary research process.[8]

The offerings of the performance score are the invitation of poetic language, sensuous becoming-together as embodied singularity, an encounter-forming contact based on the ambiguity of meanings, while simultaneously affirming its ethico-aesthetic significance and body. Our shared practice and affective and epistemological grounding go hand in hand, even though our collaborative writing process here comes out as fragmented reflections in semi-detached, de-merged perspectives, that move *Towards More-Than-One Means of Inscription*. Franco 'Bifo' Berardi (2012, 22) states that poetic language "refuses the exaction of a semiotic debt." Tapping into the contingent potential of polysemy through plural bodies (of work) and practices encountering each other, opens up play and creativeness. In the chosen episode, it is the viscerality of words and the materiality of language (See *Figure of Ventilating Meaning* referred to later in this chapter) that gives tangibility to the consequences of bringing into relations our specific constellation of practices (choreographing — drawing — writing).

In *The Pleasure of the Text*, Roland Barthes (1975/1973, 17) writes "The pleasure of the text is that moment when my body pursues its own ideas — for my body does not have the same ideas I do." For Lilia Mestre (2014, n.p.), the sense(s) of the body generate ideas and "an awareness of being in the present. It's the state of attention mingled with the desire to play." The framing of the field of action and laying bare the constituent agencies, becomes a tool for the understanding, probing and interrogation of the process. It is particularly enigmatic to articulate and unearth the decisions made when performing the score of our live explorations. However, the episodes we created had a compositional form that radiated contingent resolution and sensible decision-making among all involved, both as performers and wit(h)nesses. The shifts between practices and figures were either silent slips from one to the other or calls that were situated between instruction and recognition. As Berardi (2012, 8) states, "Only the conscious mobilization of the erotic body of the general intellect, only the poetic revitalization of language, will open the way to the emergence of a new form of social autonomy."

The focus within an episode was on the shifting cognisance of figuring, interlaced with activating practices of attention, of conversation, of notation and of wit(h)nessing. These interlaces had the function to bridge and serve as a landing site and/or springboard for *Choreo-graphic Figures* that we had distilled from the enquiry into the creative arc and flow of our situated, transdisciplinary, collaborative process. There was an accumulation of delicate adjustment as we kept practising the score we had developed as collaborators. In the later stages of the research, we invited wit(h)nesses who were implicated in our pursuit to live through and understand the compositional navigation between practices and figures. Throughout the project, the exploration of multimodal planes of composition kept gravitating to modes and differentiations of relationality as practical problems that challenged agencies and bodies and particularly their potentialities when transfiguring.

Beyond semantic and episodic knowledge, Dieter Mersch (2015; cf. Cocker 2021) emphasises the dimension of aesthetic epistemology, and it is this realm that *Choreo-graphic Figures* spawned through practising abundant openness. The role of the score was to safeguard this excess of not knowing, while being precise in terms of the contour of qualities and their transformations. The possibilities of *More-Than-One Means of Inscription*, the negotiated layerings of materials, movements and words made it a tangible search for connections, synchronicities, affective encounters through experimentation. The line between performer and wit(h)ness was constituted from both sides and formed a porous membrane for resonance. The poetics and politics of assembling and de-assembling of a range of agencies created intimate closeness or distant concessions that radiated vitality at best, or provoked renunciation. Movement between practices and figures was birthing meaning. The figuring out meant to bear its vulnerability through surrender to the score as the vessel for an encounter between concept and intuition.

The continuous striving for sharpening the compositional tool kept all involved on their toes and fuelled the research on *Choreo-graphic Writing*, where the hyphen purposefully interrupted the given, or supposedly stable, meaning of choreography. It was (and still is) the quest to deeply scrutinise how *chorein* and *graphein* come together. The *written-drawn-choreo-graphed* questions both embodiment and perception, affordances and resistances, in relation to aesthetic composition and performative epistemology.

Resonance II

Moving from how the choreography/writing of scoring operates as a compositional tool within our overall choreo-graphic processes, we now zoom in, attending to specific performative and experimental practices and figures. Within our shared enquiry, we have evolved and tested various "micro-scores" for *Reading*, *Self-reporting* and *Voicing*, alongside several conversational approaches, which we name as specific practices: *Dialogic, Upwelling, Keywords, Wildtalk.*[9] Whilst these specific language-based "scores" can be separately engaged with (in isolation from the wider project), we were interested in how they can be brought into touch (through the transitory chains of events that we call an episode) and in the sensuous and sensible materialities and relationalities (perhaps even *figures*) that this bringing-into-touch might enable.[10] For example, within our online episode[11] we begin by warming up through a *Practice of Voicing*, attending to the physicality of sounding inside and outside of the body. Sound as material, reverberations *before* words. This act of voicing might then evolve or become mutated through a *Practice of Reading*. Reading *with* the body. Reading experientially. Reading in/with time, in/with space. Reading-with. Not reading for sentence's sense; words become sonorous as much as signifying units, the soundness of a text tested by tongue and lips as much as by the mind. Certain language must be rolled in the mouth before it can be fully digested. New meanings become revealed by changed inflection, in the pauses and durations breathed between the words. When conditions are conducive, somewhere between breathing, voicing and reading, the *Figure of Ventilating Meaning* is called:

Before they can become material, words must first be rendered matter. Emptied of signification, evacuated of semantic sense. Collapse to sound, sonorous babble of emancipation. Dispersal. Disintegration. Release of language from itself: rhythmic and relational, a move beyond informational exchange. Beyond representation, beyond the symbolic: ventilation of the sign. Displace the agency of words to escape the regime of "this means this." Names can be forgotten, syntax lost, thrown to the wind. Not only words, but letting go of the meaning of things. Yet, language seems the most stable of things, so how to prevent it from becoming further solidified? Less towards density, but an enlivening through aeration; practice of resuscitation, revitalise through the bringing of air. Resuscitate: bring back to life, invigorate. Creating air holes, punctuation through the intervention of breath. Activate the intermediary zone between voice and exhalation. Hyperventilation. Not the proliferation of meaning towards meaninglessness, but a practice of sensuous soundings. To ventilate: to winnow, fan, to set in motion — not towards action but affect. Aeration conceived as quality, not the production of air. Lightness. Levity. Still not yet mutual co-production, rather an affective doing of things with words. Turning over: rotation, inversion. Permutation. Repetition whisks up, froths. Agitation empties out. To expose to wind separates as with the wheat from chaff. To wind: vente — adventure at the limits of language, uplifting, slips, taking of flight and fall. Beyond the self-expressivity of the speaking I: towards a practice of collective voicing, movement of words beyond the dialogic, beyond conversation. Passage. Relay. Circulation. Appropriation. Re-appropriation. Re-citing. Citing — again, again, an act of summoning, to call or rouse to action, towards meaning as the creation of the common.

The text above (in italics) is our performative invocation or evocation of the *Figure of Ventilating Meaning*, comprised of distilled fragments of transcribed conversation through which we attempt to get close to the figure's qualities or properties.[12] Being able to recognise a figure's characteristic qualities emerges as a prerequisite for its calling, yet our aspiration was to also remain open to being surprised, attentive always to the possibility of newly emergent figures. *Ventilating Meaning* was one of the figures identified during our project within

FIGURE 11.2   Documentation of *Choreo-graphic Figures*. Photograph by Victor Jaschke.

a broader group called *Transformative Figures*, each of which is connected through the prefix *trans-* indicating movement across or through, the act of "going beyond." We conceive each figure itself as an emergent atmosphere that can be collectively recognised, rather than a repertoire of actions that can be determined in advance. Still, within the *Figure of Ventilating Meaning*, language itself was often a recurring medium and material. *Beyond* discursivity, *beyond* words as signifying units of sense, *beyond* the linguistic sense-making of a singular *I*. Yet, *how* was language ventilated in our shared enquiry; through what means did we attempt to aerate words?

Within *Choreo-graphic Figures*, and especially within emergent figures, such as *Ventilating Meaning*, it becomes possible to observe the evolution of specific processual or process-oriented, collaborative and relational approaches for ventilating language. Here, new possibilities for choreographic writing emerge as an embodied oral and acoustic endeavour, interweaving of speaking and listening activated within acts of conversation and of collective reading. For example, at the outset of the project, I introduced a language-based artistic research practice called "conversation-as-material" as a tactic for inviting immanent, inter-subjective modes of verbal-linguistic sense-making emerging through different voices enmeshed in live exchange (cf. Cocker 2022). Conversation-as-material is a practice of collaborative writing, perhaps even choreographic writing, which unfolds through the interplay of different voices "turning about" together in conversation. Conversation — from *con-* meaning "with, together" and *versare*, "to turn, bend"; or else, from *conversare* — "to turn about, to turn about with." The practice of conversation-as-material involves a tripartite process of conversation, transcription and distillation. Phase 1 — *Conversation:* We would engage in a period of framed conversation as a way of touching upon, getting in touch with, or turning over together, some aspect of our (shared) experience. Conversation-as-material attends to the vocabulary emerging in the fragile thresholds of speech formation — the incipient moments of language on the cusp of articulation. The specific rhythm of conversation produces a different shape and texture of textual articulation compared to that of conventional writing. Bodily lettering: the tasting of words, language caress of the tongue, phonemes felt against lips, exhaled on the breath. Conversation-as-material is not only a practice for attempting to speak of and from the lived experience of being-in-relation within collaboration: it is also an ethical, relational practice in and of itself. For philosopher Alva Noë (2016, 6–7), conversation involves the "complicated activity of listening, thinking, paying attention, doing and undergoing, most of which happens spontaneously, without deliberate control [...] conversation is a fundamental mechanism of relationship building and joint living." For Daniel Stern (2010, 51, 53), conversation may be conceived as a practice of "interactional synchrony" involving a process of "affect attunement" between speaker and listener, a "communicative musicality based on the coupling of vitality dynamics between people." The act of conversation thus reflects the meeting points and moments of empathetic connection experienced within our collaborative artistic exploration, as well as the disparities and interferences emerging through excesses of meaning, points of intransigence and (in)translatability. In this sense, conversation-as-material, conceived as choreographic writing, emerges as a way for giving articulation to the meaning and weight of relations as generative forces within the making of aesthetic knowledge; the sensitivities and sensibilities of *being-with*.

Phase 2—*Transcription*: During our three-year project, many of our conversations were recorded and then subsequently transcribed: there were over 150 hours of recorded conversation resulting in over 300,000 words of transcript.[13] Significantly, the process of transcription within conversation-as-material does not seek to differentiate one speaking voice from another — the perspective of the singular speaking subject talking from their own experience is loosened in a process of generating a single text for speaking of an experience beyond the individual "I". Phase 3 — *Distillation*: Distil the transcribed conversation through a process of editing or condensing the transcription material. Within *Choreo-graphic Figures*, the transcript material was approached as a material to be *worked-with*, distilled as a live and performative event. Large piles of transcript material (typed on A4 sheets of paper) were often present within our Method Lab, to be picked up and activated as part of our live explorations, our own (previously spoken and recorded) words becoming new scripts for improvisatory readings, for playing with the orality and acoustic dimension of language at the cusp of sense. Guttural utterances. Whispered repetitions. Chanted incantations. As Brandon LaBelle (2014, 61) notes, "At times, speech runs over itself. Words twist and tense under pressure, tripped up by inertia, or with urgency [...] to produce slippages, ruptures, and even nonsensical outpourings." Emergent poetics generated through endless iteration and the chance collision of textual fragments, repeated, mutated, over and over. Polyvocal, non-linear, sensorial voicing: reading as an aesthetic act. Human (and machinic) voices intermingling: words becoming exhausted (even emancipated) of linguistic meaning, collapse of language towards pure voicing and sensuous soundings. According to LaBelle (2014, 62),

> The relation of sense and nonsense, of the semantic and the sounded, is to be appreciated as the very fabric of the voice, and it is the mouth's ability to flex and turn, resonate and stumble [...] which continually reminds us of the potentiality in being an oral body.

Our attempts at "ventilating meaning" might attest to the poetic voicing of an "experimental orality" conceived in LaBelle's (2014, 63) terms as "choreographies of the mouth." For Berardi (2012, 20, 139), "voice and poetry are two strategies for reactivation" for emancipating language and affect from the logic of capital, of finance: towards "a new space for poetic praxis, the emancipation of the word from its referential task." As Berardi (2012, 21) claims: "Poetry is the here and now of the voice, of the body, and of the word, sensuously giving birth to meaning." He continues:

> Poetry is language's excess: poetry is what in language cannot be reduced to information, and is not exchangeable, but gives way to a new common ground of understanding, of shared meaning: the creation of a new world [...] Poetry is the singular vibration of the voice. This vibration can create resonances, and resonances may produce common space.
>
> (Berardi 2012, 147)

Perhaps this might hint at what might be at stake at the interstice of choreography/writing: to re-conceive our living being as "oral bodies" alongside the possibilities for creating a "new common ground." Within the process of our live exploration, the act of writing/choreography rarely solidifies into the written, but rather remains unfinished, in a state of "contingent resolution" or what Brian Massumi (2013, 140) refers to (of dance) as "perpetual nascency, unmediated by any predetermined idea of finality." Writing remaining as verb rather than noun: not writing as a means of informational exchange, but rather as a time-based event capable of infinite permutational possibilities and translations. Conversation becoming voicing, becoming reading, becoming writing, becoming choreography.

FIGURE 11.3 Documentation of *Choreo-graphic Figures.* Photograph by Victor Jaschke.

Resonance III

Reading a drawing: choreo-graphic writing in relation to the *Figure of Translational Flux.* So, when I re-enter my diagrams and drawings and begin to breathe in this world of my own, moving in this force field of lines and textures and coming again into contact with their agencies, it is as if I am entering a scene or zone that is unfolding before me. When I visualise this scene, make it present, I become part of it, and the diagram begins to unfold in me, to operate, to live.

To translate means, first of all, to build a connection, a channel of communication, a mutual connection. A bond felt like a silken thread. Flexible but fragile. Translating also means reaching (out for) another shore, another territory, another zone, another state of being. An immersive practice. Not observing or judging something from the outside, but seeing it from the inside. Recognise. Then sharing. At least the attempt to utter. How to translate a drawing to text? Lines as words, worlds as text. What must be left behind so that the new state can (find) form?

The space is ambivalent. I do not see a centre. I am not the centre. Multiple centres form and disappear all around me. I am not in one place, but in many states at the same time, but all connected like an archipelago of possible moorings. Anchoring in time. Knots and nodes that transform and materialise in different modes only to dematerialise again.

There are back and forth movements, not linear or mechanical, more like dancing. More like touching. Connecting lines open up a field of tension.

A kind of lone black parenthesis (or is it an arch?) spans a space, a field of action for metamorphoses. Processes of formation. From (a) to (b) via (p) to (q) and (d). No immanent pull of gravity? Strange forces seem to be at work, mirror forces, forces of flipping around and swapping. Of shifting, of going astray. Small but essential nuances, but also dramatic turns. 180, 90, 360 degrees. 222 degrees back. Speeds of rotation. Turbulent but not chaotic. Following an inner path. Cycles of thought, non-linear processes of becoming — something else.

Again a small initial explosion in the middle, fanning out upwards, jumps to the side and forward again. Centrifugal forces. The temptation to escape a closed form is vigorous. To the right, a kind of foggy pipe is swelling, indicating a sheltered direction into an inverted (a). A reservoir to rest, to hide? A possible level indicator? A tube tunnels through the pipe. Inside the tube there is turbulence, a circular white movement around a small centre of gravity. Inscribing, digging deep into the ground. Particles of speech flicker out. I think aloud, a silent exclamation? The (i) turns into (!).

On the left is a filigree web of trace-like appearances. Dotted, delicate, almost tender. Volatile, light-footed change of aggregate states, fluttering from here to that to there and on, radiating further and further. Warm field, it rustles, sensory hairs overgrow an intermediate sign. Language partially flowing into a (t)(r)(a)(n)(s). Suddenly the (i) sparks out at the very top. What's next? Where do we go?

Somewhat remote, and at the same time hovering above it all, an open-ended sequence operates. From a complex moving line configuration (q) a manifest material (b) and from this, in turn, a polygonal upright sign (d) is formed that will manifest itself into something new that is not yet there. An arrow points to an empty space, a kind of clearing in the diagram. The outcome is uncertain, the becoming will come first.

Resonating resonances

Resonance: from *re-* "back, again" and *sonare* "to sound or make a noise." In acoustics, resonance refers to the prolonging or repetition of sound by reflection or through reverberation. To re-sound or sound back, to echo, re-echo, or reverberate *with*. Through three singularly authored sections (named "resonances"), we return (back, again) to our shared project *Choreo-graphic Figures*, exploring different aspects of choreography/writing, which continue to reverberate with our current individual interests. Less interdisciplinary and rather *more than* disciplinary, our enquiry has evolved towards a vocabulary that reaches *beyond* the conventions, protocols and domains of our respective disciplines. By pressuring, translating and in turn expanding the gestures of choreography, of drawing and of writing — through the cross-contamination and friction within shared research — the gestural vocabulary of each discipline becomes hybridised and roughened, inflected or even infected by the gestures of the other(s). Undoubtedly, we have been pressured and constrained by the page as both a spatial and conceptual frame within the context of academic publication. Under such pressure, the essay component of our chapter invariably slips from *being* choreography/writing, more towards *being about* choreography/writing. Yet this slippage enables us to recognise principles and qualities of choreography/writing that we may not have noticed from the performative perspective of the practice itself.

We notice that (our) choreography/writing involves:

- Relational practices.
- Compositional acts.
- Bridging of the gap between words and movements of thought.
- Manifold options for re-combination.
- Collaborative material and immaterial negotiations.
- Polysemy through plural bodies.
- Ethico-aesthetic entanglement.
- The sensitivities and sensibilities of *being-with*.
- The unfolding sense of interrelations between agencies.
- The viscerality of words and the materiality of language.
- Practising abundant openness.
- The poetics and politics of assembling and de-assembling.
- Incipient moments of language on the cusp of articulation.
- The sonorous babble of emancipation.
- A release of language from itself.
- An enlivening of language through aeration.
- A practice of collective voicing.
- Immanent, inter-subjective modes of verbal-linguistic sense-making.
- Excesses of meaning, points of intransigence and (in)translatability.
- Bodily lettering, the tasting of words.
- Polyvocal, non-linear, sensorial voicing.
- A channel of communication, a mutual connection.
- Infinite permutational possibilities and translations.
- Seeing it from the inside.
- Endless iteration.

We notice that (our) choreography/writing is (might be):

- Ethical, rhythmic and relational.
- An intermediary zone between voice and exhalation.
- A practice of sensuous soundings.
- Beyond the page, dedicated to the unfolding of time.
- A perceptive fabric of intra-actions and plurifocal relations.

- An embodied oral and acoustic endeavour.
- Not in one place, but in many states at the same time.
- Turbulent but not chaotic.
- A scene or zone that is unfolding.
- Ambivalent.
- An archipelago of possible moorings.
- Not linear or mechanical, more like dancing.
- More like touching.
- A field of action for metamorphoses.
- Delicate, almost tender.
- A kind of clearing.

Attending to choreography/writing, we borrow from Hélène Cixous and
Catherine Clément (1986, 96) by asking how we might "steal into language
to make it fly." Towards *languaging* as a material, temporal, relational becoming, a polysemic, polyfocal, polyvocal plurality — *towards more-than-one
means of inscription*. We wonder: what common ground, what new worlds,
might this choreography/writing create? For Luce Irigaray (2004, 14), "In
this world otherwise lived and illuminated, the language of communication
is different, and necessarily poetic: a language that creates, that safeguards its
sensible qualities so as to address the body and the soul, a language that lives."
We wonder: what is at stake in the interrelationship of writing and choreography? The proximity, perhaps even conflation, of choreography/writing makes
explicit a relation between language and the body. Often conceived in antago-
nism or tension, within choreography/writing, language becomes embodied,
or rather the body becomes apparent as a "linguistic body" (Di Paolo, Cuffari,
and De Jaegher 2018). For Ezequiel A. Di Paolo, Elena Clare Cuffari and
Hanne De Jaegher (2018, 3), "participation of our bodies, and participation
with others, is a given for linguistic bodies. Every body participates. What we
want for linguistic bodies critical participation […] This ethics-as-practice is
realized in keeping ourselves open to our own unfinished becoming." Here,
again, an ethical — perhaps even ethico-aesthetic — dimension of bodying/
languaging emerges as a central precept. Following Erin Manning (2012,
221), our engagement with choreography/writing "foregrounds language
not as a personal enunciation but as a collective event articulated through
relational series." As Manning (2013, 168) states, "The making-collective of
language is an ethics. Think-with, feel-with […] Compose with, participate
at the edge of meaning where language no longer holds together." Our own
experiments with choreography/writing seek to inhabit this edge, and in turn
seep beyond the edge or limits of this publication. Extending beyond the
pages of this book, we have realised our aspiration to *show* choreography/writ-
ing practices as an experimental, performative and highly visual choreographic
text through a research catalogue exposition, which allows for the alternative

layouts and possibilities of multimodal presentation that choreography/writing arguably calls for. Therein, a further challenge lies: what forms of new publication, of making public, does choreography/writing require? What new modes of reading (and of reader) do choreography/writing call forth?

Glossary

Within this chapter, we use certain terms and terminology that we developed specifically within the frame of the *Choreo-graphic Figures* project. Here we offer a glossary of some of those terms — reiterating and in places expanding upon the tentative "definitions" outlined in our chapter.

Choreo-graphic: We adopt the term *choreo-graphic* within our shared practice, using hyphenation to draw attention to (both to separate as well as to connect) the two component elements of the *choreographic*: *choreo-* and *graphic*. We understand *choreo-* in this context to mean "more than one" or "in relation to another," as in chorus, as in group, always a communication between. The term *graphic* foregrounds the possibilities and sensitivities of *inscription* (of moving, drawing and writing and the modalities in between); not just for describing — representing or reproducing that which already exists — but as much a dynamic happening, capable also of bringing about, constituting, transforming.

Episode: During long periods of live exploration, we found it necessary to provide a further sense of structure or shape to the passage of time — we call these *episodes*. We use the term *episode* for describing a designated (often timed) period of live exploration organised durationally through the scoring of real-time composition through which we explore the relation of the event of *figuring* and the emergence of *figures*.

Figuring: Figuring refers to the perception of indeterminate affective intensities within the artistic process that are often hard to discern, but which ultimately shape or steer the evolving action — those small yet transformative energies and experiential shifts, minor revelations or epiphanies. We conceive the event of *figuring* as a qualitative shift, the sense or awareness that "something is happening" perceptible at the level of intensity, experienced *as if* a change of taste, colour, or perhaps even of textural density.[14]

Figure: We use the term *figure* to describe the point at which the indeterminate or undifferentiated awareness of "something happening" (*figuring*) becomes recognisable and qualified through a name. Figures are conceived as performative, relational and contingent "assemblages" recognisable or identifiable whilst at the same time motile and unstable, capable of evolving.

Wit(h)nessing: The term *wit(h)nessing* is a neologism combining "witnessing" and "*being-with*." Within *Choreo-graphic Figures*, we use the term *wit(h)nessing* to refer to the different ways in which an individual might engage with the unfolding process of live exploration through empathetic practices including watching or listening.

Notes

1 Along the research journey, we worked closely with critical interlocutors Alex Arteaga, Christine De Smedt and Lilia Mestre, alongside guest collaborators Werner Moebius and Jörg Piringer. We also worked with videographer Victor Jaschke, who generated much of the photographic and video documentation of the project (including materials encountered in the exposition), and artist–designer Simona Koch, who has helped us translate our embodied, experiential enquiry into different publication formats, including the exposition component of this chapter.

2 On "exposition," see Schwab (2019) and Schwab and Borgdorff (2013).

3 For wider contextualisation of the project, see Cocker, Gansterer, and Greil (2017; 2018). See also https://www.researchcatalogue.net/view/462390/462391.

4 For Dieter Mersch (2015, 170), the "decisive epistemic modus" of artistic research is one of *showing*: "we are dealing with 'showings' that in equal measure reveal something and show themselves while in showing, hold themselves back [...] their métier is not representation, but presence." For Mersch (2015, 15), "reflexivity takes place as an event within constellations and their composition in order to, through them, draw something out that could not otherwise be elicited."

5 Our notion of *wit(h)nessing* draws variously on Jean-Luc Nancy's notion of being-with (Nancy 2000); Luce Irigaray's (2004, 87) model of "being with the other" where "human becoming is considered as a relation-with: with oneself, with the world, with the other." We later discovered Bracha L. Ettinger's use of the term wit(h) nessing in *Intimacy, wit(h)nessing and non-abandonment*, http://jordancrandall. com/main/+UNDERFIRE/ site/files/q-node-562.html. See also Ettinger (2006).

6 In the third chapter of his text *System of Ethical Life*, Hegel (1979/1802, 143) writes: "Intellectual intuition is alone realised by and in ethical life; the eyes of the spirit and the eyes of the body completely coincide."

7 These four kinetographic differentiations have been developed in nexus to and in dialogue with Irmgard Bartenieff's (2002) BESS categories: body, effort, shape, space. The intention was to expand the notion of *bodies* towards *agencies, shape* towards the wider notion of *form*, *space* was embraced through *direction*, while *rhythm* and *dynamics* attend to *effort*.

8 Condensed transcripts of conversations between key researchers were synthesised into *the voice of the project*.

9 The micro-scores for various practices can be found in Cocker, Gansterer, and Greil (2017).

10 In that sense, the publication *Choreo-graphic Figures: Deviations of the Line* operates as a "toolkit" of scores for others to use.

11 See https://www.researchcatalogue.net/view/1313691/1395642.

12 The use of evocative/invocative modes of writing has been informed by Della Pollock's (1998, 73–103) notion of "performing writing" or "performative writing." Phenomenologist Max van Manen's (2014) writing on the "vocative" has also become an important influence, where he outlines the vocative dimension of phenomenological writing by methods of the revocative (lived through-ness: bringing experience vividly into presence through anecdote and imagery); evocative (nearness: an in-touch-ness activated through poetic devices including alliteration and repetition); invocative (intensification: a calling forth by incantation); convocative (pathic: expressing an emotive, non-cognitive sensibility).

13 This transcript material was subsequently used in various ways within the project, including revisited as a way of discerning and clarifying the conceptual-theoretical direction of the unfolding enquiry.

14 Our conceptualisation of the event of "figuring" and the emergence of "figures" is further expanded upon within a dedicated chapter *Figuring > < Figure* in *Choreo-graphic Figures: Deviations of the Line* (2017, 69–79) by Cocker, Gansterer and Greil.

References

Bartenieff, Irmgard. 2002. *Body Movement – Coping with the Environment.* Oxon: Routledge.

Barthes, Roland. 1975/1973. *The Pleasure of the Text.* Translated by Richard Miller. New York: Hill and Wang.

Berardi, Franco. 2012. *The Uprising: On Poetry and Finance.* Los Angeles, CA: Semiotext(e).

Cixous, Hélène and Catherine Clément. 1986. *The Newly Born Woman.* Translated by Betsy Wing. Minneapolis: University of Minnesota Press.

Cocker, Emma. 2022. "Conversation-as-material." *Phenomenology & Practice* 17(1): 201–231.

Cocker, Emma. 2021. "Towards an Attitude of Openness." Keynote presentation at the 12th International Conference on Artistic Research, Society for Artistic Research, Vienna, 07– 09/04/2021. https://www.researchcatalogue.net/view/1220981/1222004.

Cocker, Emma, Nikolaus Gansterer, and Mariella Greil. 2018. "Choreo-graphic Figures: Scoring Aesthetic Encounters." *Journal of Artistic Research* 18. https://www.researchcatalogue.net/view/462390/462391.

Cocker, Emma, Nikolaus Gansterer, and Mariella Greil. eds. 2017. *Choreo-graphic Figures: Deviations of the Line.* Berlin: De Gruyter.

Di Paolo, Ezequiel A., Elena Clare Cuffari, and Hanne De Jaegher. 2018. *Linguistic Bodies: The Continuity between Life and Language.* Cambridge, MA: The MIT Press.

Ettinger, Bracha. 2006. *The Matrixial Borderspace.* Minneapolis: University of Minnesota Press.

Hegel, Georg Wilhelm Friedrich. 1979/1802. *Hegel's System of Ethical Life and First Philosophy of Spirit.* New York: State University of New York Press.

Irigaray, Luce. 2004. *The Way of Love.* Translated by Heidi Bostic and Stephen Pluhácêk. London and New York: Continuum.

Joy, Jenn. 2014. *The Choreographic.* Cambridge, MA: MIT Press.

LaBelle, Brandon. 2014. *Lexicon of the Mouth: Poetics and Politics of Voice and the Oral Imaginary.* New York: Bloomsbury.

Manning, Erin. 2013. *Always More Than One: Individuation's Dance.* Durham: Duke University Press.

Manning, Erin. 2012. *Relationscapes: Movement, Art, Philosophy.* Cambridge, MA: MIT Press.

Massumi, Brian. 2013. *Semblance and Event: Activist Philosophy and the Occurrent Arts.* Cambridge, MA: MIT Press.

Mestre, Lilia. 2014. *Writing Scores Glossary*, Supplement. Brussels: apass.

Mersch, Dieter. 2015. *Epistemologies of Aesthetics.* Translated by Laura Radosh. Zürich: Diaphanes.

Nancy, Jean-Luc. 2000. *Being Singular Plural.* Translated by Robert D. Richardson and Anne E. O'Byrne. Stanford, CA: Stanford University Press.

Noë, Alva. 2016. *Strange Tools: Art and Human Nature.* New York: Hill and Wang.

Pollock, Della. 1998. "Performing Writing." In *The Ends of Performance*, edited by Peggy Phelan and Jill Lane, 73–103. New York: New York University Press.

Schwab, Michael. 2019. "Expositionality." In *Artistic Research: Charting a Field in Expansion*, edited by Paulo de Assis and Lucia D'Errico, 27–45. London and New York: Rowman & Littlefield.

Schwab, Michael and Henk Borgdorff. eds. 2013. *The Exposition of Artistic Research: Publishing Art in Academia*. Leiden: Leiden University Press.

Stern, Daniel. 2010. *Forms of Vitality: Exploring Dynamic Experience in Psychology, the Arts, Psychotherapy and Development*. Oxford and New York: Oxford University Press.

van Manen, Max. 2014. *Phenomenology of Practice: Meaning-Giving Methods in Phenomenological Research and Writing*. London and New York: Routledge Francis & Taylor Group.

12

THE CHOREOGRAPHIC POLITICS OF A STAIRCASE

A duet by Kirsi Heimonen and Leena Rouhiainen

In this duet, Heimonen and Rouhiainen discuss their approach to site-informed textual choreography by examining its applications at the staircase of the Parliament House in Helsinki. They present the full textual choreography generated in tandem with this site, that is reiterative poetic text, and introduce the political interests motivating their undertaking. Important to their choreographic approach is a multifaceted score and the urban sites they work in. Relying on insights from Sara Ahmed and André Lepecki, they explore the political opportunities that experimental co-authored choreographic writing has as a mode of queering the familiar. The duo describes their experiences of engaging with the staircase and how it permeates their writing and text. They underline that otherness conditions both their experience and the sharing of their collaborative endeavour. They discuss textual choreography as a plan that involves others and enables the freedom to explore and initiate alternative ways of perceiving, writing, moving and being together, alternative choreographic futures. Important is that the choreographic process is repeatedly engaged with and that in reading others continue to enact the published texts as performance. The authors propose that, as a continuous and progressive collaborative practice that engages others, their textual choreography is public political activity.

Striding across the beloved nation, trauma freezes my blood. Propriety at the parliament polices spontaneity and refuses bodily accommodation.
May I exist? Frenetic teetering, an unnoticed bodily statement. A war, dare I oppose? The infinite skies are observant when harmless artists bend over authority and perform a far-reaching display.

DOI: 10.4324/9781003397427-15

Who supports the eroding shrine of might, any demonstrations of worship here? The erosion of the citizen, family, police and artist exist and are monitored here. Leaning on granite and infinite skies, the body protects the right to exist.

Bending over, reaching for spontaneity, permission is not allowed on that road. Is the demonstration a mere façade of war trauma and at the corner of destruction?

Am I written by lies of authority, teetering at the corner, a harmless crumbling onlooker? An empty view on the distant might, this scene freezes my body and blood. An invitation to a serious stride?

May I lie here on the snow, unnoticed?

A removal of this performance from the gates of authority?

My blood, my frenetic existence opposes the might of war.

The eroding body demonstrates its trauma and strides across the statements of authority.

A harmless display of propriety and spontaneity bends across the infinite skies. An unnoticed authority demonstrates a worship of accommodation.

Any nation that does not dare to oppose freezes. The police perform a display of might.

Observant artists reach far to the parliament, over and over.

At the bottom of one edge, escaped from the patterns of dominance, breathing with the wind and the flags. Relaxation is frozen, lost in between the severity of dominance and submission.

This rocky every-and-no-one's-site escapes the touch of protestors, movements forgotten, the severity of greyness does not go away.

The trace of this face is left on the snow, the site defies the safety vests.

Bending away from the sky, the head goes down.

Vertigo: lost touches and compact severity.

Pausing.

Pausing to breathe, why resist?

What to resist? Snow leaves protective patterns on the stairs. Its movements escape the dominance of the site.

Time pauses. The wind, only. Forgotten time, forget time.

The delicacy of the snow allows defiance to pause, waving to the children.

A safety vest defies the invisible protest. In the delicate snow a rocky resistance.

At the edge of dominance and submission, children. Bending over they mock vertigo, and the skies open. Forgotten, the futility of their movement, a mere curtsy. No safety when breath and touch is forgotten.

A bottom on the building, pausing in touch, relaxing.

There is a forgetting of time and all vertigo escapes.

Delicate snow, wind, like frozen movement, protest the traces of dominance.

A resistance, the grey granite of the building protects the site of everyone-and-no-one. Do not go away.

The snow, purifying the blood. War trauma. Frenetic teetering.

The resistance of everyone and none.

Bending over into vertigo, a protest, a bodily statement... Is it allowed or will the police remove me?

Who protects this all-encompassing site? I got lost.

The rocky resistance refuses bodily accommodation, its right to exist.

Who writes us as citizens, mocking propriety?

May I, can I, do I dare, anyone? Rejected spontaneity. Forgotten breath and touch submitted to monitored existence.

Not allowed to pause or relax here.

Exhausting greyness erodes spontaneity, severe wind removes resistance. The patterns of teetering by harmless artists are written on the frost, lost in an empty site.

A curtsy, a delicate submission to the compact granite house.

Defiance is frozen.

Bodily corners are visibly invisible, forgotten and futile at the façade of might. Faced by rocky dominance and all-encompassing propriety.

Surveillance reaches my breathing monitored by cameras and gazes. Can trauma be purified by lies or snow?

The head leans on an empty scene, a serious vertigo clears all traces, is all lost?

The wind and the infinite skies resist the patterns of time. Pausing to perform a display of escaped opposition.

Vertigo touches forgotten traces and traumas. Nothing unnoticed.

Frozen flags and harmless movements bend over the rocky building. The severity of statements leaves the dominance to the site. My blood, only my blood defies the eroding might.

The bottom reached, who leaves safety vests for children?

Dominance and submission leave traces on our accommodations. This building, an eroding shrine of might, is teetering.

Why resist, there is protection in the safety vests?

Bending over, we touch the stairs as bodily statements and pause. Time pauses. The wind moves the delicate snow and the forgotten flag and escapes into the infinite skies.

Severe vertigo, a protest.

Propriety freezes blood and refuses bodily accommodation. Can I escape performing this trauma?

Worship is a far-reaching display: the permission to curtsy and bend over at the bottom of some corner.

To exist is to protest, pause and breathe in the greyness of the eroding snow.

The harmless movement of all exhausted visitors opens up to the windy skies.

A frenetic visitor teeters at the edge of the lost defiance.

The severity of war trauma harms the existence of the nation.

Nothing forgotten, nothing opposed.

The stairs, the site for curtsy, reaches the sky demonstrating all-encompassing frozen distances at the scene.

The crumbling site bleeds, a corner lost, the rights of citizens removed.
All and nothing.
Only the wind clears rejection and mocking.
Breath pauses in between the granite and snow: the erosion of might?

* * * *

The previous piece of site-specific textual choreography was initiated at the staircases of the Parliament House in Helsinki. In generating the text, we drew inspiration from Sara Ahmed's (2006) contributions to queer phenomenology and André Lepecki's notion on choreopolitics (2013). In our duet, we questioned the possibility to reorder socio-cultural relations inherent to public settings and how this might involve a politics of disorientation. This thematic derived from the perplexity we experienced when European nation-states, Finland included, enforced restraints to manage the global pandemic. As we engaged with this concern, the Ukrainian war broke out. The political leadership of Finland was faced with the threat of an invasion by Russian forces. Since Finland has a 1,300-kilometre border and previous war history with its eastern neighbour, the risk became quite tangible to us. Both situations highlighted issues of governmental authority, control, surveillance and, in contradistinction, the freedom of citizens. Consequently, we decided to explore a site of political significance. We chose one that was visible in TV newscasts related to national security during the pandemic and continues to be so in relation to Finland's new NATO membership processes.

At the staircase, we examined and challenged conventional place-related actions and meanings associated with the Parliament House building. We did so by questioning how our bodies carry and disrupt timely socio-cultural meanings, values and narratives. Integral to our textual choreographic process is the aim to generate alternative forms of performative agencies (cf. Hunter 2015). Our bodily explorations and writings at the site were framed by the choreographic approach we have been developing over the past few years (Rouhiainen and Heimonen 2021; Heimonen and Rouhiainen 2022). It is a phenomenologically informed collaborative score that includes embodied and written exploration of urban sites, eventually generating detailed reiterative choreographic texts. The intention of this choreographic approach is to allow the impact of the bodily sense of being in contact with the chosen urban location to permeate our activities in writing.

We visited the staircase leading up to the parliament building twice: on February 4 and April 5, 2022. The wide and long staircase is in the open air. If lined up end-to-end, the granite stones of the staircase would be 2.7 kilometres in length. When we first spent time there, the stairs were partially covered in snow and the temperature was well below freezing. On our second visit, the weather was merely chilly and windy, typical for the time of year. On both occasions, we explored the place for a few hours, observing its features and moving in relation to it and then wrote down words and phrases evoked by the site. Our explorations began with orienting ourselves to the site, lingering in different parts of it. The staircase invited us to test how it might act as a support for our movement. We also experimented with movements and bodily actions which felt appropriate and inappropriate in and to the site. We touched, leaned, sat, lay and crawled on the stairs. We bent over, lay on our backs and threw our arms and legs in the air. We marched, crept and ran up and down the stairs. We trembled, emitted vocal sounds and spoke in gibberish. The massive stone pillars of the building at the top of the staircase, allowed us to play with both hiding and coming into view. We perceived the environs with all of our senses: the loudness of traffic, the view of downtown Helsinki, cars, buses, trams and pedestrians passing by on the main street, Mannerheimintie, tourists and demonstrators at the staircase itself.

The building is on a hill, so the staircase is very prominent in the landscape. This makes the people on it very visible too, underlining their performativity. Our intention was not to perform for an audience, yet we were clearly exposed to the gazes of the passers-by. This made it difficult, if not impossible, to avoid evoking a sense of performance. We were also conscious of the fact that we had not notified the police of our activities in the public place. The police closely monitor the staircase and the entire vicinity of Parliament House. We witnessed them too. Parked in their car on the side street, they saw us but left us alone.

* * * *

Deeds of the past, traceless and traced, are sheltered in this fortress of rock pillars. Soaring to the heights in solitude, it beholds the city with might.
The empty façade hides a shrine of false virtue, accessibility ignored except for oligarchy.
The demonstrators steadfastly feast by the temple to attain power: Paasikivi, Kekkonen… Niinistö and Marin.
The dispossessed, baffled by the King of the Castle, ever only fall.
A steadfast powerless demonstrator at the empty façade of the grandiloquent mausoleum.
The unattainable might of the stern fortress soars to the heights.
Falling away from the sturdy non-place, baffled and hiding in solitude around the hill.
Traces from the past feast, hidden from the dispossessed, accessibility sternly ignored.
The hubris of hard rock drives away? A hideout of the shrine?
Forever unattainable. Forever plain false virtue, an empty shelter.
The fortress of the oligarchy's hidden might. Rock pillars shelter inaccessible power. Deeds of Paasikivi, Kekkonen and past kings fall.
The empty façade demonstrates the castle of solitude, inaccessible to the dispossessed.

Demonstrators baffled by the steadfast castle of traceless deeds.
Only to fall, ever, only to fall.
Humbleness opens at the façade of the unbreathable symmetrical bunker.
A servant marching through the sediments of rules, silenced violence, interrupted shouting, inflexible extremities, sweat and closed papers.
Not fitting here in-between the pillars of harsh realities, breathing is silenced.
Knees follow the echo of the rustle of paper and ink structuring the citizens.
The sealed secrets from the making of the big granite monument:
shouting, sweating, gravel, spades, hail, storms and crumpled whispers from the past touch my spine.
Sharp cracks in-between the sky and stairs, isolation exhausts everything.
Now, just here, compressed into the visible centredness.
Inflexible servants march echoing the gap between realities. Untouchable citizens closed in their isolation.
Shouting through the past decades, structured violence bend knees and seal secrets.
Compressed whispers in an unbreathable bunker. The monumental granite pillars rule. Interrupted shouting sealed into secrecy.
The sky cracks. A visible storm, hail.
Violence bends knees and exhausts the spine. Unbreathable humbleness fits reality.
Servant citizens. Sealed papers and the granite monument rule.
A baffling gap of invisible traces, deeds and whispered rejections. Empty might? False rules?
A stern non-place rules the city centre, demonstrators isolated, citizens driven away.
Secrets rise from hard rock, not fitting the stairs of the mausoleum.
Hail touches the sun, the shouting of the servants openly ignored. Sturdy rejection by invisible ink.
Unattainable might beholds sealed secrets. A hiding place for the oligarchy.
A gap between realities, false virtue. The sweat, speech, swearing, shouting of demonstrators silenced and driven away. The knees of humble citizens bend in the violence.
Exhausting deeds of the past traceless, forever dispossessed.
Silenced shouting exhausts the demonstrators. The past compressed into the granite temple, sediments of isolation and violence visible to the marchers.
The granite bunker is possessed by ignorance. Extreme might falls in between the sky and the stairs. Big empty deeds hide the breathing virtues. Traceless solitude never falls.
The King of the Castle ever only falls.
Dispossession exhausts humbleness.
Past whispers touch the spine.

* * * *

Our actual choreographic process is framed by the following score:

1 Explore the site by being attentive to how it resonates in and extends your body. Move in response to it. After some time at the site, and sensing its impact, respond by writing down single words or two-word phrases in your notebook.
2 In the next few days, allowing the impact of the site to linger with you and using the words written at the site, write five to ten sentences, again conveying the sense of contact with the site.
3 Then send your words and texts to each other.
4 Allowing the silent impact of the site, as well as the resonance of the already-written words and sentences, to inform your writing:
    a Write sentences or a short text by using the first list of words that you yourself did not generate.
    b Write sentences or a short text by using the first sentences that you yourself did not generate.
5 Then send these new sentences or short texts to each other and use all the previously produced texts in the next phase of writing.
6 Again, allow the silent impact of the site, as well as the resonance of the already-written words and sentences, to inform your writing:
    a Write sentences or a short text by using the first list of words generated by both of us.
    b Write sentences or a short text by using the first sentence groups generated by both of us.
    c Write sentences or a short text by using both the first list of words and the first sentence groups generated by both of us.
7 Edit all the generated texts into one piece of textual choreography (cf. Heimonen and Rouhiainen 2022).

The score, and our intention to attend to political themes, had an important influence on our duet and informed how the textual choreography took shape. Underlining the importance of these starting points, Ahmed (2010, 245) notes that "what is reachable is determined by the orientation we have already taken. [...] Orientations are about the direction we take that puts some things and not others in our reach." However, crucial to our textual choreography are the places that we choose to explore. At the Parliament House, the staircase strongly directed the contents of the text. It was as if the site demanded which words were to be written, and the place inscribed itself in the text through our writing. Ahmed (2006; 2010) relates to this by relaying how orientations do not fully determine how we act in any given situation. Aside from our habitual comportment and the tasks we choose to do, the things we are in relation with impact us. According to Ahmed, other beings, objects and places, have agency in that they move us in certain ways and directions, often doing so without us being aware of their effects (Ahmed 2006; 2010). She continues:

> Even when orientations seem to be about which way we are facing in the present, they also point us toward the future. The hope of changing directions is always that we do not know where some paths may take us: risking departure from the straight and narrow, makes new futures possible, which might involve going astray, getting lost, or even becoming queer.
>
> (Ahmed 2006, 554)

Here, the queer relates to the opportunities we have to disturb the order of things by inhabiting things that seem to flee our grasp. The oblique approach may open new perspectives, but it also demands that we tolerate the disorientation of not knowing (Ahmed 2006, 555, 556).

The site confronted us with many challenges and made many kinds of impressions. These related to the uncomfortable contours of the stairs, our lack of formal permission to be there and do what we were doing, our personal family histories and related trauma, the societal status of citizens, marginal groups and families, the historical sediments of the building, the national war history and related politics of Finland. Directly derived from being in contact with the staircase, these impressions came to us as fragmentary moments of affect. They moved us in many ways, both in our actions at the site and in generating the initial words and ultimately the full text. The words and text seemed to continue to emanate from the site even once we resumed our collaborative writing elsewhere.

We believe our experiences relate to the embodied and gestural base of language as described, for example, by Shaun Gallagher (2006, 121) in the following manner: "Even if we are not explicitly aware of our gestures, even in circumstances where they contribute nothing to the communicative process, they may contribute to shaping our cognition". For him, gestures are expressive movements, which are activated in communicative situations. Even when they are not consciously thought of beforehand, they contribute to the accomplishment of thought. He asserts that: "[...] we do not have to be conscious of embodied functions for them to effectively accomplish thought. Gesture and language shape cognition in a prenoetic manner" (Gallagher 2006, 123). This notion points towards how our encounter and inter-relationship with the staircase intrinsically underpinned our writing. The embeddedness of writing is further discussed by van Manen (2014), who finds that writing is both a manner of making contact with the world and a process through which we learn how we relate to the world. Indeed, in the aftermath of our physical exploration, we were surprised by the qualities relating to command, subjection, control, powerlessness and power that the finished text contained. Even if our interest was to observe the political opportunities of our approach to textual choreography at the staircase, the contents of our collaboratively generated text highlighted political issues to a far stronger degree than we expected.

In one of his articles, Lepecki (2013) discusses his term "choreopolitics," describing what he views as the inherent political force of choreography. In doing so, he relies on the insights of two seminal thinkers, Hannah Arendt and Jacques Rancière. Rancière (2004/2011) argues that as experiential events, artistic works and aesthetics acts open up new ways of perceiving, and simultaneously, enact novel forms of political subjectivity. Arendt (1958/1989; 2005), in turn, forwards a notion of political action which appreciates the plurality of human life. She suggests that this activity is about engaging with common interests that set in motion unforeseeable futures. This is where she understands freedom to be actualised.

In writing about politics and art, which reconfigure our ways of seeing and speaking, Rancière opines:

> Political statements and literary locutions produce effects in reality. [...] They reconfigure the map of the sensible by interfering with the functionality of gestures and rhythms adapted to the natural cycle of production, reproduction, and submission. [...] The channels for political subjectivization are not those of imaginary identification but those of "literary" disincorporation. [...] The "fictions" of art and politics are therefore heterotopias rather than utopias.
>
> (Rancière 2004/2011, 39–41)

He, therefore, argues that art can question and decompose conventional positions in multiple ways. Co-relatively, to overcome totalising order and government, Arendt (2005, 112) asserts: "In other words every new beginning is by nature a miracle when seen and experienced from the standpoint of the processes it necessarily interrupts." She continues: "[...] the most important activity of a free life moves from action to speech, from deeds to free words" (Arendt 2005, 124). In positioning us differently in relation to reality, art thus can shift the manner in which we are actualised, are in contact with the world and indeed ways the world may open up to us. Here lies the chance to witness the previously unforeseen, which is where freedom comes into play.

What might be said in relation to our work is that the chosen site and the frame of the choreographic score positioned us queerly in relation to our conventional everyday relationship with downtown Helsinki, where the Parliament House stands. Together they called us to reconfigure our attention and confronted us with abundant sensation, innumerable observations, affects, memories, imaginations and visions of historical events we had not previously experienced in the same way. As said, these all concretely moved us. They did so affectively and emotionally, pushing us into physical action at the site as well as into a writing that revealed the complex significance the site carries. The site pushed itself into the text, a text that is characterised by strong power-related tensions and oppositional forces and the sheer magnitude of the material formation that the staircase is. The text performs the staircase of the Parliament House as a stern, severe environment.

Even though the text came into being through us, it was, and continues to be, unfamiliar to us. In writing it, we did not actively decide on its contents or quality, and therefore it practically taught us, something which relates to Lepecki's discussion of choreopolitics as an opportunity to learn. He writes:

> [...] choreopolitics requires a redistribution and reinvention of bodies, affects, and senses through which one may learn how to move politically, how to invent, activate, seek, or experiment with a movement whose only sense (meaning and direction) is the experimental exercise of freedom.
>
> (Lepecki 2013, 20)

In our site-specific writing, we were questioning, perhaps even reinventing, how we and others might relate to the Parliament House staircase. However, Lepecki reminds us that freedom requires collaboration and does not occur without constraints. He claims:

> Choreographic planning is crucial because [...] the political is not a given to the subject, it is not even a given of the human species. Rather, it is a social and personal force and a promise that must be built with others, must be set into relation, and must be dared, collectively, into existence. Once in existence, it has to be learned, sustained, and experimented with. Again and again. Lest it disappear from the world. It follows that if the political is not a given, if it needs to be (re)discovered and (re)produced, then the political is always a kind of experimentation. It comes into the world through the experience of experimenting.
>
> (Lepecki 2013, 22)

The above quotation underlines the importance of the collaborative aspects of our choreographic process, the fact that we have co-designed, co-experimented with and co-authored our textual choreographic practice over many years. However, it also points to the specificity of our co-inhabitation with the Parliament House staircase during our site visits.

We have written elsewhere about site-specificity and the collaborative dimension of our approach to writing choreography (Heimonen and Rouhiainen 2021). In addressing our previous choreographic processes, we recognised that, in the related collaborative writing, our individual authorship disappears.

The sharing involved in the writing is based and dependent on our individual experiences, yet, what we experience is always co-dependent on the relationships we acquire through contact with other people, other beings and things. In relation to the Parliament House site, our sharing depended on the interrelationship not only between the two of us, but also between us, the staircase and its environs. In general terms, the sense of sharing and community generated by our duet was contingent on us being exposed to otherness. The perceived specificity of our embodiment was momentary, situationally defined by our tasks, our collaboration and our embeddedness in the material environment.

The above quotation by Lepecki also points to planning and repetition. Our explorations of different urban sites via the textual choreographic method we have created, includes and involves practices of repetition and reiteration. At the Parliament House staircase, these repetitions and reiterations related directly to choreopolitical dimensions and opportunities. We could thus be understood to be involved in an experimental choreographic programme. In relation to the political significance of planning Lepecki continues:

> Thus planning, programming, and experimentation (always corporeal, always social, as Deleuze and Guattari insist) become synonyms of choreography, which can now be defined as the necessary *minimal condition of sociality* so that (1) the political may appear in the world; (2) the political may move across agents, short-circuiting policed systems of obedience and command; and (3) the political may surface, persist, and be performed thanks to (choreographic) planning.
>
> (Lepecki 2013, 22, emphasis in original)

He also states:

> I propose the notion of the choreopolitical as the formation of collective plans emerging at the edges between open creativity, daring initiative, and a persistent — even stubborn — iteration of the desire to live away from policed conformity.
>
> (Lepecki 2013, 23)

We stubbornly persist with and repeatedly engage with our textual choreographic score, which experimentally questions our relationships with familiar urban settings, queers their existence and performs them differently. In so doing, it opens them up for new kinds of relational possibilities. On the one hand, our work persists via our repeated site-specific undertakings. On the other, it persists through the performance of a textual choreography, which is enacted when the published texts are read by others. They may be lured, puzzled or moved through reading the reiterative textual choreography. Readers can also adapt the score to their lived environments, if they so wish. In this way, the textual chorography continues to enact and embody otherness in diverse ways. It is here that our duet truly becomes socially engaged, and we concretely enter the public realm, which for Arendt, is the dimension in which political action becomes possible. She highlights the vital importance of political activity by stating that, "Here the issue is not just freedom but life itself, the continuing existence of humanity and perhaps of all organic life on earth" (Arendt 2005, 109). On the basis of the previous insights, we propose that it is via open-ended and thoughtfully framed communal or social action that the past can move the present and yield various unexpected choreographic futures, which can, in turn, generate fresh outlooks. Our collaborative, situated, embedded, progressively extending textual choreographic duet aims at doing exactly this.

* * * *

In isolation, the sheltered traces hide a shrine of virtue: a breathable access to the soaring skies.

A feast in-between the baffling reality of the closed bunker, this fortress of rock pillars and sealed secrets.

The baffling softness of round rock, a steadfast hiding-place.

Deeds of the past whisper in the sediment of the compressed pillars. Their inflexible extremities breathe and rustle with these traceless traces.

The rise and fall of this fortress reverberate in every step.

Silent echoes of sweating, speaking and shouting by invincible citizens soar to its grandiloquent heights.

In solitude, the mausoleum beholds the hybris of the dispossessed.

The king, an architect of sheltered secrets and fallen traces.

Rock pillars hide the asymmetrical breathing.

The sky closed, sweat and exhaustion of the citizens invisible to the rulers. The city silently follows the grandiloquent power of the oligarchy.

An access to the fortress through the cracks in power, a hideout sealed. Plain humbleness belongs to the past, now hidden power of invincible persons steadfastly structures the spines of the citizens.

Inflexible followers ignored.

The visibility of virtue does not fit the harsh façade of the monument. Silenced shouting soars to the heights. If persons do not belong to the might, they are compressed into the granite.

Secrets sealed by hail.

The reverberations of interrupted silence open the invisible traces of the past for the powerless.

Forever, for the powerless.

Total silence empties everything.

References

Ahmed, Sara. 2010. "Orientations Matter." In *New Materialisms: Ontology, Agency, Politics*, edited by Diana Coole and Samantha Frost, 234–257. Durham and London: Duke University Press.

Ahmed, Sara. 2006. "Orientations: Toward a Queer Phenomenology." *GLQ: A Journal of Lesbian and Gay Studies* 12(4): 543–574.

Arendt, Hannah. 2005. *The Promise of Politics*. Edited by Jerome Kohn. New York: Schocken Books.

Arendt, Hannah. 1958/1989. *The Human Condition*. London and Chicago, IL: University of Chicago Press.

Gallagher, Shaun. 2006. *How the Body Shapes the Mind*. Oxford: Clarendon Press and New York: Oxford University Press.

Heimonen, Kirsi and Leena Rouhiainen. 2022. "In the Shadows: Phenomenological Choreographic Writing." *Choreographic Practices* 13(1): 75–96. https://doi.org/10.1386/chor_00042_1.

Hunter, Victoria. 2015. *Moving Sites: Investigating Site-specific Dance Performance*. Abingdon: Routledge.

Lepecki, Andre. 2013. "Choreopolice and Choreopolitics: Or, the Task of the Dancer." *The Drama Review* 57(4): 13–27.

Rancière, Jacques. 2004/2011. *The Politics of Aesthetics. The Distribution of the Sensible*. Translated by Gabriel Rockhill. London and New York: Continuum.

Rouhiainen, Leena and Kirsi Heimonen. 2021. "Katveen varjon sanominen koreografisena kirjoittamisena (The Saying of the Shadow as a Choreographic Writing)." *Ruukku Studies in Artistic Research* 15. https://doi.org/10.22501/ruu.848270.

Van Manen, Max. 2014. "Writing Phenomenology." In *Phenomenology of Practice. Meaning-Giving Methods in Phenomenological Research and Writing*, edited by Max van Manen, 1–10. London and New York: Routledge Francis & Taylor Group.

13

CHOREOGRAPHIC AFTERMATH

*Kirsi Heimonen, Rebecca Hilton, Chrysa Parkinson
and Leena Rouhiainen*

Here the four editors talk about co-authoring the epilogue and what it should consist of.

One Editor (OE): Is this an epilogue?

Another Editor (AE): What do you mean?

AE: Well, traditionally an epilogue brings some kind of closure to a volume, and I think it's safe to say that with *Writing Choreography: Textualities of and beyond Dance* we are more interested in opening rather than closing anything, in creating choreographic possibilities rather than coming to any conclusions.

AE: In that case maybe this epilogue needs to be something more like an afterword?

AE: Or maybe it's an aftermath? We're here together in the aftermath, sharing the feeling that something has happened.

AE: So many things have happened! This volume has brought together many diverse choreographic actions, writings and readings and hopefully will continue to do so in the future.

AE: Hmm, maybe this open-ended aftermath-ness could be expressed via something affective, something more poetic than conclusive?

AE: Like a description of a practice or a shared experience? Or a score?

DOI: 10.4324/9781003397427-16

AE: Something that we editors can work on together but separately from where we are, at the peripheries of north and south, in three different countries, three different time zones, three different weather systems, three utterly different environments.

AE: This would also illuminate something particular about the way *Writing Choreography* emerged, through our exchanges across continents with each other and with all of the contributing authors, each with a very different take on writing choreography and choreographing writing.

AE: Maybe we could use your score from Chapter 12 to explore this shared yet singular sense of being absently present?

AE: Yes, but let's adapt it a little. Let's each choose a site and linger there for a while, observing the place and our own bodies in relation to the place, exploring this idea of being absently present, settling in and moving with whatever is emerging. And afterwards, we can write down some words evoked by the experience.

AE: Then we will write some sentences using our words and each other's, and bring all the materials together into a single poetic collaboration, moving the words and phrases around until it feels like something is beginning to emerge through and with it.

AE: And then we will share it here, as a processual rather than as a complete or perfect or conclusive thing.

AE: This is so nice. After all, the body and movement are only ever absently present, as this volume attests to. And our hope is that traces of choreographic writing from each of the contributing authors will also be absently present here in our processual, open-ended, poetic epilogue, that we will all somehow come together, here in the aftermath.

Editors In Polyphonic Unison (Eipu): Yes.

We absently carry a mute knowing, the shadows of wings. Wildlife.
Longing to be part of you.

The body, marked by stone, is heading south. The call of the sea.

Damp hair, damp skin, cold hands.
Low and still, under the overpass.

Dirt, rocks, twigs, leaves.
Hair, skin, hands, tiny creatures.
Sliver of sky, cars roar across brown river.
Bird cry, birds cry.

Huge, still, golden goddess.
Tiny creatures crawl.
Damp, cold, pale, brown, low life.

Whitecaps compose the forgotten lullaby; the wind caresses the skin of the
rocks.

Brightness rocks all that is remembered, emptiness hangs with clouds.
I am stunned by the disappeared time and the heaps of yellow flowers.

The sea plants forgottenness into the waves.
Windy air clouds my existence.

Timelessness flowers on the bedrock, the wind signs,
a wave of disappearance composes the hereness.

Where does the horizon end? What can I not remember?

Then snow cut beats into the sea floor
and lichen furred you.

Brittle bones and brittle stones.
Brittle lichen and brittle fur.

This brittle wind beat a sea floor in.
This west wind boned the snow stone.

Now this snow stone bones the beat.

Remember the skin of the rocks:
The composed existence of sea plants flowering on the bedrock.
Caresses of the skin are waves disappearing into whitecaps, too.
They sing the windy lullaby of the sea.

Disappearing in the horizon, they are here, forgotten and not.

Twigs rock the dirt and leave the goddesses hair damp.
Skinning the cold, hands low and still,
She cries tiny golden creatures.

Life roars under the overpass.
Car river crawling in a huge pale brown sky.
Birds sliver.

I am not your sea, your snow, your west wind.
I am the lichened stone, the beat, your beat:
Now and then.
Then and this.
This and now.

I am not brittle bone and fur.
I am the floor.

I am now and I am then.
I am the sea floor.
I lie waiting until I become the ground.

Lichen, stone, fur, bone, wind, stone, snow, sea are all in me.
Little furry, bony, brittle creatures, beats in time, come and go.
Here they come. There they go.
They are fleet, I am forever.

Timelessness hangs in the air. The sea sings its lullaby.
Forgotten and remembered, existence caresses my skin.

At the end of the horizon, a stunning bedrock, with crowds of seagulls and
bright yellow flowers.

You, the shadow of the sea, carry the stone with you.
Your mute body longs to be part of wildlife.

The sea calls us wildly. Wings carry our absent lives.
The absent body is marked by longing.

With damp hair, damp skin, cold hands, she lies low and still, under the overpass.
Dirt, rocks, twigs, leaves in her hair, skin, hands, and some tiny creatures.
She can just see a sliver of sky, birds cry, birds cry.

Cars roar across in a brown river.
She's huge, and still, this golden goddess.
The tiny creatures crawl: damp, cold, pale, brown, low life.

The call of the sea marked in stone.
The shadows of wings, absent.

What do we absently carry? Wildlife?
I am part of your shadow.
The stones carry the sea with them.
We are marked by the sea and its knowing. We are marked by absence.
Your absent parts are called by the sea.

Wings carry the shadows of us and the sea.

CONTRIBUTORS

Emma Cocker is a writer–artist and Associate Professor in Fine Art, Nottingham Trent University, whose research practice unfolds restlessly along the threshold between writing/art, including experimental, performative and collaborative approaches to working with language. She is a co-founder of the Society of Artistic Research Special Interest Group for Language-based Artistic Research and a co-editor of "Practices of Phenomenological and Artistic Research," *Phenomenology & Practice* (2022). Her writing has been published in *Failure* (2010); *On Not Knowing: How Artists Think* (2013); *The Creative Critic: Writing as/about Practice* (2018); and solo collections *The Yes of the No* (2016) and *How Do You Do?* 2024). For more information on Emma, visit https://not-yet-there.blogspot.com/.

Marie Fahlin is a choreographer, dancer and curator based in Stockholm, Sweden. She completed her PhD in Performative Practices with a specialisation in choreography at Stockholm University of the Arts in 2020 with the project *Moving through Choreography — Curating Choreography as Artistic Practice*. Within the project, she developed an interest in dressage and its relation to choreography and curating. Taking form as text, choreography and objects, Fahlin's PhD work was presented as a series of curated exhibitions and performances. In 2023, Fahlin began her new research project *The Curative Act*. The project is funded by The Swedish Research Council and hosted by Stockholm University of the Arts.

Nikolaus Gansterer is an artist and researcher interested in the links between drawing, thinking and action. Since 2007, he has taught at the University of Applied Arts in Vienna, where he is a board member of the Angewandte

Performance Laboratory. He is the author *Drawing a Hypothesis* (2013), a book on the ontology of diagrammatic configurations. From 2014 to 2018, he worked on developing new systems of notation between drawing, writing and choreography within the international research project *Choreo-graphic Figures*. From 2019 to 2023, he was the leading key researcher of the artistic project *Contingent Agencies* for experimental diagramming of atmospheres and environments. For more information on Nikolaus, visit www.gansterer.org.

Lynda Gaudreau is an artist, choreographer, curator and researcher. Her PhD in Art Practice (UQAM, Montreal) is on the concept of asynchrony in arts. She was a postdoctoral researcher at the Performing Arts Research Centre, Theatre Academy, University of the Arts Helsinki in 2019–2021 and is now a visiting researcher. For more information on Lynda, visit https://ly86.webnode.fr.

Mariella Greil, PhD, works as an artist and researcher, focusing on contemporary performance, especially its ramifications into the choreographic and the ethical. She is a Senior Artist at Angewandte Performance Laboratory at the University of Applied Arts in Vienna, where she currently works on *Choreo-ethical Assemblages — Narrations of Bare Bodies* (Elise-Richter-PEEK/FWF). Her work explores a politicised practice that targets trans-subjective, communicative processes in performative encounters, using expanded choreography and somatic practices as compositional tools. Together with Vera Sander, she co-edited the book *(per)forming feedback* (2016) and recently published the monograph *Being in Contact — Encountering a Bare Body* (2021) and the antology "Bare Bodies — Thresholding Life" (2023). For more information on Mariella, visit http://www.mariellagreil.net/.

Martin Hargreaves is a dramaturg and writer, and his interests vacillate between boredom and hysteria. His research coalesces around performativity and includes the recent histories of dance and performance, queer practices and camp misunderstandings. After completing his PhD, he was the editor of *Dance Theatre Journal* and has worked in various educational contexts in the UK and further afield. He has been a visiting lecturer at Stockholm University of the Arts since 2013 and beginning in 2024 is Head of Choreographic School at Sadler's Wells in London.

Kirsi Heimonen is University Researcher at the Research Institute of the University of the Arts Helsinki. Her background is in dance, choreography, somatic movement practices and experimental writing. Her recent research interests have focused on the notion of silence, and the way in which written memories from mental hospitals transmit the bodily interweaving with the environment and unsayable. A phenomenological approach runs through her artistic research projects.

Rebecca Hilton is a dance person from so-called Australia. Currently working as Professor in Choreography for the research area *Site Event Encounter* at Stockholm University of the Arts, her interest in exploring the complexity of relations between aesthetics and ethics first emerged in New York City where she was part of the downtown dance community from 1986 to 2001. As an artist, a researcher and a pedagogue, her work continues to explore interactions between embodied knowledges, oral traditions and choreographic systems. Situating participatory art processes in spaces that are private, public and in flux, her working environments include hospitals, residential care centres, malls, parks and family homes.

Simo Kellokumpu is a Finnish choreographer and researcher born in Lapland and based in Helsinki. They completed the Doctorate of Arts in 2019 in the Performing Arts Research Centre, Theatre Academy, University of the Arts Helsinki based on the artistic research project *Choreography as Reading Practice*. Simo's artworks examine the choreographic relations between corporeality and materiality in various scales and contexts and they explore the entanglement of contemporary speculative fiction, space culture and site-specificity. Besides artistic work, Simo works currently as a lecturer at the Theatre Academy, University of the Arts Helsinki.

Jennifer Lacey is a dance–artist, raised in NYC. Based in Paris for 20 years, she is currently an Assistant Professor at Stockholm University of the Arts, where she directs the MA programme in choreography. She creates across fields of choreography, performance and publication, her constant project being to re-negotiate production methods in dance-anchored art projects, proposing a playful hermeneutics of bodies and their environments. Often co-signing and collaborating, her works unbind dance from the spectacular, whilst investing in the multiple ways that the performative acts on, with and in the world.

alys longley is an interdisciplinary artist, writer and teacher, whose work exists as performance, artist-book, installations, films, education curriculum, poetry and performance writing. Over the last decade, alys has explored mistranslation studies, working across languages and disciplines with the spill of ideas beyond conventional systems of meaning, through a series of international artistic-research projects. alys is an Associate Professor in Dance Studies at the University of Auckland. The capitalisation in alys's name is sometimes in capitals and sometimes undercase — references to her name across both text and reference list reflect an experimental practice with change and fluidity in what a name does and can be.

Chrysa Parkinson identifies as a dancer. She comes from North American and Northern European dance communities where she works as a performer.

Her artistic inscriptions include the proscenium stage, queer communities and somatic practices — which combination manifests in a deep respect for both poetry and camp, a queasy relation to categories, and ongoing pleasure in experimentation. Since 2011, Chrysa has worked as Professor of Dance at Stockholm University of the Arts (SKH), directing the New Performative Practices Master education. Her research focuses on how dance situates itself in practitioners' lives and how performers, in turn, author, dismantle and re-constitute worlds.

Amaara Raheem is a Sri Lankan Australian dance–artist based between Narrm/Melbourne and Black Range (regional Victoria, Australia). Her prac-tice of choreography and performance takes multiple modes, including live events, video, sound and text. She sits on the Artistic Directorate for Next Wave and is an inaugural thinker-in-residence for APHIDS. In 2022, Amaara was selected for ABC Top 5 and commissioned to make programmes for Radio National's "Blueprint for Living" on her research on artists in-residence. She is a Lecturer at The Victorian College of the Arts (Dance), University of Melbourne.

Leena Rouhiainen is Head of the Research Institute of the University of the Arts Helsinki and Professor of Artistic Research at the university's Theatre Academy. She is a dancer and choreographer whose research interests lie in somatics, choreography, experimental writing, phenomenology and artistic research. She has published articles and co-edited journals and books in these areas. She was chair of the board of Nordic Forum for Dance Research (NOFOD) between 2008 and 2010 and executive board member of Society for Artistic Research (SAR) between 2015 and 2020.

Vicki Van Hout is a performer and choreographer of Wiradjuri, Dutch, Scottish and Afghan heritage. She graduated from Sydney's NAISDA Dance College (National Aboriginal Islander Skills Development Association Dance College) and received a scholarship to attend the Martha Graham School in New York. Upon returning to Australia, she danced with *Bangarra Dance Theatre*, the *Aboriginal Islander Dance Theatre* and Marilyn Miller's *Fresh Dancers*. In 2014, Vicki was the first indigenous recipient of the *NSW Dance Fellowship*, and in 2019, the *Australia Council Dance Award* recognised her outstanding contribution to Australian dance and her impact on the cultural narrative of Australia.

INDEX

Note: *Italic* page numbers refer to figures and page numbers followed by "n" denote endnotes.

Printed in the United States
by Baker & Taylor Publisher Services